FAREWELL
TO EUROPEAN HISTORY

PUBLISHED ON THE
LOUIS STERN MEMORIAL FUND

FAREWELL
TO EUROPEAN HISTORY

or The Conquest of Nihilism

by

ALFRED WEBER

Translated from the German
by R. F. C. HULL

GREENWOOD PRESS, PUBLISHERS
WESTPORT, CONNECTICUT

Library of Congress Cataloging in Publication Data

Weber, Alfred, 1868-1958.
  Farewell to European history.

  Translation of Abschied von der bishergen
Geschichte.
  Reprint of the 1948 ed. published by Yale Uni-
versity Press, New Haven.
  Includes index.
  1. Civilization--History. 2. Philosophy--His-
tory. 3. Nihilism (Philosophy) I. Title.
II. Title: The conquest of nihilism.
CB83.W3813 1977   909   76-52396
ISBN 0-8371-9447-4

Originally published in 1948 by Yale University Press,
New Haven

Reprinted in 1977 by Greenwood Press, Inc.

Library of Congress catalog card number 76-52396

ISBN 0-8371-9447-4

Printed in the United States of America

TABLE OF CONTENTS

AUTHOR'S FOREWORD

This sketch was written during the last phase of the war when it was clear that the war was turning into an event that would fundamentally affect the further course of history. Whether this upheaval could then be seen correctly in its full outline and content is open to question. But at any rate its nature and its spiritual content could be grasped in some measure. About the fate of our country, about the fate of Europe we Germans still know nothing final.

May those into whose hands it is given not only track down the guilty, may they also, apart from imposing on us the tasks of reconstruction which they must, remember that there are living historical bodies which no man may dismember unpunished, nor keep in military or political imprisonment for an indefinite period unpunished. Not unpunished, because by so doing he only does damage to himself in view of the interdependence of all life and economics nowadays; not unpunished, because in the long run no man can prevent an actual, organically living thing from reconstituting itself as an organism at the first opportunity. May they, to-morrow if not to-day, establish a peace that will bring peace, and this means inward satisfaction, to all. Even if it be a hard peace it should still leave every nation, even the most sorely tried—and Germany is one of the most sorely tried to-day— with a future.

It would be a terrible thing if ever I came to regret having written this book, which in truth does not spare my own people. Terrible not merely for me, but terrible because it would mean that all attempts to reach a real world recovery had become meaningless.

To-day the fate of the world lies in very few hands, never before in history have they been so few. Will they prove equal to their gigantic task?

On the other hand: will the Germans, this order-loving and— as will hardly be contested—brave people, so richly endowed in the broad mass but so completely at odds with itself to-day, will they really understand what has happened to them? Not *outwardly*, merely. From this point of view even the blind will be able to grasp the fearful logic of events once they have got to know the true facts which have been largely withheld from them or presented to them distortedly. But as a spiritual body! Will they be in a position, will they have spiritual stature enough, to come to terms with themselves in their misery and affliction under alien pressure and alien rule? Will they have the power to descend into themselves and re-discover their own human depths, finding there a new ground whence run the liberating springs? Instead of—falsifying or forgetting the dread calamity they have drawn down upon themselves—eating their hearts out in bitter reaction, or worse, in hatred of the hard executioners of the fate they have merited? Will they endure the most grievous trial that history can inflict on a great people in such a way as to prove triumphant? Triumphant over their own shadow? Will they, so struggling with themselves, discover their inner richness anew in a new light? Then they would once more be the peer of any nation on earth.

February 1945

SUPPLEMENTARY NOTE

Reading through the text once again after the end of the war in Europe I find, despite all that has happened meanwhile, no cause to alter anything in it, let alone its contents as a whole. The wave of hatred that has broken over everything German and will not, after what has happened, abate so soon, we ourselves have deserved. From the last chapter of the book it can be seen *how* one is to think of the abominations that have only now been revealed or are only now coming to a climax, and of the degree of our responsibility as a whole therefor. This still stands, although one did not realize the hideous extent of these happenings.

I would like to remind readers that the last chapter was written before the post-war revelations.

The depth of the abyss which I there hinted at is now all the clearer. All the clearer too, I hope, the task we have to set ourselves, be it made lighter or heavier by our conquerors.

June 1945   ALFRED WEBER

INTRODUCTION

For anyone endowed with historical perspective it must be clear that the catastrophe we have lived through and are still living through sets us at the end of History as we know it, that is to say, history as moulded by the civilization of the West.

As has been explained in my *Kulturgeschichte als Kultursoziologie*, ever since the scientific and technological discoveries of modern times we have been living no longer on our dear, familiar old earth of wide-open spaces and infinite variety, but on a new star which in some remarkable manner combines the old geometrical extension with foreshortenings and shrinkings and permanent world-contacts, thus completely altering all life upon it. Formerly we used to hear some six months after the event, that "they were having a war far away in Turkey"; now, every day, we are immediately involved by ear in the struggles of nations for power, their world-spanning battles, their plans and actions, all in running tempo. Everything that is done, no matter where, is served up to us piping hot a moment later wherever we may happen to be, as though it were going on in the same town, almost in the same room. In short, we live in a world made great and small at once by the conquest of space.

Similarly, it was one thing to take the brave harmonies, the colours, the worlds of heat and energy, the physics and chemistry of an earlier day with their far-ranging influence, naively and innocently as the only things that mattered in the practical business of life. But it is quite another to know, as scientists first and then as laymen, that these things are only an infinitesimal part of the countless forces flashing through the immensity of the cosmos, ourselves living in their radiant energy and making use of it—factors in the form of rays, waves, quanta perpetually changing into sound, heat and light, into invisible acoustic and optical phantoms which can pierce and see through every cloud, every barrier, and put us in touch with hitherto unsuspected correspondences in the universe. We now know that the "solid matter" we come up against is nothing less than a mask, a continual disguising of energy, inaccessible to us in its very nature and hiding from us all the mysterious electric, magnetic, radioactive and other entities into which the cosmos, regarded as matter, has now been resolved; and that our poor intelligence can understand so little of this *occultation of energy* that we can only express the processes by which we are surrounded and in which we live, in formulae of probability or in terms of spontaneous activity—formulae, moreover, which cannot even be reduced to a common denominator (the corpuscular theory and the wave-mechanics theory of light being examples). We know, further, that infinity and eternity no longer exist in the archaic or patriarchal sense in which we have always, despite Kant, spoken of them and been accustomed to imagine them, but rather as a whole series of equally legitimate ways of conceiving the familiar world of our environment, so much so that if ever we want to get a little closer to or behind the material aspect of its secrets we have, in our calculations, to make use of several independent concepts at once. In short, we know that the apparent certainties turn somersaults in all directions the moment we try to seize hold of the phenomenal world. At the same time, this knowledge has given the phenomenal world so completely into our power that there is scarcely a distance in it, scarcely any independent, inviolable sphere of matter, sound or colour whose proper boundaries we cannot overstep.

A construction of this kind, containing no insurmountable barriers, no discrete fields of perception and action, and ultimately lacking the foundation of the old matter *in extenso* which we thought so solid and used to regard as at least the world's body, has in very truth become something infinitely mysterious, something that has shrunk to a little ball while yet outwardly retaining its size, something that eludes our thought and loses itself in unguessed depths and a thousand shifting transformations. It has turned into something strangely ambiguous, the material or conditional network of which seems plastic and understandable enough *in practice* through the modification of the factors at work in it, while *in theory* its body—matter—has grown as it were transparent, a sort of curtain through which there shines the Transcendence lying immanent within. We still speak of the force of gravity, of the affinity of elements, we speak of entelechies which unfold biologically in organic matter; we know of collective, purely biological and psychological forces of tremendous chemical valency, so to speak, on this new and newly conquered

earth of ours. But are we really aware—though probably men of
deeper vision have seen it long since—that we are only juggling
with words, playing with powers and agencies which, in their
very nature, are sealed to our understanding, using a kind of
mental shorthand in order, so we think, to explain things, but
behind whose symbols there lurks only our ignorance and,
always, everywhere present, that same Transcendence? Faced
with this Transcendence we have, in the last analysis, not only
to gain practical and minute control of the network of material
conditions in which its functions, but we have also to look upon
it as active, ultimately indeed as the one active and spontaneous
thing that exists. So doing, we shall be able, perhaps, to order
our picture of the world in accordance with it, and, in the spiritual
sense, acquire that bold frame of mind to which we must cling
fast if we are to find our bearings anew and overcome the prevailing Nihilism of our time—that same Nihilism which is the
deep-seated cause, as greater minds have already realized, of the
historical catastrophe which we of the West, and particularly
we Europeans, have brought upon the world. It is as imperative
for us to overcome this Nihilism as it is to overcome our old
historico-sociological conceptions regarding the possible outward
patterns of human life, which were rooted in the now obsolete
spatial conditions. We have acted on these conceptions right
up to the present as though we were still living on the old earth
—with the result that, with this last war, we have laid our life
on this world as we have known it hitherto, finally in ruins.   .

*   *   *   * .   *

Let us make a tentative sketch of this vanished pattern of
human life, showing just how we have destroyed it and what this
destruction means, speaking purely objectively at first.

For more than five thousand years, ever since the first great
civilizations of Egypt, Babylonia, Northern India and China,
the recorded life of man has been organized in historical groups
widely differing from one another politically, economically and
spiritually. For the first few thousand years they were stable,
non-expanding structures situated for the most part on the banks
of navigable rivers. Owing to the irruptions of the equestrian
tribes about 1200 B.C. these aggregates were, in the East, converted into large-scale organisms which, in the case of China,
actually underwent territorial expansion at certain times. But

on the whole, partly for geographical reasons and partly for reasons connected with their psychological structure, they remained static, without any history capable of profoundly modifying their innermost nature, subject only to the formative processes of alteration and repetition taking place within their own being. In the West, on the other hand, that is to say, west of the Hindokush, what we call "history" emerged with the invasion of the equestrian tribes—that crystallization of States, kingdoms, and spheres of culture whose mutually alien modes of life oscillated between conquest, subjugation and destruction. Though they knew a certain interchange and cross-fertilization they nevertheless found themselves, from 1200 B.C. to A.D. 1800— a period of 3000 years, therefore—in a state of continual rivalry which in the last resort could always be decided by war and which aspired to all-embracing, but never completed, Empires. In the fruitless struggle to build them, however, this rivalry resulted in never-ending mass-upheavals and new power-groupings with new cultural contents. This grandiose interplay of forces has cast such a spell over men's minds that Ranke and his successors, closing their eyes to the whole Eastern panorama with its very different character, have called it alone "history". It seemed to debouch into two main channels following the collapse of the last attempts by the Romans, Arabs and Franco-Germans to establish universal Empires, namely, a tremendous territorial conquest by Europe and, in Europe itself as promoter of this conquest, a self-regulating balance of the great political and economic bodies existing within it—a system lately character-ized in so singular fashion by England as the "Balance of Europe", as though the whole thing had been invented apparently for her benefit. As certainly as Great Britain tipped the scales very strongly and, because militarily unassailable, enjoyed the usufruct of this Balance almost without cost to herself, above all taking full advantage of it to overrun the earth and build up her Empire, it is equally certain that this system was the only mode of tolerably peaceful association for the expanding military and economic Power-States which composed this world-conquering Europe. After the disintegration of the European kingdoms and the dis-appearance of their sanctions it was, indeed, the only thinkable form that such a system of European States could possibly take in their efforts to establish certain conventions of peace and war grounded in international law. For, despite having been born of the equestrian spirit and thus being furnished with an insatiable and wolfish hunger, they did at least make sporadic attempts to bring about a general settlement. The Balance of Europe was the last type of external political structure to offer Europe and the world tolerable conditions of peace right up to the end of the Nineteenth Century.

We shall be speaking later of the political and economic shifts of emphasis and the complex spiritual changes by which this system was undermined after the final third of the Nineteenth Century. Its roots atrophied. Consequently a new, not merely European but a wholly novel world-order had to be discovered.

In history we can only see external conditions together with the possibilities latent in them, and the exploitation of these possibilities by spontaneous acts. What happens is contingent; it is the fulfilment of but *one* of the numerous possibilities inherent in a framework so constituted.

From this point of view, therefore, it would seem that in the situation existing before the first World War the old system of a balanced Europe could, since it was manifestly obsolete, have been transformed into a balance of great imperial world-bodies and hence into a World-balance. To do this, however, it would have been necessary to fit one of those economically expanding, highly unstable States, namely Germany, whose weight was constantly changing owing to the folly of her rulers and who, moreover, regarded herself imperially as a "Have-not" Power, into a new system of Great Powers with equal rights. The opportunity was missed, no matter whose the blame. The first World War was the result.

Historical opportunities being, like all opportunities, unique and, once missed, giving rise to a wholly new configuration under the stress of subsequent events, there was at this juncture, therefore, only one thing possible: the creation of something entirely novel. There followed the attempt to bring together, through some kind of international organization, the various States of the world on a basis of (formally at least) very considerable equality. But owing to the isolationist policy of America and also, for some time, of Russia, and owing further to its own peculiar structure which failed to take sufficient account of the balance of power, the attempt checkmated any effective results if it did not actually aggravate the decisions necessary for this. Consequently only an elaborate paper negotiation was possible on all the vital questions, and the attempt simply led to a sort of side-show behind the trappings of which the old game of power-politics continued, a little more obscured, a little more variegated by being decked out in public discussions which might, perhaps, take the edge off the recurrent crises but could not in practice prevent them.

Despite which, even on this basis a tolerable grouping of States might have evolved politically, composed of the still independent competitive Great Powers, especially after the admission of Germany when, following the breakdown of the Disarmament Conference, her right to arm could no longer disputed in fact and the bonds of war-guilt were struck from her, if only—well, we all know how the violent feeling of resentment and the grave economic situation were exploited by the unscrupulous new rulers who came to the top in Germany, and what happened.

Now that, thanks to the seizure of Czechoslovakia and the assault on Poland, to whom England had pledged her word, the Second World War has broken out in so frivolous a manner—a war which, despite its (apparently) specific causes must, like all great wars to-day, necessarily become global—there is no going back to the old forms. This war, which has been cried up in certain quarters on account of its "total" nature as the inevitable event of the future, has become so total, indeed—that is to say, so destructive of the continued existence of the nations it has engulfed, and of their whole cultural heritage accumulated with such pains through the centuries; it has proved so over-whelmingly that a major war these days cannot possibly be confined, in our diminished contemporary world, to a few big States only, and that its rage halts at nothing, not even at those things most worth safeguarding, things which nearly all previous wars have held inviolable ever since the age of primitive barbarism; further, the horrible engines at its disposal have made it so utterly different from the wars of the past, no longer a "war" at all but a systematic process of mutual annihilation carried on with the utmost refinement, in very truth a universal butchery masquerading in war's clothing; it has demonstrated at the same time that, given this mass-carnage and the limited alternatives on an earth grown so small from the global point of view, only *two* combatants can possibly survive in the end to struggle for world-supremacy: it has shown all this and the nature of modern warfare as mass-suicide so clearly, I say, that something entirely novel, a completely different kind of world-organization such as has never existed before, must surely result. This world-organization cannot yet be foreseen in all its details. It will pass through many intermediate stages and will only reach its final form very slowly. But the basic principle of it can be clearly discerned in the light of the conditions which must be mastered, and from the alternatives with which we are obviously confronted on so shrunken an earth. It can only be this: to compose these alternatives in such a way that, as far as is humanly possible, no new "war", no new mass-murder—which, with the instruments then to be expected, would necessarily attain prodigiously destructive dimensions quite inconceivable even by our standards, and would probably mean the obliteration of whole peoples—shall ever break loose again. And this means that all forms of power-politics, since these, as Clausewitz might say, carry war in themselves as the continuation of statecraft by other means, must be exterminated at the root. This in its turn means that the principle of open rivalry, which has long been eliminated over a wide field of economic life and replaced by the syndicate principle, will have to vanish from the stage of foreign policy as well, and that World-syndicates, made up of a few paramount Great Powers and in one form or another comprising or annexing the lesser ones, will arbitrate on the great world-questions.

Before approaching any of the vital problems of to-day we must recognize first and foremost that this is the irreversible result of anybody having been frivolous and blind enough to unleash total war on this shrunken earth, thus threatening and blighting the lives of all its inhabitants to the very fibres of their being—the most irresponsible licence history has ever witnessed. By this act and the now inevitable consequences of it the history of the world has been changed for ever. The old system based on the free competition of large and small, relatively loosely-knit contiguous States, and the old "history" inaugurated by the equestrian tribes 1200 years before Christ, are at an end.

Well may we regret much of what must now sink from sight. I confess that I am one of those who do regret it. For in a certain respect these endless struggles between the various power-groupings did help us to keep, if only in a crude and elementary way, a sense of value. Such struggles prepare the ground for a true "agony" as the Greeks once meant it; they beget initiative, sacrifice, courage. This has been said a thousand times and it has been proved if not a thousand times then at least a hundred times right. The loss, the unquestioning effusion of the finest blood of manhood in voluntary sacrifice is bitter indeed for those large portions of the earth which will in fact be drawn into the mass-politics of the future, if not for those excluded by it. One of the prime tasks of the coming era must be somehow to make up for this loss suffered by nations which have hitherto played a leading role politically or spiritually, by giving them opportunities for nobler forms of self-sacrifice.

For far more will pass away than merely the outward pattern of human life as we have known it, which found expression in the stresses and strains of power-politics and had its centre of gravity so long in the West, above all in the one-time leadership of Europe. The instinct for power will remain the same as when this instinct sought an outlet in the balance or expansion of Great Powers. Nature cannot be changed. But in the age of mass-politics this instinct will largely become the monopoly of a very few Power-colossi of global proportions, barely five in number, who will uphold the political World-syndicate. And their power-instinct, their inevitable rivalries among themselves will have to be curbed by something very different from the checks we have tried to put upon the power-drive of individual States so far,— that is, by ideal or extremely real forces, if the breakdown of such a Syndicate and its backsliding into war are not to bring about something perilously akin to a decline of the West, indeed, of the world.

That is to say: just as the once free States are now more or less dependent on these colossi and are thus in reality no longer sovereign States in the old sense, no longer power-formations with their own freedom of action, but, viewed objectively, are international authorities controlled *de facto* or *de jure* and them-selves exercising control to a greater or lesser degree—so the syndicated "world-mammoths" will have to accept a common basis of ideals and adhere to its principles unreservedly and in good faith, both for the sake of world-administration and also to ensure that the smaller States follow suit, and above all for the sake of their relations with one another. Quite apart from this, however, their mutual interests, assuredly very strong, will tend to knit this Syndicate, like any other, more closely together. But should the mammoths fail in these measures and the bloc collapse, a third World War will inevitably break out with all its incalculable consequences, one of which would in any case be the creation of a new World Syndicate on such ruins of human life as still remained. No matter what course history takes, the old, freely competitive sovereign State with its assemblage of neighbouring power-formations great and small, has reached the end of its tether, at least as a political archetype.

Already in 1914, with the first clash on a global scale in this new, diminished world of technology, history had reduced the sovereign State to absurdity, so that even then it was only a mask for mass-formations of a totally different order. And now, with the second clash whose temporary end we have reached, history has laid it bare in all its impossible weakness. The State as an independent entity, even the small Power-State, will no longer survive in this form as the dominant type of political system, whether this happens now or is occasioned by another and still more appalling catastrophe.

Historically speaking, however, nothing very remarkable will have happened. For it was in itself quite fantastic, something that was only made possible by the absence of equivalent countertensions outside Europe, that for the last five hundred years we Europeans have, for reasons of expediency in the Fifteenth, Sixteenth and Seventeenth Centuries, then, from 1800 on (thanks to the pernicious State-fantasies of Hegel) as a matter of principle, and now, backed by the tendentious so-called "Historical School" of Ranke, quite consciously and deliberately, placed the sovereign State completely outside the moral sphere, in other words, beyond any effective control of its actions. This was the cardinal sin which the West committed against itself. It was a sin that cost it dear, since in this way the whole body-politic which, all through the Middle Ages, had been under the sanction of the Church—the individual ordering his life, his happiness, his fortune, his spiritual being by this and this alone—became something quite arbitrary, and, although allowing itself outwardly at least to be forced by the humanitarian ideals of the Eighteenth Century into certain moulds that showed some respect for the human decencies, later threw aside not only these moulds but also, appealing to "National interest", all respect whatsoever for decency and honour—particularly when this latter word was in everbody's mouth. Finally the whole *raison d'être* of a-moral State-action with its plausible self-justifications collapsed, since its own actions, as the present war and present breakdown abundantly show, inevitably brought about the end of all autarky based on power alone.

The modern State, which will in future be adjusted first and foremost to the norms of ordinary decent behaviour, will not, as I shall show in the sequel, lose appreciably in its inner administrative significance but only in that external sovereignty—and this applies to great and small States alike—which has been imputed to it ever since the time of Bodin. This loss will, however, favour the growth partly of overlapping international structures standing outside Statehood as understood hitherto, partly of new aggregates, really political in character, superior to the State and virtually depriving it of all concern with power-politics. We shall witness an epoch altogether novel in its political configuration, as different from the Europe of the Fifteenth Century and after as this was from the mediaevalism that preceded it—which was, in fact, anterior to Statehood as such.

So transformed, the body-politic will find room for a new kind of social and economic structure, and a new world of technology and culture. All this will be dealt with later and at length; I am only mentioning it here.

As regards the change in the structure of society, the masses will have altogether more weight than has been the case so far, except in Bolshevist Russia or under National Socialism with its demagogy and techniques of corruption, which could only keep its hold on the masses by pandering more and more to their material and emotional greed. To the extent that the new world will nowhere countenance privilege or the sanctity of big holdings, and will have as its guiding motive the security of the masses, their life, work, and wherever possible their welfare, by means of large-scale planning, it will be "socialist" in a variously watered-down sense, taking the word at its broadest. With the gradual trend towards the kind of mass-organization which will be inevitable in the world of the future, government will be impossible, as all mass-organizations have found, without a ruling class or a permanent élite of leadership. Like all societies this too will be marked by a synthesis—for there can be no question of separating them in the future—of the intellectual and spiritual qualities of its ruling class and the innate strength, the emotional stamina, of its substrata as represented by the masses, who will now be very influential. In this way it will discover its characteristic cultural physiognomy. But whatever this physiognomy looks like it will always and everywhere result in the formation of a new *average type*, and there will always be an élite which, to the extent that it is effective in practice, will be the quintessence, the sublimation, the epitome of this average type. So that the question is at once: what sort of human being will set the tone in the new world of the future, this diminished earth of ours?

Whatever he proves to be he will certainly be conditioned very largely by his history and culture, above all by the technological considerations already stressed. But at the same time and within these limits, the form he will assume will be the result of *our* initiative, *our* will, and *our* undrestanding of the depths which we unlock in ourselves and from which the new man will emerge.

If we desire men of a noble stamp we must realize that these depths in ourselves are the background, the matrix of all the human coining that history ever does, and as such can only be transcendental in nature. Once more they open out before us, shadowily, in the abysses of the fearful transition-period we are now going through. As for myself, I can only indicate, hint at them fragmentarily. Fragmentarily also because, from a "metalogical" point of view they cannot be pressed into the service of any system, and, from a logical one, insofar as they replace the old myths, they are fundamentally contradictory. To reduce them to reasonable order will be the purpose of the last section of this book. It is not to be regarded as a vademecum, rather as a sort of spiritual injection which may stimulate us to further enquiry and to examine our experiences in the full light of consciousness.

It is preceded by the main bulk of the book—a "farewell to history" as we have known it, a farewell taken mainly on sociological and historical considerations but intended in an equally transcendental sense, since it offers a survey of immediate data of experience in historical form. This, as an expression of Transcendence, may well prove more adequate to our understanding than the final section. An historical presentation is also necessary and important because, in the first place, "the new" will not simply drop into our laps but will somehow have to use "the old" as building-material, and because, in the second place, turning our gaze within, we discern a question that is vitally important for our new spiritual orientation: what is the significance of "the old" for us to-day, who have lived in its spirit up to the first World War and—at least over wide portions of the earth—to all intents and purposes right up to the present? In what sort of relationship does "the new" stand to "the old", and in particular what does the Nineteenth Century mean to us, which, in many ways, even though it witnessed the breakdown of all previous history, was also the time of its fulfilment? In what proportions are outworn and outmoded traditions mingled in it, like portents, with the emergent Nihilism in which we now live? But the Nineteenth Century itself can only be understood in the light of the 800 years which led up to it from A.D. 1000, when the West came to spiritual consciousness. This period corresponds in a sense to the three centuries through which Greece passed from the time of Homer to the Nihilism of the Sophists, that is, from 750 B.C. to about 430 B.C. In these 800 years, when the West rose once more to historical leadership, we shall only concern ourselves firstly with the essential features of Western development, the manner in which it evolved from an initial situation of unparalleled complexity, full of spiritual paradoxes, of rigid theological and philosophical dogmas, and then attained a spiritual freedom which enabled man to break through to an age-old understanding of his essential *human being*—something completely free of dogma—and secondly with the break-through itself, which may yet prove to be a torch gone on ahead of us lighting the way to a deeper discovery of ourselves.

So that thematically the work is divided as follows:

1. Farewell to History.
   (a) The Nature of the West and Personal "Breaks-through" to the Non-dogmatic Deeper Level of Being (A.D. 1000–1800).
   (b) The Dynamics of the Nineteenth Century and the Road to Nihilism.
   (c) The Contemporary Situation: Can Nihilism be overcome?
2. Intimations of Transcendence.

CHAPTER I

THE UNIQUENESS OF THE WEST

1. *The Awakening into Dogma. The Manner of Western Dynamism*

What does history tell us of the historical and sociological peculiarities of the West and its development, which I have described elsewhere in considerable detail?

A small peninsula of Eurasia stands to-day, it would seem, together with all the glories it has brought forth, in the midst of a crisis similar to the one in which its still smaller spur Greece, with its equally multifarious cultures, once stood after the great military decisions fought out in the Mediterranean Basin, namely, the Peloponnesian War, the Persian and Punic Wars and the later crises which made Macedonia and then Rome the dominant factors in that area—such would seem to be the future picture, as seen within the global frame of the present, of the Europe which once ruled the world and history. It shows us a forlorn, diminutive particle threatened, after its fall from power, with the fate of pumping its "culture" into others, as was the case with the Graeculi. The picture is by no means wholly unjust and yet the comparison is deceptive if we want to see the peculiar nature of Europe's past, its economic role in world politics and its spiritual role in history, in true perspective and also recognize the fundamental conditions for its role in the future.

About the far-reaching effects of the external factors which made Europe with its two capitalist nuclei, England and Germany, the industrial centre of the world second only to the United States; its position of economic dominance woven out of the imperialisms of England, France, Italy, Belgium and Holland all supplying the world with industrial goods and capital; the position of Germany on whom, as the centre of Europe's economic integration, the emphasis of world supply fell, above all in respect of machine tools and products dependent on science and highly skilled labour—about this planetary power-position occupied by Europe we shall speak later. It has recently been regarded as

1

something ephemeral, but in reality it is based on the strongest forces of endurance and recuperation; and neither in the Mediterranean position of Greece at any time in the classical period nor in the whole history of the world does it possess a parallel. For the moment, however, we are interested only in the qualities of will and the spiritual and mental attributes which led to this dominance, and their future.

The part Europe has played in world politics by reason of her will and spirit springs from her dynamism. Thanks to this unique dynamism she has been mistress of the earth ever since A.D. 1500 and has made it dependent on her—something that Greece was never able to do in the small Mediterranean area. She has initiated a process of emigration which has europeanized two continents and the southern portion of a third. On these foundations she has not only built up the world capitalism already mentioned; she has created at the same time that which can best be called "The Western World", a veritable global structure not so easy to dissipate at a breath. For to this Western World there belong, in the sense that an originally European human type holds sway there and forms, with certain psychic modulations, a spiritual territory more or less congruent with that of Europe, North and South America, Australia and South Africa as well. But not, be it noted, Hither Asia and the Russian territories of the "white man". For not only does Hither Asia, the region primarily of the Arabs, Persians and Turks, not belong to the Western World, but neither does Russia despite many spiritual, economic and power-political ties with it. They are worlds of a completely different spirit. They have not the dynamism of Europe which is, indeed, nothing but a symptom of her peculiar spiritual and psychic essence; and this in its turn has become the source of the westernization of the whole world.

Europe is alone in having witnessed, even before the final complete manifestation of her dynamism, the spectacle of a graduated series of social structures only to be understood in relation to this dynamism of hers—a gradation which ultimately led to the eruption of capitalism all over the world and the technology serving it. After the far-spreading conquests of the Arabs and the assimilation of portions of the preceding classical culture the "white world" of Hither Asia and North Africa remained fixed, like India and China, in a unique social form well-nigh unalterable even to-day for all practical purposes and extremely conservative as regards European influences, immobilized in its sheikdoms and sultanates. Allowing for certain differences an analogy is to be found in the world of Mediterranean antiquity which, even under the Roman Empire, never discarded the basic structural forms of its metropolitan, urban and municipal constitution. And although she appears to have passed through so many convulsions Russia, until the advent of Bolshevism, has in reality always been an immense, primitive peasant country, almost untouched, labouring under various forms of tyranny and exploitation and, latterly, with sprinklings of industry, but without any gradual development deriving from her own self.

Such gradual development above all of social form, an innate process of crisis-like transformation until in the end an expanding capitalism emerges—this is what constitutes Europe's uniqueness in so far as her nature has been tentatively assessed here. This gradual process has been concocted into all sorts of general theories of economic stages, the view being strictly confined to Europe, however. In general there are no economic "stages" apart from those which result from civilization adapting itself to newly invented technical procedures. But there does exist in Europe this absolutely unique conversion of the money economies and the latifundia surviving from ancient times, into the political and economic complex of feudalism, with its characteristic diversity of great and small structures based on serfdom and developed partly through barter and partly through the medium of monetary exchange. There is also the growth of cities within this feudal net, cities quite peculiar to Europe in that all are given over exclusively to crafts or trades, as such constituting small economic units on their own; the modification or permeation of feudalism by city-economies originating in the cities themselves and sustained by the stream of currency; the rise of the modern States, mass-formations equipped with standing armies and officials, all struggling for a unity over and above the small units; and finally the emergence of capitalism as foreshadowed in the cities and then fostered outright in the States, with its well-known stages and consequences which were ultimately to transform the world.

Each of these phases which together act like a series of superimposed set-pieces in a drama, carries with it not merely a new spiritual stage—there also correspond to it, continually, new human types which stamp the whole scene. And not only successively, so that the artisan follows the knight, the feudal courtier the ártisan and the capitalist entrepreneur or worker the feudal courtier, but in such a way that an entirely new world of human types comes into being each time. Beside the knight the obdurately proud peasant, thirsting for liberty although a serf, waging a ˙ stubborn warfare shoulder to shoulder with the emergent artisan in an attempt to free himself from feudal overlordship; beside the court noble another peasant—La Bruyere has described him—ground down into complete passivity; or an artisan formerly his own master but now sunk to a mere bourgeois; the brave mercantilism of a precapitalist age cheek by jowl with an aristocracy; and an educated class ranging from the priest through the professor, now rapidly gaining in importance, to the learned official. And so on—a great diversity of worlds not merely behind one another but always side by side in the same period, continually changing through the centuries with kaleidoscopic effect. No other region of the earth knows anything of the kind. Nor does any other know the volcanic outburst of energy which, starting from a single area, overspread half the earth and not only conquered other peoples and countries but irresistibly transformed them by settlement.

What are the causes of this dynamism and its diversity? They lie in the paradoxical manner in which history shaped the spiritual beginnings of the West. Young peoples, the Germanic and Romanic tribes to be, were flooded through by an older and superior intellectuality, and also by a faith which, properly understood, was explosive in the highest degree. Both these had been elaborated to the limits of speculation and were already encrusted with dogmas of the most hair-splitting kind when they became the spiritual nutriment of the young emergent peoples. The latter assimilated the faith on account of the immense superiority of its values. And as soon as they themselves started inwardly to thrive on it, it in its turn was flooded through by fresh juices the more greedily it was sucked up, was rejuvenated and yet remained old. History had thereby placed the West at the very *beginning* of its development in a situation which had only come at the *end* of other epochs as, for instance, of the classical epoch preceding it; the situation of being immediately and initially implicated in the spider-spinnings of an over-intellectualized world which imposed casuistic laws, rules and taboos of its own. The result was that in the West the mythopoetic faculty with which other periods had begun, only shaping their myths anew right at the end or throwing them off completely, perished as in an utterly alien spiritual element.

It was a situation in which mankind was imbued with a code of ethics that had once been taken rigorously enough but was only very laxly observed by the type of man who had evolved in the meantime. Such an ethos, other-worldly in its highest ideals, demanded for its attainment a deflection of the most vital instincts. A deflection of this kind was inevitable if the ethos was to be taken seriously by the new and powerful life-forces at the moment of the West's spiritual awakening. And this very deflection is the underlying cause of Europe's dynamism, the key to its unique nature. From the tremendous explosion of the Crusades and the rigorous new monasticism onwards we can as little understand the repeated spiritual explosions to which Europe has borne witness ever since—that is, since roughly A.D. 1000—or its proneness to revolutions for idealistic rather than merely material ends, as we can understand the sequence of scientific and technical explosions or indeed the irruption of European capitalism into the world at large, unless we proceed from this deflection of the most vital forces. Everywhere accompanying this deflection we can discern the overspill of powers which had been voluntarily taken in hand and guided in a certain direction, powers which with other peoples were left to ebb away peacefully and impartially, discharging themselves into Nature and thus into the slow cyclic rhythm of historical occurrence.

In Europe, on the other hand, everything was tense, concentrated, charged, seeking the path either of fundamental change within or of explosive action without. The first great inner tensions of the West between the Church, which had acquired a certain piety despite its preoccupations with power, and the Emperors, to whom the Church appeared almost as a force of nature, worldly for all its spirituality; the further tensions between the ecclesiastically consecrated feudal knights and the peasants and cities; the struggles for freedom on the part of the latter two with the nobility and the Princes—successful in Italy and terminating in the north with the territorial supremacy of the State; all these tensions and polarities between freedom and unfreedom which with their powerful undercurrents have constantly shaken Europe and characterize her political being, and lastly the yawning disparities between the privileged and the unprivileged ending in conscious revolution—grew out of and flourished on the hot-bed of that original paradoxical antithesis between the homogeneity of straightforward youthful instinct and the schismatic and ascetic tendencies that later supervened.

Christianity and its derivates were assimilated by other young peoples contemporaneously with the West, chiefly by the Arabic and Russian spheres of culture. The Islamic derivate that gave shape to the Arab world, however, was in itself so adapted to reality and allowed all instinctual life such free play that, precisely because of this adaptation and the cults that accompanied it, nothing could evolve but the exact opposite of dynamism, namely the most powerful traditionalism that exists outside the cultures of the Far East, one that maintains its continuity unbroken even to-day. For Russia, on the other hand, the case was again very different after her assimilation of Byzantine Christianity. She remained anti-dynamic because virtually only ritual superstition and Christian magism were taken over in the beginning; hence it was only on single sections of the people that piety shed its radiance to any depth. The great masses remained a gigantic body sporadically shot through with deeper veins of Christianity, but on the whole and in all essentials they kept their aboriginality almost untouched, their natural paganism.

And to complete the tensions of the West and all the schisms that resulted, pagan antiquity, with its high philosophical speculation, its myths which still went to the heart of reality even in classical Christendom, its smiling acceptance of life and its earthly orientation, was absorbed by the Arab world as a dynamic agent that might loosen the doctrinal crusts gradually forming on Islam, and was soon incapsulated. But when Russia assimilated Christianity pagan antiquity gave her nothing more profound than certain classical modes of expression, sculptural and architectonic, strongly modified; nothing basically anti-Christian, nothing markedly different from the Christian solutions of the eternal problems of life. The West, on the other hand, while absorbing Christian antiquity, also drank in great draughts of the pagan antiquity that had permeated the latter in the form of syncretism ever since the end of ancient Rome. Like Christianity, pagan antiquity too became authoritative and, again like Christianity, the absolute authority. The more the men of the West understood it and the more they came to know of it chiefly through Byzantium, the more there grew up, side by side with the deflected instinctual life that came from Christianity and the spiritual attitude pertaining to it, a completely different configuration of instinct and spirit, one that went far beyond the customary outward acceptance of ancient myths and archaic forms of speech—there grew up, in fact, *a second world*, in which people lived and in which they were inclined to seek refuge if they wanted to free themselves from the distorting tendencies of Christianity. This and this alone is the cause, spiritually speaking, of the never-ending succession of classical Renaissances which accompany the history of the West. This is also why, having regard to the original constellation of events whose significance grew all the stronger with each recrudescence of antiquity, we must speak of an increasing *dichotomy* in the soul of the West: a turning to the Beyond that springs from Christianity and a delight in the Here and Now that is nurtured by the classical world. Not to mention the tensions which Christianity itself had produced, an over-abundance of conflicting and collaborating forces in which the West was involved the more forcibly with every development, until its position became unique.

Assuming that man, as regards his instinctual and psychic structure, is and has always been built up of many layers under the stress of the various forces that rule him, this inner stratification must needs amount to something extreme in the European; he must be a field for countless operations, a veritable whirlpool of forces, in which every great man of the past, every man who lived life to the full saw himself implicated if he wanted to live from the depths of his nature, take a stand and express himself. If, quietly safeguarding his innermost soul, he did not seek refuge in a superficial compartmentation of mind, a harmless versatility, where all the numerous alphabets he had in him, as it were, lay peacefully side by side each speaking its own language (and this was very often the only way out of the dilemma)—he then in very truth found himself shut in all round by blank walls, by an array of dogmas built up in him through his European origin and its history, theological, philosophical, speculative dogmas, classical dogmas that bid fair to offer freedom but proved to be rigid in their embrace—all of which he had to clear to one side or burst asunder so as to come to the core of existence, the original source of Being which lies behind all dogmatism and is there for the grasping; so as to contemplate it untrammelled in thought and express it in symbols or howsoever he wished.

One thing came to his aid. Ever since its appropriation of Christianity in a fit of youthful enthusiasm Europe had been shot through with Absolutes like no other culture-area in the world. Apart from Buddhism and Yogaism, both very different, there is no great world religion of such extreme absolutism as Christianity taken at its face value. And its absolutism streams like that of no other religion into the earthly side of existence, shaping our life, making personal demands of a very high order, thus rousing the mountain-moving energies of the soul that thirsts for the Absolute. All the other absolutist cosmogonies that streamed in upon the European and activated him, were in their turn galvanized into activity so that their absolutism awoke from its long slumber in the midst of Being. The significance of this is clear: since the man of great spiritual stature, standing as he did in this medley of newly awakened absolutist dogmas, could only find an independent way out by *himself* breaking through into depths of Being as yet undogmatized, nearly all the great men of the West were confronted with this question of a personal breakthrough as soon as Europe achieved spiritual independence. There is a spiritual history of Europe in terms of dogma. But what her great men saw in absolute values that were non-dogmatic, what the values were that they clung to and how they understood or modified them, *that* is Europe's real spiritual history. And that, too, is the reason—which is still being borne in on us—why Europe, when it gave up the search not only for the dogmatic Absolute but for the non-dogmatic as well, collapsed during the Nineteenth Century and, for all its material wealth, sank into the arms of a long process of Nihilism which was to dissipate its soul's harmonies and utterly destroy the mighty music of its deepest being.

We shall have to indicate the sort of break-through achieved by certain representative Great Europeans during the eight centuries of vital European history if we are to find the signposts already mentioned and, groping our way out of the spiritual nihilism of our time, win to a new orientation, a new and deep-seated apprehension of Being. Starting with the period when the dynamics of history and sociology effectively conditioned the material and spiritual problems of the present, we shall have to take these problems into account also. It is necessary, however, to see them as being overshadowed at the outset by a question which is supremely important at least for us Germans to-day: the imperishability of the soul's past experience which, let us hope, is capable of recapture. This question, therefore, will undergo a comparatively broad analysis.

We can understand without difficulty why the road leading Europe out of her tradition-ridden beginnings to an untram-melled view of life was longer by so many centuries than that of Greece. It was because of the presence at her cradle of certain fixed orthodoxies which speculation had squeezed spiritually dry, whereas the Greeks, awakening in freedom, found themselves wrapped in a dense cloud of mythical interpretations of Being which, either in part or as a whole, were extremely protean; a cloud that was to become still denser before it was irradiated by enlightened consciousness, after which, however, it fell an easy prey to the whirlwind of philosophical, rationalist and sophist speculation. But in Europe every step from the path of dogmatism was impeded not only inwardly (despite the incentives of youthful self-interpretation); outwardly as well, dogmatic and ecclesiastical barriers being almost everywhere, it was extremely dangerous for a very long time, since each step was threatened by excom-munication and proscription and ultimately even by inquisition and death. Courage was demanded or, as was mostly the case in the earlier periods, the apparently harmless interest in pagan antiquity—tolerated by the Church because the vision it afforded into the depths of the soul had been assimilated and sublimated by her own theologians—if the individual was to come into his own and express his individuality.

And the demonstration of an Absolute immediately appre-hended, of some Ultimate Being—a task which, in classical Greece, could only be undertaken by the greatest individuals and thus, accepted without question, woven into the fabric of the age—was bound to come about almost invisibly in Europe, at the hands of individuals inwardly isolated from each other by the gulf of current opinion. These spiritually lonely great men stand there like light-houses, pointing out the path we seek.

It is only with them, and only with the greatest and most notable of them, that we shall concern ourselves.

2. *The Homeric Period of Europe (A.D. 1000–1250)*

In the first period, which saw the awakening and growth of the substance and human content of Christianity, the rise of the monastic orders such as the Benedictines and the Cistercians and later the Franciscans and the Dominicans, the expansion of the ecclesiastically consecrated chivalric orders following the Crusades, the period that one reckons roughly from A.D. 1000 to 1250, there was unfolded, running parallel and supporting all this, a process of strongly speculative spiritual activity known as Early and High Scholasticism. This activity became, of course, the high point of dogmatism; but on the other hand, apart from the religious impulses which culminated in Gothic art and sagas like Parsifal, it settled down into an attitude of impartiality, an attitude that was even critical of the Church. Impartial as in the case of the Troubadours and in the poetry of the wandering monks, for instance. Critical as in the sphere of poetry exemplified by Gottfried's *Tristan*—not to speak of the various heresies and such-like—so that the pagan, pre-ecclesiastical view of life, the epic and tragic vision comes once more into the ascendant, certain peaks of which are caught by the poets who, in Germany, paint for us—albeit in colours that are almost too vivid—the splendours and terrors of the *Nibelungenlied*.

But all this, like many more of the things born or reborn, so to speak, of "the Mothers", remains naïve, naïve as everything was naïve in the Homeric age of Greece: probing, guessing, but bearing in itself no fully conscious, independent, universal interpretation of existence. Magnificent as the achievements of this period are, significant as many of its life-symbols have remained for us, we shall find very few signposts in it pointing a way out of our distress and our questioning. Our only guides, in fact, are the alone-standing individuals we encounter, who chart the way for us.

CHAPTER II

THE LOOSENING OF DOGMA AND THE BREAK-THROUGH INTO THE DEPTHS[1]

1. *Dante*

This begins in a highly remarkable, almost paradoxical manner in Italy, with the end of the Thirteenth Century already touched by the dawning Renaissance, and with the loneliest of all the prophets of the West—Dante. In a paradoxical manner for, in conscious striving and formidable artistic ability, Dante is the last great architect, and the genius of his imagination the last great bastion, of the one supreme Christian conception of Being which was dogmatic down to the minutest details of speculation. One can, if one likes, find the main burden of the medieval thought of the three preceding centuries reflected in him, just as one can find in him the last sublimations of classical dogmatic philosophy in so far as they were spiritually relevant. Nevertheless Dante wished or was compelled willy-nilly to say something quite different, something new, non-medieval; something that from now on was to be eternal in a Western sense. We are not thinking here of that marvellous plasticity which gives us such a realistic vision, sunlit and shadowy, of the medieval "other world" as known to Dante. This objectivity of his makes the reading of the Divine Comedy a rare artistic pleasure despite the often very abstract and scholastic passages which are alien to us, and it could only come from the hand and eye of a Renaissance man, post-medieval and moving freely in the world of antiquity. Nor are we thinking entirely of the peculiar humanism—lit by an earthly yet sublime radiance—that binds the leading figures together, the poet and his patroness Beatrice, Virgil and Sordello the

[1] When Hermann Keyserling in a brilliant but unfortunately hitherto unpublished work throws light on the progress "from thought to the source of creativity" he is illuminating something other than the phenomenon we are concerned to represent, which has its roots in the historical stuff of the West—the phenomenon of the break-through to the immediate transcendental background of life. Transcendence in our sense is on a more earthly plane than the experience communicated by Keyserling.

poet's other guide and companion, and unites them all with the unhappy damned, thus raising the work to a spiritual cosmos of the highest order.   What is crucial for us is that the poet sees this cosmos permeated by divine and darksome powers wholly non-dogmatic in nature, which are directly apprehended by himself as existential data.   He knows about these powers, he incorporates them into the meaning of existence as he understands it in the Christian dogmatic sense, and outwardly builds them into the structure of Christian retribution.   But at the same time he sees them as subsisting in themselves, as simply given by existence, and even when they are bottomlessly disastrous and only redeemed by a few noble streaks he has such a compassion for and feeling of obligation towards their human protagonists that, quite regardless of the fearful punishments of hell, he makes no secret of this fellow-feeling; indeed, he tearfully laments the fate of the condemned and some of the most beautiful passages in his poem are actually about these outcasts, Francesca and Malatesta, Ugolino and others.   It is the first great Western vision of the contradictory, inscrutable transcendental forces underlying existence; a vision steeped in humanism and rising by virtue of its own paradoxicality to a completely different interpretation of life.   Its intriguing originality and directness of approach make the poem a landmark for the West and one of the first signposts into the future.

2.   *Leonardo and Michelangelo*

At the end of the long path through the blossoming Italian Renaissance, which had drawn the curtain of dogma aside and led to a clear vista of the Undogmatic, there stand two contemporaries: Leonardo and Michelangelo.

Leonardo, an insoluble enigma of fascinating complexity, but certainly an example of a man completely free of illusion, gazing into the depths regardless of the consequences.   The masterful scope of his knowing and doing is probably without parallel in his age.   At the same time he is unique in the way he permits the transcendent and immanent forces of Being, as though behind veils, to insinuate themselves into the phenomenal reality he is depicting in the greatest of his pictures, partly by means of landscape suffused with a metaphysical radiance and partly by making such forces the immediate object of his representation, as in the St. Anne, Mary and Jesus or in the Mona Lisa. In the latter the Sphinx-like yet perilously sweet smile of these dark powers is the real theme. It is so concentrated, this smile, that ever since Leonardo symbolized it people have fluttered round it out of some obscure compulsion, drawn by some mysterious force in themselves like unwitting moths.

To speak adequately of Michelangelo from the standpoint appropriate here would demand a whole book. For even in his youth he harboured in himself such depths of world-wide vision, expressing it in his work as in a hall of many mirrors which serve to reveal his meaning though they do not always give it perfect shape. He is a man of extreme complexity that comes quite naturally to him; gazing deeply upon the multitudinous, contradictory symbols of Christian and pagan antiquity gathered about him he sates his fantasy, transforms them and visibly shapes them in such a way that never before or since in history has Primordial Being, with all its conflicts and contradictions, been represented with such overwhelming sculptural and plastic force.

Though regarding himself as a pious Christian, not only in old age but quite early on at the time of the Sonnets, he was still just as much under the spell of Platonism and Neoplatonism and was unfeignedly classical in experience and expression. The classical world of symbols was as real to him as the Christian and its Judaic predecessor. In his heart he wrestles continually with paroxysms of pure daemonic possession occasioned by the physical beauty of Man or Woman. Right into green old age he was in the grip of this most actual, objective daemonism which enthralled him. At the same time he studies, experiences and fashions out of his own resources—always, however, under the aegis of beauty —the multitude of very different powers which sustain life in the as yet unplumbed depths. Himself a devoted son and brother, never wearying in his help of relatives, he is subject in abundant degree to the ties of common humanity which he has expressed so overwhelmingly in his Holy Families and his Madonnas with the Christ-child. These ties are typified most sublimely, however, in that wondrously daemonic feature of the Medici Madonna, which shows the Mother being mysteriously sucked up into, absorbed into the Child. Gentleman and practical fighter for freedom and for the free government of his country, he is aware of the presence of super-virile powers, which disengage in his mind marvellous battling figures, beginning with that transcendent yet earthly incarnation of youthful lordliness, moulded as though by a God's hand, which radiates from the *David*. This virility revealed itself to him in innumerable ways. It begets those tormented masculine groups of wrestling and climbing figures, plastically beautiful in their taut strength. It is bodied forth in massive representations of inexhaustible potency, it concentrates in the personal symbols and portraits; one only has to think of the *Brutus*, of the two sovereigns in the *Tombs of the Medici*, of the tremendous *Moses*, the law-giver, lord of supernatural powers, restraining weak and pitiable humanity with the lightnings of his will—or of the apotheosis of all this in the magisterial Christ of the *Last Judgement*, who is nothing less than the daemonic ruler of the destinies of all created beings. Michelangelo's superhuman creative strength brims over in the images of the Sistine Chapel, where a world magically steeped in silver-grey, absolutely ours yet exalted infinitely above us, a world full of ourselves, of the tremendous presences within us, addresses us as though from an overarching Beyond. But it is probably in the *Tomb of Julius*, in the figures incarnate of Morning and Evening, Day and Night that he gives us the depths of his soul, for each one of them expresses the knowledge that he himself had of the invisible powers and their struggles, the sufferings he himself endured at the hands of life, which is in very truth continually ravaged by such powers, whose terrors—one can almost feel the hammer and chisel trembling—he finally enthralled. At the other extreme, man's thraldom to the dark and the daemonic is manifest nowhere more simply and grippingly than in the slave-figures, which seek vainly to loose themselves from some hidden doom but are not even capable of bursting the inert matter that imprisons them. Everywhere the mightiness of the Transcendent has been apprehended in a manner that will never be repeated, clothed in the visible bodiliness of mankind and at the same time pulsing with daemonism.

Summing up what shines out, as though through fissures, in and around these mythical symbols, what witness they bear to non-dogmatic, non-mythological vision and experience, we can say that it is evidence of our being shaped and sustained within a zone of Transcendence, which Michelangelo makes symbolically captive in his human individuals and collectively embodies in his groups, endowing the visible manifestations of its power with plastic form and at the same time raising them into something superhuman. Not, however, into any unearthly world; rather personifying the interplay of quite earthly forces which he experiences so mightily that nearly all his figures are magnified by it, become over-life-size, yet are informed through and through with the deepest humanity. Restrained as these figures almost always are in expression the same transcendental animation courses through them all; none of them is simple and, even when they seem filled with a sweet melancholy despite the violence of their feelings, all are quick with complex life; and since they are so much in correspondence with reality they exercise an uncanny power over us, without any mediation. They are like a melody of Being played near at hand yet with heightened intensity.

Darkness and brightness, dissonance, the diapason and the overtones of life are continually mixed; but their harmony shakes us and sets us free. For they are all echoes of some fundamental ground-tone, the vibrations of which in the phenomenal world transformed Michelangelo's inner being into a whirl of excitement, or as he himself says, "Kindling every spark to a consuming flame": manifestations of Beauty everywhere mingled with Cruelty, whose presence he recognizes and experiences with such deep pain. This Beauty is nothing fortuitous, for him it is the positive and transcendent force underlying all existence, which we are much too feeble to endure fully unveiled:

> Thus beauty burns not with consuming rage,
> For so much only of the heavenly light
> Inflames our love as finds a fervent heart.
> This is my case, lady, in sad old age:
> If seeing thee I do not die outright,
> 'Tis that I feel thy beauty but in part.

Beauty is an objective force that withdraws into its transcendental domain in order to shine forth once more:

> That thy great beauty here on earth may be
> Deathless through Time that rends the wreaths he twined,
> I call on Nature to collect and bind
> All those delights the slow years steal from thee,

And keep them for a birth more happily
Dowered, and more auspicious, and refined
To a more heavenly frame, a nobler mind,
Yet blessed with all thine angel purity.

But he himself can be so smitten with Beauty as to cry out:

Souls burn for souls, spirits to spirits cry!
I seek the splendour in thy fair face stored;
Yet mortal man that beauty scarce can learn,
And he who fain would find it, first must die.

All his figures are shaped by the shattering experience of this
force, even the dark and dreadful ones. And only in a single
fragment did he visualize in an image those shuddersome powers
which Transcendence *also* discharges into life—without calling
on the maieutic help of Beauty:

My soul hath fallen from her state of bliss,
Nor know I under any flag but this
How fighting I may flee those perils sore
Or how survive the rout and horrid roar
Of adverse hosts, if I Thy succour miss.
O flesh! O blood! O cross! O pain extreme!
By you may those foul sins be purified
Wherein my fathers were, and I was born!

It is an undisguised admission of horror on the part of the
sculptor of that superhumanly beautiful *Night* on the Medici
monument, of which he himself had written:

O Night, O sweet though sombre span of time!
All things find rest upon their journey's end.
Whoso hath praised thee, well doth apprehend,
And whoso honours thee, hath wisdom's prime . . .
Thou shade of Death, through whom the soul at length
Shuns pain and sadness hostile to the heart,
Whom mourners find their last and sure relief!
Thou dost restore our suffering flesh to strength,
Driest our tears, assuagest every smart,
Purging the spirits of the pure from grief. [1]

The experiences of the terrible and the daemonic that came
in with the Renaissance passed by this greatest of its sculptors
as little as did the overwhelming experiences of Beauty, which
sustained that marvellous efflorescence of all life's sunniness and

---

[1] Quotations from Sonnets XLVII, XXXIII, LV, LXXI, and XLIV as translated
by J. A. Symonds.

earthliness. We are blind if we do not feel everywhere in Michelangelo his obsession with a Transcendence immediately present
and quite undogmatic, to which he gives expression so superbly
that practically all his symbolizations of Christian, Judaic or
classical mythology seem to detach themselves from their origins
and, no longer dependent on their mythological meaning, can
be apprehended as something purely human.

3. *Shakespeare*

What is there to say about Shakespeare, who lived in the same
Renaissance climate of dissolving dogma and gave birth to a
whole world of fates and figures all proclaiming with loosened
tongue the same sort of message that apostrophizes us dumbly in
the figures of Michelangelo? About him, whom we must examine
in greater detail because he is the embodiment of all the questions
that are decisive for us, Fredrich Gundolf has said the last word. [1]
Shakespeare passed through two periods separated by the
crucial personal experiences of his thirties and early forties during
the decade preceding 1600, which he wrote down in the Sonnets.
The first is the more "ethical" period, as Gundolf calls it, the
second "tragic". In the first, which saw the birth of the historical
dramas and then, on a sunny upland of life bursting with strength
and affirmation, of *Romeo and Juliet* and the comedies grouped
round the *Midsummer Night's Dream*, life, with all the powers
working in it, is still accepted as a whole, just as it is, with no
deep questionings as to its value and meaning. Whereas the second
period, which begins with *Julius Caesar* and leads via *Hamlet*,
Othello, *Lear* and *Macbeth* to *Anthony and Cleopatra*, *Coriolanus*,
Timon of Athens and *The Tempest*, is sustained and permeated by
the experience, often amounting to terror, of just these questionable powers which are the vehicle of existence. Sometimes, as in
Troilus and Cressida and *Timon of Athens*, this experience takes the
shape of paroxysms of mordant irony, but at its highest it releases
those crowning tragedies suffused with melancholy, until in *The
Tempest* the master, weary of his doing and with a bitter-sweet

[1] *Shakespeare: His Life and Work* (Berlin, 1928).

incantation, breaks the wand with which he had held the world and all its spirits and powers spellbound—transforming them into figures of fate and revealing the immanent Transcendence within them.

It is with this latter mode of conscious seeing and forming that we are concerned, hence with the peaks of the second period. But it is important to recognize that Shakespeare, however plastic and actual, individual and unique his characters are, never uses them as "I's" standing by and for themselves. His "I's" and their destinies are rather, in all their unmistakable characterization, as Gundolf says, "powers become Man, the incarnation of various elemental forces, tensions, colours, masses". And all of them are raised, by the might of his creativity, out of "the General Being which we humans by origin are", in order to "make this Being manifest in many figures by means of the mimic, corporeal word; to represent unity as a plurality of 'I's". For "in every true man the whole of humanity reigns; and though in most of us it slumbers dumbly and blindly except for an ever-watchful special self or 'second I', in the man who is graced it lives as a whole multitude of figures". These two things, the unity, universality of Man, from which the individual, even the mightiest of them, can only lift himself as the concretion of something everywhere present like an undercurrent—and the incarnation of suprapersonal powers grounded in universality, their tensions and their struggles in the phenomenal world as manifest in the entanglements and antipathies of us all, including the individual conscious of his own character: these two things are the key to the Transcendental in Shakespeare, from which level he created as a dreamer in the first period and as a visionary in the second. At the same time it is the key to the heart-stirring effect which his fates and figures have had upon us the world over. Always men could experience anew and can still experience to-day with unparalleled force the tremendous objective powers through which personal destiny is moulded into something universal. For Shakespeare always feels it and represents Fate as something profoundly common to us all, something completely devoid of social form but for that very reason binding each to each, since in it every man rises up with every other out of the same element.

It is first and last a field of human destiny that Shakespeare gives us, not simply the workings and counter-workings of individual character but, as Gundolf has already pointed out, always destiny and character mysteriously fused into one. And even if destiny is not personified mythologically or regarded as an independent construction, rather incorporated for the most part in the complexities of situation and character, nothing could be more erroneous than to speak of processes of which the characters are the mere vehicles, in alleged contrast to destiny as conceived in classical tragedy. But, just as the characters are the incarnations of certain powers, so the situations are symbolic of our general human situation, of our being woven into the very fabric of existence. This is so even in the first period. It begins with the historical dramas. We cannot fully understand Richard III, neither the sequence of events nor what he embodies unless we see him as the final culmination and summing up of all the evil powers that had accumulated in England during the struggle between the Houses of York and Lancaster and had shaken the country for generations. It shows a field of destiny overcast by the unchaining of the powers of darkness, where goaded ambition and mutual hatred bring about one murder after another, where—as also in the three parts of *Henry VI*—an evil fatality is represented so concretely that the very earth seems to shake. Out of it there rises in *Richard III* a monstrous hump-back in whom all the fearful powers that have ever reigned come, as it were, to consciousness of themselves and, after having justified their action (in the famous prologue) by the ugliness which Nature has wreaked upon them, find incarnation in Richard, undergo an uncanny transfiguration, superbly daemonic, which shows the last scene of the struggle with its grisly murder lit up like an apocalypse by some sublime spectral power. The one-time queens, the magnificent Margaret and others, robbed of their husbands and children, follow this scene of devastation with their chorus of maledictions reminiscent of classical tragedy, until everything dissolves in ghostliness in the midnight apparition of the whole band of the murdered before Richard and his good antagonist Richmond. Yet, despite everything, the process is not yet at an end; for, as though to indicate that it can still go on working in another direction after withdrawing from this spectral field, the incarnate power of evil calls with ungovernable pride again and yet again for a horse to carry it to safety. The entire play is the most marvellous representation of the elemental powers locked in combat against the arching background of destiny.

And what else is the high-light of Shakespeare's still unclouded middle period, *Romeo and Juliet*, but the same struggle transposed on to a seemingly sunlit plane where the forces of human love hold sway? Once more it is a family quarrel, once more a fate-like process of destruction through a power which rules the lovers from outside and from which they cannot at the outset escape, drawn as they are into the pitiless maelstrom of this quarrel.

And yet it is probable that Shakespeare at the time saw this transcendental background, which he actually depicts everywhere in the play, quite unconsciously. His hand was only guided instinctively, by the inspiration of genius.

But at the time at which the Sonnets were written, at least the second part of them, he had experienced in the relationship between himself, the beloved aristocratic friend who ill-treated him, and the "dark lady" who ensnared both this friend and himself—obviously a not particularly beautiful but evilly seductive creature who, in some incomprehensible way, held him in bondage body and soul—the terrible force of those entanglements that rule even the strongest of us and the boundless sufferings produced by those transcendental powers, so deeply that, like Michelangelo, only in an even somberer tone, he cries out in despair:

> O from what power hast thou this powerful might
> With insufficiency my heart to sway? . . .
> Whence hast thou this becoming of things ill,
> That in the very refuse of thy deeds
> There is such strength and warrantise of skill
> That in my mind thy worst all best exceeds?

A devastatingly honest wail of anguish from one relentlessly buffeted by the gusts of love.

The court grouped round the splendid figure of Elizabeth, almost perverse in her need of love and her vanity, pullulated with ambitions, intrigues, denunciations and reeked of executions —the spiritual crypt of England's outwardly so glorious Eliza-bethan Age. It was the everyday experiences culled from the most intimate contact with this court that, together with experi-ences of his own, brought the transcendental background most easily discernible in the dark powers of the world to Shakespeare's consciousness in the way shown by the tragedies of the mature period that followed. In these he pierces through the foreground processes to complete objectivity; his vision is turned to those spheres which mould mankind out of "such stuff as dreams are made on". And his experiences are such that although he still knows serenity, warmth, sunlight and all the things that are woven into our human dream and although he portrays not only the louring forces that drive us to despair but the sparkling, soul-liberating ones as well, the ground-melody is still a profoundly melancholy sadness over the lot of humanity, and the sublime expression of it. Such is the spiritual cast of Shakespeare's experience of life, his most personal and deepest possession which must be distinguished, however, from what is universal in trans-cendental experience and, therefore, has quite another tinge. The vision of non-dogmatic Transcendence itself and the particu-lar tint lent to it by the personality of the seer and the age he lives in are not the same thing. But there is no other such out-standing example of world-wide vision made word and flesh as the vision of this greatest of all non-dogmatic seers.

For Shakespeare the transcendental zone is not something that merely exceeds the upper and lower confines of the human realm. Rather is it inextricably bound up with the form and being of the cosmos itself. It is no mere theatrical device, it is simply to make plain the bond between the cosmic powers and the man of supreme historical or spiritual importance when, on the occasion of the greatest event in history that Shakespeare portrays, namely the murder of Caesar, the whole cosmos announces its agitation as in sympathy; when one of the con-spirators, the utterly sober Casca, says sepulchrally:

> Are you not moved when all the sway on earth
> Shakes like a thing unfirm? O Cicero!
> I have seen tempests when the scolding winds
> Have riv'd the knotty oaks; and I have seen
> The ambitious ocean swell, and rage and foam,
> To be exalted with the threatening clouds:
> But never till to-night, never till now,
> Did I go through a tempest dropping fire . . .
> Besides (I have not since put up my sword),
> Against the capitol I met a lion
> Who glared upon me and went surly by
> Without annoying me: and there were drawn
> Upon a heap a hundred ghastly women
> Transformed with fear, who swore they saw
> Men all in fire walk up and down the streets. . . .

It is another reflection of the same warning that Calpurnia calls out to Caesar in the night amid thunder and lightning, against the danger that threatens him on the morrow; but Caesar, after a brief hesitation calculated to please her, sets out for the Senate despite her conjurations, despite the cosmic uproar, despite all the omens and portents, in full consciousness of the doom hanging over him—sets out to be Caesar and to die there as Caesar.

We do not have to take all these events and representations quite literally. It only means that the tremendous incarnation of life-forces that Caesar *is* cannot perish without these life-forces themselves being violently shaken.

It is the same in *Lear*. The tempest that sets in as the abysmal heartlessness of Regan and Goneril unfolds before Lear is not only the objectification of the cruelty with which the two daughters abandon their old father without compunction and toss him out into the night and the raging elements like a bit of driftwood. Neither is the elemental uproar itself, which forms the setting for their outcast father's and benefactor's madness, a mere accidental accessory heightening the theatrical effect. It is the deliberately intended expression of a profound cosmic derangement, the trepidation of world-forces which, stimulated by the monstrousness of his human fate, have given birth to the phenomenon Lear.

The theme of *Macbeth* is of a man, good and noble in himself but darkly disposed, caught up and entangled in the elemental forces aroused in him, and made dominant, by his encounter with their ghostly incarnations in the shape of women. Twice they appear at the critical moment. But it is not only Hecate and the witches who play a decisive part—the whole power-apparatus of existence is set in motion. For, it is rumoured, the horses of the murdered king Duncan have devoured each other. All this, far more gripping and significant than the apparition of Banquo, which lacks objective reality, is an expression of the mysterious concatenation of all the happenings on some deeper level. This steeps the play in a strangely pregnant atmosphere in which the fate of Macbeth and his lady, tormented though they both are after their deed by inner uneasiness and pangs of conscience, affords the most expressive—and hence also impressive— instance of the interplay of fate and character in man, as Shakespeare saw it. The transcendental powers give a word, a sign—

and the man who bears them in himself by disposition is instantly delivered over to these powers to such an extent that, although fully conscious, he is capable of doing something horrible, something contrary to his nature as dominant hitherto, something atrocious—and then does it, unable to escape from it. These powers, both the dark ones and the bright ones they have mastered, are painted as something quite real and actual not merely in their outward workings but in their essence as well. In his crucial struggle of soul Macbeth says:

> And pity like a naked, new-born babe
> Striding the blast, or heaven's cherubim hors'd
> Upon the sightless couriers of the air,
> Shall blow the horrid deed in every eye,
> That fears shall drown the wind. . . .

This is assuredly no euphuistic locution meant to express the nature of pity in baroque form; it is fetched up, absolutely real, from the deeps of Being, just as are the words of Lady Macbeth, swiftly succumbing to the same forces of temptation and still more swiftly to the torments of their soul-spotting foulness:

> Come to my woman's breasts,
> And take my milk for gall, you murdering ministers,
> Wherever in your sightless substances
> You wait on nature's mischief. . . .

The essence of the Transcendental, given express name here and so forcibly evoked, is everywhere present in the works of Shakespeare's peak period if one looks closely enough. It endows all his characters with their sublimity and is the source from which they come and act. It is there in the characters themselves and in their destiny, with which they are fundamentally identical. And it is there in their actions as a sort of hereditary incarnation of all the forces bound up with their destiny.

Othello is not simply and solely a drama that has become the type of the jealousy play, though it is this too. As Gundolf has already realized it is, in its truest sense, a play about the proud and illustrious "outsider" who is assailed by the powers inherent in a station of life to which he does not really belong, and finally crushed by them. Jago is not a villain engaged in developing his individuality to the full like many of Shakespeare's other villains. He is, in Gundolf's word, the "executioner"—the executioner who springs out of the ground in order to meet

Othello at this very spot and to destroy him there, just where he has rooted himself most deeply but at the same time precariously on alien ground: in passionate union with the beautiful white woman, the highest human expression of the surroundings in which he is placed. Once uprooted he must perish in this environment, destroying himself and her:

> But there, where I have garnered up my heart,
> Where either I must live or bear no life,
> The fountain from the which my currents run
> Or else dries up; to be discarded thence
> Or keep it as a cistern for foul toads
> To knot and gender in!—turn thy complexion there,
> Patience, thou young and rose-lipp'd cherubim,
> Ay, there, look grim as hell. . . .

Everything else is so much trimming; but this is the precise spot hit upon by the executioner of fate whose task is to unleash to their own destruction the forces of jealousy, which are almost independent of Othello's temperament, simply given by the toils of the situation itself.

So we could continue right the way through *Anthony and Cleopatra* and *Coriolanus*, demonstrating this transcendental groundwork and its fatal emanations. But it is not necessary.

For the clearest and most obvious example of what we are concerned with here is to be found in Shakespeare's two most comprehensive and illuminating works: *Hamlet* and *Lear*.

Hamlet, in outward form akin to a classical destiny drama and to this extent the modern continuation of the tragedy of Orestes, is first and foremost the play in which Shakespeare offers us such an awe-inspiring vision of the powers throbbing beneath the skin of events that our heart quails at the sight. Hamlet is not by nature a weakling in action. He could devise the unmasking of the amorous king and his own mother very skilfully, just as he could secretly contrive his return from the exile in England planned for him, which would have meant his end. A resolute man through and through he embarks on the final duel and, clothed with determination, vigorously carries it to a triumphant conclusion. But the devastating appearance of his father that fills his dark presagings with unholy reality—although he stands his ground fearlessly and without trembling—suddenly opens his eyes to the incomprehensible powers in the depths, which now set about laying his life waste and ravage his world. This hardens

his heart and at the same time makes him daemonically clairvoyant to all the relativities which, so he feels, surround him like
masks for the secret play of these forces. Scarcely able to endure
this clairvoyance of his, he masquerades behind a feigned madness
which hides both himself and the deed he has to do, so that the
pure current of his feelings only runs openly to his friend and
fellow conspirator Horatio. Meanwhile, in desperation, he has
destroyed the thing dearest to him, Ophelia, who had evidently
become but an empty shadow for him; and as regards his mother
he positively wallows in the horrors he has experienced, so that
the spirit of his father himself has to bring him to his senses. So
overwhelmed is he by the monstrous Unknown and what it
reveals of the chaotic in life, that he is driven to reflect ceaselessly
on the meaning and content of the powers that move him and his
being. We have only to think of the gravedigger scene. He finds
it easy enough to base his action firmly and factually on the
little drama partly devised by himself with a view to unmasking
the king. But he fails to act when the possibility of action comes
to him as he takes the king by surprise from behind, on his knees
in repentance. He fails to act because action has been magnified
by reflection to such symbolical proportions that his avenging
deed and the crime he is about to commit stand there like extremes
balanced against one another:

> Up, sword, and know thou a more horrid hent;
> When he is drunk, asleep or in his rage,
> Or in the incestuous pleasures of his bed;
> At gaming, swearing; or about some act
> That has no relish of salvation in it:
> Then trip him.

With flashing irony and a mordancy of wit unequalled anywhere else in Shakespeare, this overburdening vision of the
nether powers discharges itself in a paralysis of action. As though
incidentally, "like a rat", Hamlet stabs Polonius; and as though
incidentally too, himself at his last gasp, he finally wreaks the
vengeance on the king that has been enjoined upon him.

The vision of the abysses gaping behind appearance can be so
overwhelming that it tempers the finest, most delicate and most
noble human material to razor-edged steel capable of dazzling
and wounding, but no longer capable of human feeling or the
punctual thrust demanded of it. Such, very roughly, is the
message that comes from the depths of the great poet's heart.

The message is the other way about in *Lear*: not to see the hidden powers of evil at the back of phenomena means that a streak of stupid vanity, a heedless burst of anger and its consequences are enough to crush the kingliest among us, to show him the veiled terrible truth of reality in the glare of madness— and show it not for his eyes alone but for all men. That is the magnificence of *Lear*. The truth is shown but—this is the exalting thing about *Lear* in contrast to *Hamlet*, for all its terribleness—it is not a simple truth, not purely and simply dark, rather is it light and warm even in its darkness. Never have the daemonic and evil powers of existence been portrayed so unmistakably, so actually, so full-bloodedly as in the two spiritual twin-sisters Regan and Goneril who are quite prepared, for the sake of their own comfort and lust for power, to cast their father out into the void and let him perish. The same daemonism is apparent in Edmund, who does the same by his brother Edgar and with cold cunning sacrifices his good father to his own ambition and the limitless brutality of the two sisters. The dark powers naturally exercise a mutual attraction and together spin a web in which those finer and nobler than themselves are caught and martyred. But on the other hand never have these fine and noble natures, outwardly subdued, been delineated with such force that they will always stand as examples to the world as in the proud and tender love of Cordelia, grim and bitter but bold in action; in the open and manly love of Kent for Lear, taking on itself the extremes of patience; in Edgar, magnificently simulating madness and inwardly triumphing over the void into which he, like Lear, has been cast, in the depths of his own distress yet succouring his old blinded father and tending him like another father; and, last but not least, in the Fool, never wavering in his attachment to Lear, giving off an indescribably fantastical mixture of loose nonsense to cheer the fallen king but ever and anon trying to bring him the comfort of soberer human understanding, so as to rouse him from the blindness of his wrath.

All these are figures drawn with an extravagance of poetic fantasy that makes them the denizens of another, almost a good, a holy sphere. And as their restrained lovingness and warm, open altruism works through existence like a second, all-pervading melody alongside the hell-risen forces of evil that destroy the symbolical figure of Lear, and as they nevertheless *stand their ground* in the midst of the human and cosmic uproar, we can well say that never have the transcendental powers that shape our destiny been made so tangible in their ever-present duality and innate nature as in this play. Shivering, we do not experience them only as dispelling all heart's warmth with their frosty breath. We experience as the core and kernel of them their concentration of themselves and everything else into their own "I", wonderfully symbolized by the fact that at their very first appearance the two sisters, each obsessed with her own dark selfhood, immediately try to conquer the *third* force which is akin to them in this respect, namely Edmund, striving, no matter how, to swallow him up in their own narrow selves and ending by mutually devouring each other in their rapacious hunger, since one poisons the other from jealousy and then, seeing that all is lost, kills herself. And who cannot but feel the soul-quickening breath of the other powers, triumphing over all outward destruction and warming the heart even amid the gloomiest terrors? Lear and Cordelia, about to die, are victors despite everything when both are caught at the end and Lear, embracing his daughter, says:

> Come, let's away to prison;
> We two alone will sing like birds i' the cage.
> When thou dost ask me blessing I'll kneel down
> And ask of thee forgiveness. So we'll live,
> And pray and sing, and tell old tales, and laugh
> At gilded butterflies and hear poor rogues
> Talk of court news; and we'll talk with them too,
> Who loses and who wins; who's in, who's out.
> And take upon 's the mystery of things
> As if we were God's spies; and we'll wear out,
> In a wall'd prison, pacts and sects of great ones
> That ebb and flow by the moon. . . .

Radiant, pure humanity so at one with the heart-warm powers, so magical and overwhelming that imprisonment and death seem almost matters of indifference. The spell of the dark powers is thereby broken in reality; and the manner of their overcoming has probably never been portrayed in such tender lines or so unforgettably.

When he wrote this Shakespeare knew full well the deep-seated nature of the Transcendence that wrestles with itself within our own being and so shapes us. And in that profound world-soulfulness from which *Lear* proceeded he saw despite everything the sublime soul- and world-liberating strength of the warm, bright and noble powers, to whom the vicissitudes of external events are less than nothing.

His testament he has given us in *The Tempest*, where all that is mean, low-down, the whole shadiness and daftness of life is derided and rendered innocuous by the spirit of levity and the wand of the noble-hearted. This is not merely a wistful farewell, when the master breaks his interpreting wand; it contains in its clear cadences a pronouncement on the nature, order and inner consistency of the powers which make up our human life and in the midst of which we can, if we will, triumphantly win to an ascendency of mind and spirit. It is the tail-piece to Shakespeare's knowledge of the Transcendental, which is his wisdom; and this clearly calls to us: "Do you not see? Here is the Above and here is the Below; behind everything breathe these two".

We may still add, perhaps, one thing. Though the Transcendental releases in Shakespeare figures fashioned from the reservoirs of its power, figures that are always rounded, unique personalities with the breath of life in them; yet in the great majority of cases, it would seem, the core of their being is associated closely with a complex, hereditary force which dominates them so uniformly that they often remain in the memory only as exemplars and incarnations of this one thing. On closer examination, however, ·this is characteristic only of his villains, from Richard III and Iago to Edmund and Cornwall in *Lear* and Claudius, the lecherous king in *Hamlet*. But the really great heroes nearly all have contradictory congenital forces in themselves which, goaded by their fate, battle against one another in them. Consequently the rarest and richest of his gifts often comes to us precisely through this struggle, not only in *Hamlet*, where this is the prevailing motif; not only in *Anthony and Cleopatra*, where it is likewise at the heart of problems entangling the two lovers, though in a less explicit and less calamitous way—but also in the Brutus of *Julius Caesar*, most grippingly, and setting the tone of the whole play. This Brutus is of noble stature but he is torn between his love of Caesar and the will to freedom of the Romans; it is virtually in this struggle that he is broken rather than by external events. Shakespeare knew this and made it quite plain in another play, *Macbeth*; knew that behind every blow of fate there are *recessive* hereditary forces that are made *dominant* by fate itself, and forces that, hitherto dominant, likewise sink out of sight. A *mutation of character*, therefore, is brought about in this way. The noble, fair-minded Macbeth becomes in the end a wild murderer and almost a villain. The witches knew that the power of ambition which would so change him was slumbering in him. They knew the secret of rousing it within him by prophecies of power and nourishing it on further prophecies until they had both Lady Macbeth, his impulsive alter ego, and himself at the edge of the pit. He still struggles in his heart after the initial assault, but in reality he is already changed at the first prophetic summons, because of the affinity existing between the powers that dwell in him unknown to himself and those that approach him scintillatingly from without. Hence, apparently powerless against himself, he becomes the victim of a mutation of character or, to speak more precisely and abstractly, the victim of the dark, congenital forces now fully awakened in him which unite with the core of his being and drive out the other, higher potentialities.

It will be shown later that such seemingly over-subtle and pedantic formulations have a very far-reaching explanatory significance; for whole peoples, whole ages may succumb to the fate of Macbeth, and the transcendental and at the same time personal background of it can be illuminated by these examples.

The Shakespearean figures are great, always on the verge of the tragic, because when—speaking abstractly again—the congenital forces seize control over them they allow this process to run its entire course in them, accepting the powers which assail them or to which they fall victim, fully and unreservedly into the core of their being. If these congenital forces are themselves a spontaneous emanation of the phenomenal world with all its concrete conditions, which become the substance for their incarnation and expression; if they are something fundamentally different, hence something *pre*-conditional, absolute, in the last resort transcendental, then Shakespeare's figures—whether the core of their being is wholly bound up with such forces from the very beginning or whether they ally themselves with them at the behest of fate—are in either case steeped in Transcendence. Individual though they may be they are at the same time embodiments of transcendental absolutes. Since this is in fact the case with practically all of them they are a realm from the natural features of which and the processes going on in it we may read, have we but eyes to see, the nature of the transcendental powers that reign in man. Similarly, in practically all the plays —and this is what makes them so magnificent—we can feel the universal human background against which these powers rule in us; the zone of Transcendence itself that unites all mankind; and we also feel its living and positive breath, within which all this soaring and struggling proceeds—the profound and inexhaustible space of our human being.

4. *Cervantes*

Only one other Renaissance figure voiced warm Humanity and the Absolute in the same uncompromising and unforgettable tones, and that was Cervantes; although outwardly he appeared to deride them by making both the butt of the comic. What an inimitable idea it was to hale the transcendent nature of the Absolute and the glories of Humanism before the world, each clothed equally in the caricature of an earlier dogmatism! At the same time, however, Cervantes allowed them sufficient strength to cast a spell over the most out-and-out champion of mundane common-sense and everyday selfishness and drag him through a series of misadventures. Because of the fascination that his boundless altruism has for Sancho Panza, there paces, side by side with the mad Don Quixote of the novel, the shadow of a second Quixote, high-hearted, noble, kindly, capable of the utmost sacrifice for the really great things, whom we accept as the author's picture of the true man, painted with mysterious power—so that, because of the human warmth and absolute devotion that emanate from it, there is no more heart-quickening and enchanting book than this ostensible parody of Man and the Absolute.

It represents the first loosening of dogma, the first candid glance into human life stripped of all trappings and, thanks to this extensive freedom, the first peerings into the yawning chasms where reign the powers that tear and rend mankind only to bind and unite them again. It was the courage of youth gazing on all this face to face and expressing it that gave rise to these never-to-be-surpassed glimpses of the transcendental view of life at so early a stage of Western development. The Renaissance is often charged with mere individualism; and indeed it was then that Europe knew for the first time if not exactly a universal individualism at least a passionate cult of pure personality, with disrupting consequences for life. The Renaissance stands or falls by this; for suddenly the men of profoundest vision beheld in the midst of all these disruptions, but uniting them deep down, the "human constant" and its fixed relationship to the Transcendental; it became the object of their creativity, and as in an age of transcendental revelation they spoke of the objective, suprapersonal entities that inspire and rule us. We must strip this revelation of all dogmatic disguises if we are to find the essentials of the message we need to-day.

As we shall see these essentials had not been fully perceived then. There still lacked one or two vital points, but these were grasped in an access of reflectiveness during the next two centuries and were so deeply experienced, even behind the mystifications of a new dogmatism, that they became the frame of reference for the spiritual activity of the West and the whole world.

Let us investigate this reflectiveness and its environment, since they underlie all the problems we meet with in life to-day; and let us pursue the spiritual bitterness and painful refinement which mark the road to the Eighteenth Century—the century whose widened consciousness enabled it to pierce through the veils of dogma to fundamental principles and hence to a more universal understanding.

CHAPTER III

REDOGMATIZATION; REFLECTION; ISOLATION

1. *The Return of Dogma and the Naturalistic Approach to Life*

Concurrently with the recrudescence of dogma arising from Christianity itself, which resulted in the great religious wars of the sixteenth and seventeenth centuries, there emerged at the beginning of the Seventeenth Century in one and the same historical breath three evolutionary forces born of renewed tensions within Western dynamism and of the collapse of the old dogmatism: the modern State, modern capitalism, and modern science. All three were essentially naturalistic, all three mutually reinforced one another and dominated human life to an increasing extent, and all three, rising higher and higher over the burst dams of dogma and resisting all attempts at re-dogmatization, swept life into purely biological or purely intellectual backwaters no longer embraced by one unifying spiritual stream. Just how they arose and how they came to be inwardly connected has been shown by me elsewhere. The historical significance of their combined impact is that purely vital emanations of power such as these, no longer possessing or acknowledging any higher sanction, now lodged themselves behind and above all the subsequent developments of the West as a kind of all-environing material and spiritual influence. Thereby the West was plunged into that disharmony which, despite Europe's outward conquest of the world, harboured a peril within and finally led to nihilism and the present catastrophe.

With those three evolutionary forces, therefore, certain purely biological principles dominated the historical movement of the West from then on, no matter how much these forces masqueraded as spiritual tendencies or sought to hide beneath them. Knowledge, says Bacon—and knowledge now meant modern science—is power. And it makes no difference how many other factors contributed either initially or later to the field of knowledge, now taking shape as power. Capitalism, the economy that followed the natural acquisitive instinct, growing out of it at first slowly and then upsetting all life in suddenly accelerated tempo, was nothing other than a purely organic display of power. And the modern State? There is literally nothing that people have tried to swathe more in wrappings of a supra-biological character. In vain. True enough, all political forms of rule are primarily and essentially power-formations, whether they are products of violence from birth on—as they invariably were the world over before the period here under discussion—or whether they grew up confederatively, as had been the case in classical times and in the city-states of the Renaissance, in the Swiss League and the political groupings of towns north of the Alps, the type being reproduced later in the states of North America. Power, born either of violence or of free will, is always the essence of political rule and its aim from the beginning; it is the vessel into which is poured whatever one wishes to give further shape to under the stress of politics, to create or safeguard—rights, freedom, wealth, public welfare, expansion. All this is a truism. But in Europe, the embryo of the now developing "West", all political configurations till then had been intimately bound up with supra-biological forces deriving from ecclesiastical sanction or feudal loyalties. The whole of Europe had been overlaid with political organisms of this type which were, as a general rule, clothed with the authority of the Church. The State as a pure power-entity, as a simple organism capable of concentration or expansion did not exist before the epoch we are now considering gave rise to it on the pattern of the Italian city-states of the Renaissance after the collapse of the old feudal and monarchical units. Hence Europe, hitherto united by a higher sanction, now became a field for innumerable competitive political groups great and small all preying on each other, all claiming for themselves the idea of unlimited sovereignty within and without, the right to act regardless of any higher spiritual authority, and all immediately translating such arbitrary action into restless expansionism. The idea of the "raison d'etat" appeared. This is a subject that lends itself to witty treatment, which has been done, and rightly, by Friedrich Meineke in his *Idee der Staatsraison*. Stripped of its theoretical trappings the "raison d'etat" in Europe is no more than the materialization of the ravenous hunger of the powers which were then incarnate in the absolute princes and which developed into the modern States with the rise of capitalist economy: their hunger for more and more territory and peoples to rule over, be it inside Europe or beyond its shores. True enough, a concentration and rational consolidation of human rights hitherto unknown made their appearance, leading ultimately to the idea of public welfare; but above all this there emerged, thinly disguised by the hereditary claims of this or that dynasty or court, an absolutely unbounded drive towards expansion or war. Europe and, through it, the world were swept by a wave of political violence, a sort of power-biology that built up the world dominion of the West regardless of anything and everything outside it, and in the West itself the same process of ruthless tyranny and enslavement was only arrested by rivalry existing between the various centres emerging as "modern States".

Modern capitalism and modern science are cradled in these political structures, the sister forms of the new biological "beast-world" of politics now gaining supremacy in life. For we must be quite clear about it—such a world is a biological one, a beast-world, a world of Leviathans as Hobbes properly called it, filled with monetary acquisitiveness and intellectual power-trends cultivated as ready tools and auxiliaries; a world of purely vital forces and evolutions within which the spiritual current of the West has run ever since, hemmed in as by banks and often rebelling against them, but more often playing over them with the marvellous reflections of its transcendental visions and thus all too frequently falling into high-minded self-deception.

Only from such a clear understanding of the profound disharmony thus set up and the ensuing duality of the course and dynamics of subsequent history can we form a picture of the whole: the rise of the West, its encirclement of the entire globe and its fall to-day.

From all this we have only to extract what primarily concerns Europe alone and the reflective understanding, despite all hindrances, of the spiritual powers latent in it together with the forces of will they release. There are three great groups of spiritual consequences that are significant for us. The first concerns above all the Seventeenth Century; the second and third are unfolded in the Eighteenth.

2. *The Seventeenth Century*

The return of dogma, chiefly of the ecclesiastical sort, coincided in this century with that "naturalistic approach" as reflected in the State, which I have briefly sketched. This meant the veiling off of the deeps of human life, into which the Renaissance had gazed without fear and whose abysses its great men had plumbed. But when Milton sings so magnificently of the abysses of Being and the dark or bright daemonic forces that reign in them, he is no longer using the old forms of faith merely as poetic clothing. He is wholly inspired from within by the dogmatic forms invented by Christianity to render them visible; he paraphrases and proclaims the dogmatic vision with the greatest earnestness, portraying it with all the pathos of faith. And he is only the greatest example. The rigid conventions of Christianity as the frame for all vistas into the world and life are clamped on everywhere we look.

But over and above this the new science fostered by the State was an explanation of the world in terms of mathematics, physics and astronomy. With its mathematical formulae and laws it tended to disrupt whatever had been consolidated with the return of dogma, and at approximately the same speed. Dogma and faith might try to recapture practical life and men's outlook in their close meshes and outwardly to impose the net with the help of inquisition and state coercion; but simultaneously the scientific and mathematical thinking fostered by that same State unravelled it again. As a result not only did the old theological picture of the world waver and grow dim, but men's *inner* picture changed as well, because their whole experience was permeated by the fundamental principles of this geometrical and mathematical view of things, hovering between the infinitesimal and the infinite. Further the "I", man himself became a point in infinity. The same man became a point, an atom in a mathematically conceived Whole, whom the return of dogma attempted to fit into another whole by means of a completely different, qualitative view of things—the same man, moreover, to whom the Renaissance had also conceded qualitative form, brimming with personality and bound wholly to the earth!

Thus a new element came in: the "I", feeling itself but a point in infinity, began to ask, "Am I real, how can I know that I am and that I have knowledge of others?" In this wise must Descartes, himself very pious in this age of newly-acquired piety, have asked questions for himself and for the world, thus inaugurating an interpretation of existence, humanity and its forms in terms of the individual understood almost abstractly, solely as a thinking entity—an interpretation running historically parallel to the astrophysical view. Together they acted like a magnet, attracting to themselves all the potentialities present in the form of individualistic philosophies of other kinds, religious, classical, naturalistic, etc. It was a long-drawn process the consequences of which were incalculable as regards the self-knowledge of the West and its political will; indeed they could never be lost even if the West were to perish because, so long as the "I" of the average individual —filled as it was with all those other individualistic potentialities—continued to be not a mere infinitesimal *point of departure for knowledge* as in the early stages, but rather evolved a qualitatively complete Self by boldly taking up a *central position* in life, a momentous spiritual revolution was bound to occur sooner or later, ultimately becoming practical and political as well.

All this was still far distant in the Seventeenth Century. But the inner upheaval which this originally mathematical view of life and humanity entailed was very powerful, even though it was hidden under outward forms. Its effect was immense when it touched the great men of the age, the real seers and soothsayers. As a result, the political power-groups associated with the new dogmatism developed, in those spiritual fields rapidly winning to independence through the concentration of State power, a markedly aristocratic culture based on an ampler conception of society contemporaneously with the collapse of the free cities and the peasantry and the summoning of the nobility to the courts. These new power States used their central position —as was the case in Spain—to tighten up the laxities of earlier times and make room for the tense intellectual classicism of Calderon, which ran the whole gamut of piety. Velasquez peopled this new dimension of the spirit with his realistic yet sublime figures. And the power-State of France which arose at the same time gathered round the court all those creative forces which, radiating out from the Louvre, from Versailles, from Corneille, Racine, Molière and even from the customs of the day and their paragon "l' honnête homme", served as a model or all Europe. A model every bit as compulsive as the Gothic had once been. Despite all this, however, the profound problem occasioned by the mathematical view *vis-à-vis* the human situation, remained unsolved. It undermined the new classisistic and Baroque society which was consciously steeped in the re-affirmed dogmas of Christianity, just as it was bound to call into question all dogmas, Christian or otherwise, and make a problem of them from the standpoint of a wholly new and original experiencing of man's own being and nature. But it was disguised, if thinly, by the culture of the times. The problems of the soul were seen in exclusively social terms even where the deepest aspects of human life were touched on; such was the plane on which everything was set now and on which the drama was played out. "There is no universe in him", the Frenchman Suarez said at the end of the Nineteenth Century, of Racine. The same is true even of Moliere, despite his concern for human problems. The universe breaks through in Calderon, but caught in the toils of dream. Neither is it directly expressed in Velasquez, though it can be felt hovering behind all his grandeurs.

It is, however, directly tackled and expressed by the two greatest figures of this age, both of whom originate in the problems posed by the new science—the "I" in relation to the "All". The one gives us a paradoxical answer, the other an answer so tragic that it shakes us even to-day. *Pascal* and *Rembrandt* both speak from the tension of "I" and Infinity set up by the new mathematics. Both are beset by a brooding isolation of the Self such as had not been known before. Both feel, as they glide into consciousness, that they are standing before the immeasurable and the incomprehensible, hence on the brink of the void. That is the unprecedented thing about them; it vibrates across the centuries, and its vibrations strike us and disturb our being even to-day.

3. *Pascal*

It is deeply disturbing when Pascal, the intricacies of whose thought we can only lightly touch on here, although affirming in practice all the social patterns that surrounded him, is yet driven to say in the end that "society, like the State, is no more than custom, a poor compromise for escaping chaos". And when, observing humanity and infinity behind these conventions, he says: "The whole visible world is only an inconspicuous fold in the robe of the Infinite. No idea of ours comes anywhere near it. We may inflate our conceptions beyond all imaginable space, but we only produce atomies in comparison with the reality of things". And so he asks: "What is man in the Infinite?" And answers: "A Nothing in comparison with the Infinite, an Infinity in comparison with the Nothing, a Mean betwixt Nothing and Infinity". The consequences for the soul are as follows: "He who sees himself in this light will take fright of himself, and observing himself sustained in the body given him by Nature between those two abysses of Infinity and Nothing, will tremble at the sight of that enigma—himself". Speaking of this enigma in psychological terms he says: "What a Chimera is man! What a novelty! What a monster, what a chaos, what a contradiction, what a prodigy! Judge of all things, imbecile worm of the earth; depositary of truth, sink of uncertainty and error; pride and refuse of the universe! If he extol himself, so I humble him; if he bow himself low, so I exalt him and so shall continue till he comprehend that he is an incomprehensible monster". What are the further attributes of this monster? Amongst other things, "Man is only disguise, deceit, hypocrisy, both in his own eyes and in the eyes of others". And, "If all men knew what each were saying about the others, there would not be four friends left on earth". What is our moral orientation? "Those on board ship turn towards harbour, but where find this point in morality?" Answer: "As custom determines what is agreeable, so also does it determine justice". "Justice is what is established. Being unable to cause might to obey justice, men have made it just to obey might so that justice and might may go hand in hand". "Thus we call 'just' that which we are compelled to observe". "There is hardly anything of right or wrong that does not change its nature with a change of wind". "Theft, incest, infanticide, parricide, all have had a place among the virtuous actions". "The only certainty is that nothing, judged by reason alone, is of itself just; everything wavers in time". "Thus the Self is fundamentally hateful". "The true and only virtue, then, is to hate the Self".

From all Pascal's vision and its various nuances of expression which cannot be presented here, there proceeds an unexampled pessimism and a terror, rooted in reflection, of the abysses of nihilism. In face of this, his only salvation lies in the same paradox which Kierkegaard in the Nineteenth Century deemed necessary for his soul—the plunge into Christian piety and the dogmas preached by it. He, Pascal, the great mathematician, the inventor of the calculating machine, therefore sews a testament into his jacket, a deposition of the faith that illuminated and saved him as from Monday the twenty-third of November, 1654, which accompanied him everywhere as a talisman, a protective motto; one which, in view of all his annihilating observations of life and mankind, in view of the failure of "reason", was needed to attest those "vérités du coeur" wherein alone lay salvation—both for himself and, so he proclaims, for humanity at large.

4. *Rembrandt*

These "vérités du coeur" also spell salvation for *Rembrandt* who, in his youth, stood without reflection in the different light of Protestantism and was later overcome by the reflective powers of his thought as an artist. In this capacity, experiencing the whole world in himself and expressing it, he comes in the end to feel, like Pascal, that he is standing alone in the Infinite and exposed to its perilous questions. But he solves his experience of abandonment and the immersion of the naked Self in the "All" in a totally different way. This immersion of the Self, this standing alone bring to birth in him the peculiar transcending quality of his chiaroscuro, the unique lighting of his pictures. It is responsible for his strangely intensified light, which wells out from some mysterious spot in him and falls like a series of beams, now broad, now narrow, on the things and people crowding the half or total darkness. Such a light-principle he may have taken over from others; but it was only in his maturer years, after such tragic experiences as the death of Saskia in 1642 and the threat to his means of subsistence in 1657, that it acquired metaphysical significance: the opposition of infinity and nothingness, from between which the world of men and things is lifted out, a visible reality fashioned by that transcending light. There is thus a profound parallel with Pascal.

But with what a totally different effect! Rembrandt stands his ground in this humanly isolated centre between All and Nothing.

He does not succumb. The spiritual trials with which life pursued him, from the auctioning of his property in 1657 down to his final refuge in old age with his beloved and his son in their art-dealer's shop where he died in 1669—all this he has laid down with devastating force. He has reproduced it stage by stage in his Self-Portraits—those conscious autobiographies— which end with faces wherein all the pits and chasms of life are engraved (viz. *Self-Portrait* in Aix en Provence)[1]; the most moving among them being that constrained attempt at an old man's smile over the shadow that lies upon all existence (*Self-Portrait* in Cologne). No other artist before his time had done anything comparable—given such pictorial and auto-biographical expression to the lonely darkness that was closing in on him. But he differs from Pascal in that he still doggedly persists in the hard hither-side of life. Year by year life reveals more of its shuddersome depths to him, but also, embedded in these, its tender, delicate veins of human mildness and heavenly compassion and, it must be said, the beauty of its sensuality which— in this he resembles Shakespeare—is an integral part of his being even when he is wrestling with the dark in agonised awareness. He uses classical antiquity, Jewish and Christian mythology just as, on the other hand, he uses landscape and even the *genre* to express the immense range of his experience, always relating it to the Infinite yet clinging fast to the earth, and always brimming over with that world-melancholy Shakespeare knew.

All these riches can only be hinted at here. It must suffice to state what is the salient feature in Rembrandt: just as for Shakespeare or Goethe, so for him all myths of whatever kind are only a medium through which the particular can be raised to the general and a universal statement be made, in which respect he differs absolutely from his contemporary Milton. Hence it is no accident that the stories and legends of the Old Testament with their highly personal but inexhaustible wisdom should have offered him, particularly in the years of his maturity and deepening distress, pictorial material of the grandest as of the tenderest quality—without, however, being taken at their mythological face value. Unforgettable is *Manoah's Sacrifice*, with its mystic

---

[1] This, and the following titles in italics, are reproduced in the two volumes of Rembrandt's paintings in the Phaidon edition. The plate-numbers are, in order: 58, 61, 509, 511, 519, 525, 526, 528, 591, 598, 611, 622-4, 595, 614, 410-13, 416, 415-17.

surrender to the Unknown; *The Reconciliation of David and Absalom*, full of kingly majesty; *The Vision of Daniel at the Brook Ulai*, unsurpassable in the tender loveliness of the gesture with which he interprets the miracle of the ram. *Jacob Blessing his Grandchildren* shows Rembrandt's humanity in all its splendid abundance, and lastly the two pictures which are, perhaps, the most powerful of all: *David Playing the Harp Before Saul*, who weeps, and *Jacob Wrestling with the Angel*. The latter is a painting of such magical beauty that we cannot touch its secret and can only say that all defences against southern forms of bodily beauty have broken down, since this beauty enters whole into the unity of the picture and that nevertheless it foreshadows, subjectively, the dark fatality hovering over Rembrandt himself.

It is no accident, again, that in Christian mythology the most extreme spiritual situations pointed the way to the Sublime for him: *Christ at the Column* and the justly admired *Return of the Prodigal Son*. Further that in his mythological portraits he could paint alongside the marvellous, seer-like *King David*, *Christs* of such mysterious, world-brooding melancholy that no painter has equalled them before or since—once seen, those eyes can never be forgotten. Even in scenes like *Pilate Washing his Hands* or in the mythical personifications such as *St. Paul* or *An Angel Dictating to the Evangelist Matthew*, he renders the mystery of life with imperishable force, vibrant with his own personality. Life's mystery as revealed in the greatest human individuals—that is what he is ultimately seeking everywhere. It is his favourite theme which always grips and shakes him, and its atmosphere suffuses even such famous groups as the *Night Watch* and above all that remarkable *Jewish Bride*. On the other hand, again like Shakespeare in his later tired years, he shows himself in the *Staalmeesters* a past-master of superb clarity and sobriety.

So, if he sees and gives us not only the abysses and the mysteries but the smiling plenitude of life as well, like Shakespeare, what distinguishes him in the lonely lostness of Self from the latter as also from Michelangelo, whose equal he is in expressive force, derives precisely from that lostness of the Self and immersion of it in the Infinite. The difference is this: with Rembrandt even the most general, the universal qualities which he represents in myth, metaphor and symbol are still radiated out, broadcast by the individual "I" alone, are a message coming from the "I" as the ultimate power and source of suffering, a message of universal significance yet, as it were, drowning the universal in itself. Here the individual always confronts the Infinite *immediately*, whereas with Shakespeare or Michelangelo, he finds himself in an *intermediate* realm of Being, a realm of objective, transcendental powers all round him, whose struggles with one another flood through him, quicken him, shatter him, annihilate him but at the same time exalt him. Lostness of Self in, and unity with, the Infinite—those are the two counterpoints. There is nothing between.

This attitude is by no means a narrowly Protestant one. Shakespeare, in whom these transcendental powers are also operative—and how mightily!—proves it. But with Rembrandt they have vanished, because the prevailing atmosphere of the new mathematical view of life had scared them away. They are scattered like dust. And man, lonely, homeless, caught in the beams of the Infinite, must endure his central position in the midst of an oppressive chiaroscuro as on the brink of the void.

That is the real key to the message of this great spirit, this the situation so painfully and unsparingly defined by Pascal. A splendid message, hard almost to excess, only to be borne at all by the infinitely tender humanity that proceeds from this Self lost in the unboundaried universe as from a wondrously self-nourishing fountain of warmth. It was, or so it seems to me, the profoundest, the most crucial utterance of the Seventeenth Century, which, with its mathematics and its will-to-power, had virtually blocked and dried up the streamings of non-dogmatic, non-subjective Transcendence and made impossible the immersion of the Self in its dissolvent fluid. [1]

---

[1] Spinoza does not affect the issue. For his Transcendence is purely dogmatic and apart from that it yields all too easily to a naturalism in terms of power. We have only to think of his politico-theological *Tractate*—especially chap. 16; and his *Ethics*, chap. 9.

CHAPTER IV

DOGMATISM AND VISIONARY VISTAS

1. *The Eighteenth Century*

The Eighteenth Century could no longer endure the hardness of this utterance. Neither did it need to feel it any more. It stood on the same foundations of power-political rivalry and continual argument over the old ecclesiastical and new philosophical dogmas; hence it was in a state of spiritual reversion—albeit powerfully checked—to the archaic origins. But it was also surrounded by conditions which, politically and spiritually, were very different from those of the Seventeenth Century. For the damming or at least regulating of the ravening hunger of the State by the Balance of Europe which William of Orange introduced, and in which people soon saw a new, seemingly eternal principle for the life of the West, altogether superseding the old supra-biological sanctions, facilitated—despite its being only an emergency measure in view of the insatiable rapacities on every hand—the influx into life as a whole of harmonious conceptions linked with this feeling of balance. There was a second influx of astronomical, physical and mathematical ideas, all quite different from those of the Sixteenth and Seventeenth Centuries, flowing into man's interpretation of life and giving form and content to his spirit. A tendency to conceive a universal harmony based on universal balance—such could be the motto of the new apprehension of life, far more than, as is generally held, the apotheosis of reason.

This view of existence coursed down the century, branching into three great streams, each different, of which one remained more or less isolated while the other two swallowed each other up.

The first stream, which has been very much neglected so far by the observers of the great age this century was, had already started on its course at the end of the Seventeenth Century. It had its origin ultimately in the fearful repercussions of the Thirty Years' War. It was an *emotional* movement, rising steadily from the simple church music of Paul Gerhardt to Johann Sebastian Bach and Handel; an emotional movement which then seized hold of the transcendental quality of Catholic Baroque and not only became identical with the outward forms of the latter but also gave eternally valid expression to its ultimate truths. The essential mode in which this movement expressed itself was the new music which, steeped in the Infinite and, in the structure and animation of its polyphony, seeming to come from other spheres and yet to linger in them, made men newly and vividly aware of the wrestling of transcendental forces which were already saturated with human feeling. With Richard Benz we can call it the "eternal" music of the West—eternal because it rises to the extreme heights of beauty and, in Beethoven and Schubert, attains unimaginable proportions.

I am not qualified to speak of it. But the German Baroque, imitative at first of the architecture of the South and West, then acquiring more and more of an individual style after 1690, tells its own story. Whoever has a receptive understanding for these buildings (and it is a measure of the achievement of Winckelmann and others that we really can have to-day) with their majestic, hooded air, becomes conscious—even in the stairways of the castles, the nave and choir of the churches—of an unlimited extension which then, in the ceilings and domes, seems to burst the confines of space and allows infinity to pour in through the windows. He who understands this is led from the mighty harmonic order of the outside into an interior which everywhere vouchsafes a break-through into the Infinite—in the vibration of every line, in the bearing and draperies of the sculptured figures, themselves like ciphers pointing raptly into the measureless Unknown, in the ecstatic soaring of the whole interior to pure melody. Infinity has been made captive on earth, and a multitudinous music turned into colour and stone. This had already begun at the end of the Seventeenth Century. It is intensified during the first half of the Eighteenth, but from the outset it had a graceful and delicate offshoot in the Rococo which later, about 1760, began to smother the yearning sublimities of the Baroque under a playful worldliness.

It is as though the mighty sound-structures of Bach and Handel, the two Protestants, had sprung from these Catholic churches at a time when these churches were still austere; as though the purity of Gluck, the candour of Handel found echo in them; as though the animation of Mozart filled them, playing over the depths; as though in Beethoven and Schubert, whose music almost bursts with their gigantic struggles with the Unknown, mankind were speaking a new language proportioned to this architecture.

That is the one great contour, the great achievement of the latter part of the Seventeenth Century and the whole of the Eighteenth. It signifies the opening of an era of non-dogmatic language comprising and exemplifying in itself all the depths of the soul; a language developed to its highest capacities and one to which humanity as a whole (for after a short initial period it became intelligible to everybody) can and will always turn back, because it opens the door to the universe and allows feeling to pour forth unchecked. Once it was there it became, like no other human creation, detached from time and place because detached from everything conceptual and particular. Its effect on the spirit, stirring it, loosening its bonds and liberating it, was unsurpassed; in this sense it is a symbol of that Transcendence we have been speaking of.

All the same it had *one* limitation: the limitation of its own particular kind of universality. The experience of the transcendental realm, of the struggles going on within it, and of the harmony which, in these great musical structures, over-arched it, is still an elusive experience, even though it speaks of some indefinable bond between man and the cosmos. But it cannot speak an entirely concrete language, cannot give answers to entirely concrete questions. It could not resolve the practical business of living and its conflicts into a harmony, wonderfully as it could do this with everything else.

Thus it comes about in the Eighteenth Century that this universal language of humanity, the gift of music, could exert hardly any influence on the way in which the spiritual and intellectual currents of the age were being consciously held in check. It could not, from its side, free the second and third lines of development—the ideal and the poetic-visionary—from the shackles of dogma imposed on them by the concepts of earlier times. Unfolding in full strength the stream of music flowed majestically on, speaking of human values; but the apprehension of these same human values in the form of words proceeded separately, at a remove.

It is customary to label the purely verbal and conceptual achievements of the Eighteenth Century as Enlightenment, Deism, Rationalism, Optimism, Rousseauesque idolization of Nature, *Sturm und Drang*, German Idealism and such like. What is at the back of these words in the way of transcendental values such as we are concerned with?

Of the "optimism" of the Eighteenth Century we should speak with reservations. It is true that as the oppressive and brutal struggles of the Seventeenth Century for power abated, and even before the practice and then the notion of a Balance of Power announced itself like a gospel of deliverance, there had arisen with the theodicy of Leibnitz a complicated sort of optimism rooted in the old religious principles but exhaling a new breath. Simultaneously it initiated in England, under the inspiration of Neoplatonism, Shaftesbury's impressive and enthusiastic doctrine of the all-sufficing beauty of the world and its parts; while somewhat later, in the Moral Philosophy of people like Young and Adam Smith, the sombre pessimism of Pascal resolved itself into the not exactly shallow but highly positivistic emphasis laid on the innate affections as the basis of human life and society. Yet how cuttingly Voltaire (who, drawing on Pierre Beyle, Leibnitz's great opponent, likewise asserts the moral sense to be as innate in us as the proportions of our limbs), attacks in his *Candide* the deistic-pantheistic conceptions of the existing world as the best of all possible worlds, and with what withering sarcasm does he not pursue these observations in other works, such as *Zadig*. The great Hogarth begins his labours with those well-known satirical "Progresses". And it would be difficult to outdo Swift's devastating mockery of man in the Yahoos. Hence the dark and abysmal aspects of human nature so powerfully felt by the Seventeenth Century have by no means been forgotten by the Eighteenth. Neither are they forgotten during its second half, after Rousseau's optimistic-pessimistic leap into Nature-worship. In Herder's ideas on the Philosophy of History, 1784—on the positive side of which we shall have to say a few words directly—the following two sentences occur: "What a fate it is that exposes a man to the yoke of his generation, to the weak or crazy will of his brothers". And: "This teaches us the truth that here on this earth of ours wild violence and its sister malignant cunning are triumphant". Here at any rate nothing is veiled. On the other hand Kant, although asserting the existence of "radical evil", still opines that "the wickedness of human nature is not so much *malevolence*, taking the word in its strict sense, namely as the intention to make a maxim of *evil as such* and turn it into a motive (for that would be *diabolical*); it is rather a *perversity* of the heart, which, because of its consequences, we also call an evil heart".[1] This is certainly a strong toning down, a sort of abstract levelling out of the bottomless depth-dimensions, since it does not see and acknowledge the innate powers of evil in man as such, as independent entities. It can only understand them as an inversion of the moral order of human motives, a consequence and correlative of the fanatically held orthodoxy taught by the Categorical Imperative as the sole datum of existence.

We have already seen that the Seventeenth Century with its logical thinking influenced by mathematics no longer had room— strongly as it held to the dark view of things, indeed wallowed in it like Pascal—for any directly apprehended, supra-subjective, meta-rational forces. At the very point where, as with Spinoza, such thinking preserved its supra-individual quality and started in a grand manner from a conception of the Whole, evil became pure negation for the reason that it could not be logically apprehended otherwise or fitted into the positive attributes of Divine Totality. The devil became a nonentity, as was expressly stated. Logical dogmatizations ousted the former meta-logical view of the background of life. Except in its great artists, musicians, writers and poets who were in a class by themselves the Eighteenth Century could not shake off these superstructures of logic when it tried to interpret life and its secrets. From Leibnitz's theodicy with its virtually grotesque justification of evil, and onwards by way of Voltaire, who regarded the dark element and all life's basenesses as stupid perversities on the part of Being, and Rousseau, who merely projected these perversities into society, to Kant, from whom radical evil was ultimately only a conceptual negative which, as we saw, merely leads to "perversity of heart", and even beyond Kant—the whole dark-daemonic realm remained outside interpretation even where the Transcendental was approached. It remained outside because they all tried to comprise the Transcendental in logical categories and interpret everything in terms of logic. Inevitably, therefore, the positive

[1] *Die Religion innerhalb der Grenzen der blossen Vernunft.*

transcendental forces were formalized and attenuated to mere concepts, and the brimming, daedal world of the Beautiful was associated with the bald idea of expediency (*Critique of Judgement*). Further, even where the great triumph of thought and experience was staged and what we can call the "realm of the Good accomplishing itself in spontaneous freedom" grasped as the mysterious irruption of Transcendence into the world of "phenomena" understood in mechanistic and causal terms (*Critique of Practical Reason*)—here too those values which had been apprehended and revealed *in all their immediacy* by the great visionaries were only schematized and made the maxims of a deontology laid on the will, which existed in its own right (Kant's "Neigung"), *from outside*, as it were. It was obvious, therefore, that faced with a world in which the "powers of light" had everywhere been deprived of all virtue and substance, converted into logical constructs, the world of the "powers of darkness" should appear only as its shadow, as is the case with Spinoza. Even where the existence of this dark world was hinted at, as with Kant, it was still saddled with an innate tendency to vanish, to become unimportant if not actually invisible because understood in a merely negative sense. So that to the ideas and mental structures of the Eighteenth Century, even where they pressed forward to great depths as in German Transcendentalism, there always clings this peculiarity, namely that they see things only with one eye, not with two; that they do not comprehend life as it were plastically, in all its multiplicity and contradictoriness, but only touch it from one side. It was this that brought about the much quoted tendency to bloodless, rationalistic desiccation and optimistic platitudes, at least in the case of littler minds.

Since, in this age, the whole manner of thinking was based on the mathematical logicism of the Seventeenth Century such a tendency, in the midst of all the deep speculations about man and society, ran the risk of formalizing and idealizing the individual and, instead of regarding the individual and totality impartially, as a natural relationship conditioning and of advantage to both, regarding them as a logical pair of opposites. Consequently there was a danger of accommodating the contractual view of the State to this opposed pair, of drowning the postulates of "Natural Right" which, as we shall see, were profoundly justified from a metaphysical point of view, in this kind of formalism. Though the rights of the individual might be stressed in the name of Humanity, the nature of the State undoubtedly received too much attention in the name of Rationalism. When it came to formulating the nature of the individual and that of the State which, in this century, was as deeply saturated with power-tendencies as before, the optimistic spirit of the age brushed too lightly past these abysmal forces and their relation to the formation of ideals. It is perhaps the weakest feature of the Eighteenth Century that conceptually it never bridged the gap between its humanistic ideals about the remodelling of life and society and the brutal power-individualism of its States. On the whole hardly any restraining influence, ideally speaking, was put on the State's power-drive. Without elucidating the matter further the age kept it within bounds through the fortuitous operation of the Balance of Europe which from 1763 to 1793 brought about, quite accidentally, an interim of undisturbed sunniness, apparently no longer overshadowed by the clouds of power politics and war.[1]

In this period the tendencies of the age, so critical for history, could develop to the full and it seemed that mankind could now really set about understanding and shaping life from the standpoint of Humanity and the individual. If the *dangerous* sort of optimism now came to fruition, so did the great *fruitful* optimism which makes this century in truth immortal. It consisted in the idea of the perfectibility of man through the agency of what they called "Enlightenment".

"Enlightenment" Kant, in 1784, calls the way from immaturity to maturity—in other words the way from unfreedom to freedom. By this he postulates primarily freedom of thought, but at the same time he adds: "This should enable the citizen to acquire freedom of *action*, and the Government to find it conformable to

---

[1] Even Kant, who sees and boldly attacks the problem in his *Perpetual Peace*, is unconscious of the force of the "power-naturalisms" which have to be taken into account in such a peace and built into it. Thanks to the increasing dependence of all nations on trade and money, "Nature" is supposed to bring about the gradual atrophy of the bias towards war that is born of malice, and thus to make perpetual peace possible as the goal of an expanding community based on State Contract. This is a strange anticipation of Herbert Spencer's so wrong-headed sociologico-evolutionary thesis that the fighter was being replaced by the merchant, which was offered as a practical background to the solution of the problem. But what would Kant have said had he experienced the outbreak of dæmonic forces precisely in the epoch of advanced capitalism—the most involved of all in the toils of trade and finance! But he was blind to dæmonisms.

treat man, who is now more than a machine, according to his dignity". It was put more boldly in 1793, in the demand for a Constitution aiming at Liberty, "mutual dependence" and Equality, "based on the idea of original (State) Contract"; a demand at the best for a Representative Constitution founded entirely on liberty. One can see that these are Locke's postulates of Natural Right and Montesquieu's Constitutional ideas; they are the echoes of the great movement for freedom that sounded throughout the Eighteenth Century and culminated in the French Revolution; echoes of it far removed from the storm, sounding only in the sheltered studies of savants in the distant German east that had remained fixed in its absolutisms.

Enlightenment, Liberty, Equality! The source of the strength of these words that stirred the Eighteenth Century with mounting intensity is not to be found in the hair-splittings of the savants or in scientific statements, nor in the social problems that were certainly present. It lies in the fact that Western humanity, after its terrible submergence during the Seventeenth Century, rose up from a new plane of consciousness and expérience and returned to its true self, to its old spiritual values, and rebelled against the brutal political naturalism of the despotic power State. It is a stupid and disastrous habit very popular in Germany, based solely on Hegel or the Romantics, to regard this great new departure as the result of some "atomistic" or "individualistic" Rationalism peculiar to the West. It was something totally different—namely, the rediscovery of the old Western, above all Germanic, bedrock, which showed itself in a fresh light thanks to the new understanding of man and the trend of the age. Locke, the founder of Natural Right which had released such revolutionary tendencies, appealed in the teeth of reactionary Jacobitism and Patriarchalism, both as old as Adam, to a mankind free and equal by God's grace, that is, equipped with equal claims to Right. He appealed, therefore, to a religious foundation deeply believed in. Rousseau's emotional outburst, born of optimistic enthusiasm for Nature and pessimistic rejection of existing society, and demanding, in his *Social Contract*, the surrender of everything and everybody for the constitution of a political whole and the creation of "volonté generale", is for all its rational dress the exact and essential opposite of rationalistic atomism. And the formulations of human rights which, in the separate

States of North America—themselves born of effective Contract—were laid down for the first time in 1775 as something that came before the State and was to be guaranteed by the State, were of a fundamentally religious origin as with Locke.[1] They were created and legally established by men who carried in themselves Old Germanic conceptions of liberty and of the restricted field of State action.

It is not necessary to give further details, either of the concrete distinctions between the ideas in use at the time or of the guises in which they appeared. What underlay the spiritual ferment that could lead to so tremendous a thing as the French Revolution with all its consequences for both good and ill, was nothing less than an actual and factual break-through on the part of mankind into a new, deep-lying layer of Transcendence. It was completed and made effective in that intoxication of optimism with its notions of man's perfectibility. But when even the biologist to-day[2] defines man, in contrast to animals, as "the life-carrier born to freedom", we should be quite clear by this time that the capacity to use freedom properly, and the way *special to and specific of man* by which this capacity may be reached, are two different things, and that the Eighteenth Century performed the service of having disclosed this way and made men conscious of it. It may have been optimistic and sometimes precipitate in its belief in the immediate perfectibility of freedom, although its great ones, like Montesquieu and Kant, were extremely cautious in their pronouncements. The important thing is that man was seen anew. He was understood anew in his specificity.

*   *   *   *   *

On this new level a broad wave of deepened human understanding swept the Eighteenth Century at the very spot where it was still very uncertain and limited in its ideas of political freedom: Germany. Here the flood first of all burst the old spiritual and intellectual conventions—flowing, therefore, in the direction of *Sturm und Drang*. But then its waters piled up and grew clearer. It is, to anticipate a little, timely to-day to recognize aright the marvellous breadth, depth and variety of the German humanitarian ideas of the Eighteenth Century, ideas which are supposed to be so stale and fly-blown, although every-

[1] Cf. Georg Jellinek, *Die Erklärung der Menschen-und Bürgerrechte*, Leipzig, 1895.
[2] Richard Woltereck, *Ontologie des Lebendigen*. See also last chapter.

thing that has happened since and is happening now only proves, even to the blindest of us, what their abeyance means. Anyone who reads a book like Herder's *Ideas on the Philosophy of History* without being stirred by the breath that blows through it, without feeling that here, in a form that is inwardly true, is a new, deeper vision of man, graced in piety but profoundly affecting in its ecstatic acceptance of the "Purposes of Nature and Providence"— anyone who does not feel this knows nothing of that larger vision which the close of this German century was to call "Humanity". To-day, in all probability, we are no longer disposed, like Herder, to understand man purely and simply as a stepping-stone to beings of a higher species and, from just such a devout and hopeful love of Nature, to explain his inadequacies, his imperfections, his vain endeavours and the horrors of his history as so many blunders. We have behaved too badly for that. But who will deny Herder when he shows us so enthusiastically just how and why man is the only creature on earth to have free will and to mould his destiny for good or ill, how he knows no law on earth save that which he imposes on himself? That is what this age grasped for the first time, that is what it introduced into our common store of experience, and that is what the fullness and rounded beauty of its works grew out of, their unity which is almost incomprehensible to-day.

The prime question we have to ask is not where the limitations of this age lay and what the men in it did *not* see. What the age saw was in truth a revelation. It was from such a revelation that Schiller wrote, coined sayings like that of the "laws that hang inalienably up aloft", created dramas like *William Tell* which glorified that saying in fact, others like *Wallenstein* which made plain the complexity of human nature; or else he could swing along triumphantly with the last movement of Beethoven's Ninth Symphony, music of gathering shadows and yawning abysses, and the animation of his soul was so exalted that his oratory gave birth to a thousand forms which have haunted our lives ever since and will ever continue to haunt them.

Of the greatest of them all, Goethe, we can only say one thing here. His imperishable greatness rests on the fact that, though wrestling right from his first *Sturm und Drang* period with the culture of his time and also, as Gundolf rightly says, largely shaping its cultural experiences; though busying himself without cease with its central problem, that of perfectibility, and finally becoming the champion of a quite specific cultural programme—he still towers above and is incomparably more than all that. because, almost alone in his age, he is in touch with the origins, perceiving their nature and their workings with open eyes. He sees them, like the great men of old, immediately and grasps them unhesitatingly, as they did, under whatever symbolisms they appear—Christian, pagan, no matter what. His grasp of them is as true in *Iphigenia* as in *Faust*. Without the aid of any mythological trappings he makes the dark weavings of a fate of which he his fully aware, his subject, portraying it with profound emotion and beauty as in the *Elective Affinities*. He was not afraid to leave a documentary record of some of the things he. beheld and experienced in all their immediacy, as in his well-known utterances on the Daemonic—albeit adapting himself somewhat to the "cultural formulae" of his time.

Here, then, is the last of the great; one who, making free use of imagination, culture and religious forms, gave undogmatic expression to the ultimate experiences he had reached entirely on his own; the last and only one to cling fast to the absolute values of old while immersing them in the discoveries of the new humanity. Thus he strides on like a solitary torch-bearer for another thirty-two years into the Nineteenth Century, towering head and shoulders above it.

The Goethean Age would have been great enough, even without Goethe. In music it had not merely invented a new language for mankind, it had brought it to culminating-point. In the realm of feeling it had fostered an immensely enlarged understanding of man, actively communicable and productive of action. In the world of ideas based on this Humanity, in its conceptions of human destiny and human freedom it had discovered eternal truths. It had felt its values fixed for ever. In Germany, where the old social forms, because they were not yet decayed, still held under the assault of the new ideas and were elastic enough to accept the new view of man, and where this served to break up an area of feeling that had been lying fallow for almost a century—the vision soared to heights of splendour undreamt not only in music and ideal philosophy but above all in poetry, whose message is still valid for us of to-day. Goethe's age, coming at the end of a century of purely reflective development and thus standing

in a highly conscious epoch, was remarkable in allowing no disintegration of the Absolute; rather it felt that its task lay in
declaring the Absolute with all the strength of its instinct and
consciousness (itself bathed in instinct), and thus providing the
Absolute with intellectual foundations, as seemed wholly
possible. By dint of dissociating the ultimate human Absolutes
from the historico-mythological, redemptory and dogmatic
features of Christianity and thereby effectively marrying Christianity and Antiquity, this age fulfilled in a manner that, in a certain
sense, is unsurpassable, the spiritual task of the West.

The type of man the upper classes produced at this time was
of a breadth, depth and delicacy of feeling and fellow-feeling
unexampled in any age. His receptivity went out to everything
without, however, allowing it to disintegrate chaotically in
himself. He was capable of making it an integral part of his own
substance, of assimilating and transforming it to the last possible
degree.

He paid for these high personal and formative capacities with
certain elements which, to use a photographic metaphor, never
appeared in his exposures at all or were sadly diminished in size.
Even with the greatest men of the age there was often a dogmatic
and over-simplified fixation of the many new aspects of man which
had been discovered in the meantime. But its weakness lay
not in its belief in progress, which was no trite *laissez-faire* attitude
like that of the ruling classes during the second half of the Nineteenth Century, rather a winged will, a thirst for perfection born
of high human vision. Its weakness lay, as our hintings have
probably shown, in the circumstance that in its eyes the supra-
personal, transcendental powers of darkness and light, already
dimmed by the mathematical thinking of the Seventeenth
Century, were further de-substantiated by idealization and,
from being factors of immediate experience, were changed into
notional structures divorced from the ground of Being. These
might easily, as we shall soon see, become empty phantoms or
even the playthings of a capricious dialectic, since with the
divorce from life the vision of the dark deeps of existence also
faded; and the experience of the dark and the bright as forming
an indissoluble nexus of a transcendental nature might yield to
a facile uprush of idealism which, not being tempered with the
necessary admixture of resignation—Goethe would have said

"abandon"—could not continue to hold its own against the bitter realities of life.

So that what is, practically speaking, the most important product of the Eighteenth Century—the "religion of freedom", as Benedetto Croce[1] calls it—faces the Nineteenth Century like an angel with all too diaphanous, all too ethereal garments. This angel was a fit object to rise, and cause others to rise, on the wings of enthusiasm. But though he grew into one of the strongest forces of the century the increasingly realistic chill of its atmosphere was bound to be dangerous for one garbed as he was—dangerous because he was not clothed at the start in a tougher, more weather-proof philosophy.

2. *Transition Period*

On the threshold of the Nineteenth Century there is a highly remarkable, rich and yet confused transition period which lasted until 1830 and cannot be ignored because the frontal positions of the Nineteenth Century cannot be understood without it, and because it alone shows us at what point and at what moment the road branches off into Nihilism.

The French Revolution was, apart from the equally momentous establishment of the United States, the first great historical act of the religion of freedom prior to the Nineteenth Century. It had substantially destroyed the old historical forms in Europe and justified their destruction by the postulates of freedom and equal rights. At the same time it had ended in violence and, through the agency of Napoleon, threatened the tense, multifarious structure of Europe with both fundamental upheaval and progressive uniformity. The spiritual effect of this phenomenon unprecedented in the whole history of Europe was extraordinary.

Side by side with the Revolution and more or less consciously in opposition to it and to the whole corpus of eighteenth-century dogmatism there had grown up in Germany—nourished, as we know to-day, by the emotions emanating from that country's great music—a conglomeration of forms which we now sum up under the term Romanticism. The Romantics felt the tension between the "I" and the Infinite in a much more un-abstract

[1] *European History in the Nineteenth Century* (Zurich, 1935).

way as contrasted with the ever-recurring rationalist and dogmatic tendencies of the Eighteenth Century. They felt it more nebulously but at the same time they felt the world and the self to be less in peril of exhaustion, more pregnant with form. Their marked sense for totality and also for the diversity of the individual and of history attacked the roots of the mathematical, rationalist thought of the Seventeenth and Eighteenth Centuries more powerfully and more consciously than did those eighteenth-century undogmatic elements we have already mentioned, on account of a completely different grasp of reality. This new grasp, which peopled reality with shadowy forms as a corrective to the preceding Rationalism, poured forth from Germany like a warm blood-stream across the frozen wastes of Western Europe. But, although many of its literary leaders such as Friedrich Schlegel knew that instead of saying "ideas" we ought really to say "forces"; and although it had flung up great individuals who divined anew the existence of transcendental powers glimpsed from a non-dogmatic plane, this new attitude was too superficial in scope and too fragmentary for such individuals to have broken through to a really great and inwardly coherent experience of the Transcendental, and thus liberate the instinctive visionary insight of earlier days into the spiritual depths from the intellectual shackles of the Seventeenth and Eighteenth Centuries. Save for the very greatest of them, they saw fantastic and phantasmal worlds like E. T. A. Hoffmann, instead of mighty groups of forces comprising both the dark and the bright; or else they ended up by accepting the myths of Christian dogma.

And so, because it was much more homogeneous than all this and of growing practical importance, the last flight of super-conceptualism in the Eighteenth Century, the transcendental apparatus of Hegel, emerged alongside and against the waves of freedom that were everywhere sweeping Europe after Napoleon, fed by nationalism and emotionalism. Just after the spell of dogmatization had seemed finally broken a super-dogmatism established itself as the strongest breakwater against the religion of freedom, a dogmatism of the State's omnipotence, of the unfreedom of the individual, giving free rein at the same time to the power-drive of the State which, as Hegel said, should be unimpeded by "all philanthropizings and paltrinesses of that ilk", a dogmatism which cast its shadow at least over Eastern and Central Europe. Historically speaking this was a complete paradox. Nevertheless, here was the one great position to take up against the French Revolution, a position far more radical and attractive than that of the Romantics—one, moreover, round which all the Napoleonic phenomena could crystallize.

Under the influence of these three factors new alignments took shape kaleidoscopically or old ones, shorn of their former naiveté, took on different colours. The tremendous impact of Napoleon precipitated the cloudy idealizations of freedom down to earth. The heterogeneous and venial dynasticism of Central, Southern and Eastern Europe was suddenly struck at the roots by the idea of freely integrated nationalist formations such as the West already had in practice and which these nationalist aspirations for freedom everywhere postulated. The old cosmopolitanism was swept away, only finding refuge in that world-literature for which Goethe, its promoter, yearned. And the old haphazard dynastic State order that had re-established itself in the wake of Napoleon, faced with this libertarian and nationalist cast of thought, looked round nostalgically for help. It found it partly in the Romantics, from whose individualist notions it could, not without justice, derive certain historical ideas about the State as "a cultural substance" and defend it as "organic"; partly and principally in the legitimization of power and the State advanced by Hegel. The old order in the guise of the so-called principle of legitimacy confronted the spirit of freedom which, having become flesh and blood in the new nationalisms, now threatened the greater part of Europe with revolution. Such was the "modern" form of the old European conflict between freedom and unfreedom, and politically it dominated the foreground of the Nineteenth Century. As a rule the historians over-emphasize the part it played in the course of events.

*   *   *   *   *

In the finer and deeper regions of the spirit which interest us here something more general had been happening, of which we will note two things. Among the younger generation, born since about 1770, which had experienced the Revolution, its aftermath and collapse, and the Restoration with all the freshness of first impressions, the wonderful naiveté of the Eighteenth Century —a naiveté which was there despite all the subversive ideas—was swallowed up in the tremendous upheavals that followed. This generation saw what it did see, critically, and at the same time, since it felt the lack of any great and secure form to hide in,[1] with a certain disequilibrium of soul which might easily become eccentric. And to the extent that it refused to abandon in any way, its more forceful realism notwithstanding, the great values of the strong Eighteenth Century, there echoed in it— and this is our second point—as an undertone to its clear-headedness another note which indicated a peculiar, unconscious attunement to transcendental experiences; a note of different pitch and timbre from and more marked than that given out by even the greatest figures of the Eighteenth Century under the aegis of reason. This disequilibrium and this susceptibility to the Daemonic were capable of infinite modulations, but together they gave rise to a characteristic nuance in the great interpretative figures of the age, which made them appear remarkably discordant as compared with the quiet, full tone of the previous century, so that such persons stand on the threshold of the Nineteenth Century either misunderstood at first or else exercising an oblique influence. Names of no European or universal significance can be passed over. But the extravagances and often deliberate violences in Heinrich von Kleist, whose spiritual power and force of expression stamp him as an artist of genius, are a case in point. No more than his infatuation with death are they the outcome of a mere abnormality of disposition, though something of the sort was there. Neither are they the consequence of the tardiness of his success. We can trace in them quite clearly that disequilibrium which cannot find and does not want to find any escape from the age which isolates him, or from his own particular daemonisms; which drives him at his best, as in *Penthesilea*, to inordinate and daemonic displays of passion and causes him to disappear in a gust of shrill disharmony with his time.

This disharmony with the time is the occasion, one could almost say, of an elevation, an ascent into the bright realms of daemonism, into the Divine on the part of Hölderlin. How much he is repelled by the everyday life of his age, his *Hyperion* shows. Here the letter about the unendurableness of ordinary existence in Germany reveals the impulse of the whole book, which is to pre-

[1] I am deliberately employing here the excellent terminology of Rudolf Kassner.

figure a world wholly animated by the gods in contrast to the world of our dailiness, so obviously pulsing with the powers of darkness and therefore to be rejected. It is the same in the lovely and magnificent fragment *Empedocles*. The "high" man, inspired by Divine Nature and partaking of over-normal powers, cannot, once unmanned by the gods and disowned by the dark mass-daemonisms of earth, remain in life, even when his people calls to him. He casts himself into Etna as the priest of Nature, "drunken with the last raptures". That is no pessimism; it is an aloof but positive feeling for the heights and a repudiation of the sinister chthonic forces—the same feeling that in his later poems spilled over into radiant visions of Nature, of the high-points of history and also, felt at last as wholly a part of Nature and seen as though with the eye of a bird, of our daily life on earth now redeemed of its darkness.

Very different is the second figure of universal significance that sprang from a daemonic rejection of the time—Byron. Nearly everything Byron wrote in his maturity is, overtly or covertly, polemical, with a daemonic motive behind it. Overtly polemical in the manner of those half sprightly, half mordant satires on the stupidly reactionary and bigoted society grouped round Wellington after the defeat of Napoleon, or in the manner of *Don Juan*, a work of genius despite everything, but vitiated by the polemics that obtrude throughout and only readable to-day for the few very beautiful love-passages it contains. In reality this work signifies a profound renunciation of life, born of Byron's insight into its darker recesses. The same renunciation is explicit in the "Mysteries" and culminates in the most important of his mature works, *Manfred*. Though an entirely personal experience *Manfred* is probably the most devastating indictment of human life as part of existence in general that has ever been penned. Human life as part of existence grants the man who is ensnared in its daemonisms no *forgetfulness*; and for him who feels branded by his own actions within the setting of this daemonism there is no escape, no salvation, however much he imprecates it. Better, therefore, not-being, finis.

No wonder, then, that this extreme attitude, starting with a renunciation of society and ending with a grandiose rejection of life altogether, was epoch-making—especially when evinced by a man of daemonic genius who had ideals withal and knew how to die for them. We find traces of him in Italy in Leopardi, and in Russia in Pushkin; not to mention all the languours and *Weltschmerz* that have paled the brows of lesser spirits.

On the threshold of the century which we shall get to know as the Century of the Will and of unleashed Power there stands, arising out of and still imbued with the objective values of the previous century, the great question, wrestling with reality: Should we say "Yes" to everything we experience? Such is, philosophically speaking, Schopenhauer's question, or at least the practical side of his questioning. In its conscious return to Kant and its speculative elaboration of Kantian transcendentalism his philosophy, marvellously lucid in form, is in the last resort more *felt* than in any way demonstrable. And that is its merit. For here, stimulated by the atmosphere of the century dawning behind Napoleon, Schopenhauer views a Power—which we can all apprehend spontaneously and which he designates with the term "Will"—for the first time as the essence of the objective world, as the Kantian "in-itself" of existence. Thus, in a different and profounder way compared with the scholastic thought of Hegel, he causes a reanimation and unfolding of what was an immediate datum of perception *behind* the intellectual fixations of the Seventeenth and Eighteenth Centuries. Untenable as is the antithesis in Schopenhauer between "representation" as represented world and "will" as a thing-in-itself, something active and spontaneous is apprehended for the first time in philosophy as the transcendental background, even though the designation of it as "will" is imperfect. And this way of looking at things was to prove to be the subterranean stream that flowed along underneath the unmetaphysical and increasingly positivistic Nineteenth Century and exerted a fructifying and liberating influence on a few great spirits during the latter half of it.

For the first half, however, this doctrine, with its echoes of Kantian Transcendentalism garnished with Indian wisdom, was ill-timed in the manner of its presentation, despite the fact that it was a true child of the age and that, like the utterances of all the great men of this transition period, it clung to the objective values of the Eighteenth Century, particularly to its humanity values. But if one wanted to get away from Hegel and his scholastic abstractions, then by all means go to the conceptually vague forms and individualisms of the Romantics, but not to a new ground-apprehension of existence which, although in a sense introducing something pre-conceptual, harnessed it at the same time to rigorously logical categories of Transcendence. Thus it came about that the great philosopher of Will who arose at the beginning of the Nineteenth Century to stress the shadow-side of existence, was not recognized by this same "Century of the Will".

Though not unaware of the daemonic, the agonized—or, to speak in anticipation of Nietzsche—the Dionysian depths of existence, none of the great figures of this critical period managed to exert a lasting influence on the course the coming century was now shaping.

CHAPTER V

CONSUMMATION AND DESTRUCTION—THE NINETEENTH CENTURY

1. *Fulfilments*

From many points of view the Nineteenth Century, the Century of the Will, as we have called it, is the time of the fulfilment of all previous centuries of Western history. It saw the fulfilment of the world domination of the West that started in Europe. At the end of it two continents had been settled by Europeans, a third made dependent and partially settled, the East flung open and dotted with Western strong-points. Year by year a mighty stream of people poured forth from Europe in hundreds of thousands into the unlocked spaces of the globe, a stream that kept these annexations and infiltrations suffused with living blood. In the earth-spanning single whole that had thus sprung up there whirred a gigantic centrifuge, which extended its radius with every beat—world capitalism. It deposited people far and wide, threw open areas of raw materials, supplied them with goods and capital investments, correlatively with this piled up greater and greater concentrations of people in its expanding centres of industry in England, Germany and North America, supplied them in their turn with commodities and profits thanks to the expanding areas of raw materials and emigration, continually intensifying the inner concentrations of population and enlarging the orbits of expansion, the one always conditioning the further progress of the other and so on *ad infinitum*.

Thus an unprecedented, dynamic world-totality arose, at once fulfilment and something entirely new, in the place of that world which the European forces of capitalism and the State had been throwing open, slowly, bit by bit, ever since the Sixteenth Century—the world of illimitable horizons where, even in Goethe's time, Alexis took touching leave of Dora as if for all eternity, when he set forth on his travels. Not, as yet, a new star, but an infinitely smaller earth had come into being, overspread as regards technics and organization with a net of domestication. For the Nineteenth Century had also fulfilled the dream of Science, whose ambitions had been growing ever since Bacon's time. Not only had its connections with capitalism and the State established the new world-totality; it had also, and far more so, thanks to its technics and organization, played the very devil with almost every process of life. Intellectually, too, this century accorded science a position which seemed all-devouring. It was the fulfilment of a dream of power when science, creeping into countless fields of specialization, tried to put not only all Natural History, not only the universe and its remotest recesses, not only biological growth, not only human life down to the very fibres of its physical and psychical formation, nay but all that had ever happened in history, no matter where or when, into its seemingly never-ending catalogue of new entries and corrections. It was a sheer display of power when one special institute after another arose, each with a great staff of research-workers. And the professor who, venturing beyond his speciality, reached out for ever greater syntheses and wove generalizations out of them, seemed on the way to replacing the priest, the philosopher and the visionary poet.

This century, particularly during its second half, also appeared to offer extensive fulfilment of two ideas—of the utmost importance for man's destiny—which developed out of the history of the West in the Eighteenth Century: Humanity and Freedom. It championed the minimal demands of humanitarianism wherever its powers sufficed, and not only did it abolish serfdom and slavery but it also struggled to realize a social minimum for labour in the capitalist industrial apparatus and, by means of universal and compulsory education, tried to give everyone the basis for the greatest possible determination and orientation of his own life. And if it could only partially realize political freedom and self-government in the old legitimist corners of Europe there has still never been a century and, except for the classical age of Greece, never an epoch in which such unlimited spiritual and mental, and such well-nigh unbounded personal, freedom of movement obtained. In this respect the world was a whole. And it would be unjust not to see the fullness of spontaneity which had free play in this whole for practically all classes and very wide scope indeed in some of them. Never before has there been such a rich variety of literature as in the peak period of the Nineteenth Century; never such a spate of artistic and musical productions; never such a receptive understanding which often, in individual cases, embraced the whole world and its history; and hardly ever so many harmless semi-productive undertakings working in countless ways for countless purposes. In brief, in quite definite respects this century was one of fulfilment and at the same time of transition to the process which, already latent within it, was to transform the earth into a new star.

2. *Explosive Dynamism: Spiritual Fragmentation: Loss of Depth*

With all this, however, even the spiritually valuable things which, thrown up by such a fullness of life, were bound to the time and so vanished with it, we are not concerned here. For us there stands the question: to what extent and how and why did this in every respect remarkable century bring to birth the catastrophe that now covers the whole world? What were the forces that compelled it in that direction? If it really did comprise the transition that was to change the earth into a new star, why did this transition come to an end, or how was it possible for it to end in the most hideous contest and the most frightful devastations the earth has ever seen? So much so that the Nineteenth Century and practically everything it thought it had won now lies in ruins and, it is to be feared, will perhaps never rise again in its positive aspects—with its negative aspects we shall become sufficiently familiar in the course of our enquiry. Only after we have settled these questions can we face the present from the right angle.

We shall try to approach them firstly by making clear to ourselves the peculiar nature of the dynamism that operated throughout the century, at the same time always taking full account of the spiritual impulses and seeking to answer the question of the continued operation of these forces even to-day. Secondly we shall try to catch sight of the spiritual heritage the century has left behind for us, and this culminates in the question: can we do anything with this heritage now? And should the answer prove preponderantly negative, our next question will be: what have we to remember, what have we to evoke in ourselves in order to re-acquire the strength and the will to face the mountainous problems of contemporary life?

Only at the end, therefore, will it be appropriate to outline the external problems with which we are confronted.

We have chosen the word "Will" as the emblem of the Nineteenth Century. That means to say, in physiological terms, energy and the discharge of energy, and in sociological terms violently eruptive dynamism. And in actual fact the acceleration of all the evolutionary trends inherent in the long history of the West and its fundamental tensions, a mounting tempo of development operating, in some remarkable manner, according to laws of its own, a peculiar eruptive rhythm that led to continual upheavals when two or more of these lines of force met and reinforced one another—such are the salient features of the Nineteenth Century. None of us knew, while we were being borne along on those revolutionary waves, what exactly was happening to us and where it would end. To-day, after the tremendous collapse that is the direct result of them, we can see one or two things clearly, one thing above all.

We see that the whole of history until then had been like a slow and dogged river with currents of migrations, conquests and struggles generally leading to new concentrations that lasted an appreciable time. Though the ground-swell was continually on the move, it was constant. Throughout the historical eras we know, the earth's population increased but slowly. A high birthrate, fantastically high for to-day, but combined with appalling infant mortality that accounted for a third or even more, early death, particularly of men at the height of their virility and of women in their best child-bearing years in child-bed, decimations by war and plague—these are the factors which bring it about that the human population remained static in some places for thousands of years, in others increased only under favourable conditions and even then only temporarily for the most part and very slowly. And then the other factor—the intermediate realm of technics which this relatively constant mass of humanity interposed between itself and nature. It was more static than progressive; it had indeed a development, but hundreds, often thousands, of years lay between each decisive advance. This intermediate realm was still as it were transparent, thin; it did not sever man from nature, it joined him to her only in the way he wanted and did not release him from her rhythm. Even in the second half of the Eighteenth Century it was not fundamentally different from the technical realm of classical antiquity or that of any other part of the earth. On these two foundations—constancy of population and constancy of technics—there arose, by migration, conquest and struggle, sporadically, those newly created political absolutisms whose social structure was in the main everywhere constant and, once established, carefully preserved,—from which, as will be remembered, only the West, charged with peculiar tensions of its own, differentiated itself in the gradual development of its structural forms. But how slow had been the great steps, each hiding in itself a new crystallization: feudalism, urban economy, mercantilist State!

Except in the West where, amongst other stresses and strains, it harboured the crucial tension between freedom and unfreedom, the world of ideas had nowhere been disruptive of the social structure in the long run, not even in Greece and Rome, since it left the basis of their existence—slavery—untouched and only concerned itself with the superstructure. Historically speaking, all the political and social ideas up to the birth of the West and, with short interruptions, in the West itself, still had binding sanctions at the back of them of a religious or transcendental, if not of a magical, order—sanctions which fixed the existing state of things just as it was. Ideals were not revolutionary in the great majority of cases, they were highly conservative, almost everywhere a powerfully mortising cement for the existing framework of life.

All this was suddenly changed, both really and ideally, for the Nineteenth Century on entering into the legacy of the centuries preceding, as if a mass of explosive accumulated during the previous epochs had gone off in one blast. An explosive of gigantic power had already been set at its threshold—the revolutionary idea of freedom which had been touched off for the first time in the Eighteenth Century and which now, fully developed, led not only to the abolition of privilege but, with the demand for equal rights, to democracy as well and could easily, if put into social effect, turn into equalitarianism and anarchy. Accordingly, political revolutions break out one after another in a crackling series during the Nineteenth Century, with the social revolution always looming behind them. This was no less the case in its second half, when political revolutions disguised themselves as radical reformism; but that only means that *social* revolution follows its own path: assassinations, putsches, terror, subterranean or sometimes even quite open preparations for revolt.

And how had the real changed, as distinct from the ideal? The two historical bases of life—population and technics—had gone into a galloping tempo overnight. Science and the spread of humanitarianism and hygiene, by lowering the infant mortality and raising the longevity rate, had accelerated the speed of population first of Europe, then of the whole world to proportions never before imagined, so that people began to count on a regular doubling of it within twenty years—a tendency which gave rise to the Malthusian nightmare of a shrinking margin of subsistence in face of a birth-rate advancing by geometrical progression. The population of Europe, Russia included, actually rose in a hundred years from 180 millions to 450 millions; that of the United States, thanks to immigration from Europe of about 32 millions, from 5½ millions to 76 millions. Even the present population of India with its 352 millions, and the swarming 440 millions of China, are very largely the result of the impact of hygiene and the sudden universal flooding of the human tide connected with it. Concurrently with this there occurred—the most important product of science, practically speaking—the technical revolution that set in during the last third of the Eighteenth Century and broke into a mad gallop after the middle of the Nineteenth, driving an intermediate realm like a wedge between the rapidly multiplying numbers of men on the earth, and Nature—a realm that no longer united them to her but, like a hiatus, separated them from her completely. Technologically it created a new world of the machine and, from the point of view of communications, opened up unheard-of possibilities; and since it performed both functions in ever renewed outbursts of activity it was continually offering the rising flood of mankind, now released from stagnation and caught up in the general movement, a new earth and a new environment, until in our own day man has at last—with the complete disappearance, in the *auditory* sense, of the significance of space—been made the veritable inhabitant of a new star which this realm of technology almost wholly overspreads. Nor must we leave out of account those other two lines of evolution, apparently unconnected but actually in close relationship from a certain point on. The first is the eruptive development of mechanized capitalism, already sketched in outline, continually ·drawing the human flow into its ever-widening orbit, distributing it over the face of the earth, concentrating and enclosing it in industrial key-points, and at the same time revolutionizing the stratification of classes throughout the century. The second, less noticed but no less important, is the evolution, inspired by the engineer, of a now fully mechanized militarism which, once drawn into the current of technical revolution, turned the army from a purely subservient instrument of the State into an independent political factor gradually pursuing its own policies and entering into its own alliances, with its own expanding power-drives and more and more monstrous apparatus of destruction. And there finally you have that system of world-spanning power politics, imperialist evolution, ̇which, based above all on the alliance between exclusive capitalism and an equally exclusive militarism, precipitated the world from the moment the markets of the earth began to shrink, into the age of new, planetary conflicts. There are, of course, numerous other lines of evolution, all more or less disruptive in the form and manner of their working, for which place cannot be found here, although they run disquietingly and disturbingly all through the century.

All these factors have their own driving impulse and rhythm. In their initial movement they pay scant regard to one another, but gradually each instils its revolutionary consequences into the other and is thereby reinforced. And from about the middle of the century on the various currents, borne along on the space-conquering technology of movement, had been steadily converging within the ambience of a fully developed and powerfully expansionist capitalism, carrying the multiplication of peoples and military technics with them, till the former little eddies and whirlpools grew into a single, mighty, perilous flood encircling the whole earth and changing its face from one decade to the next. For anyone endowed with superhuman hearing and powers of perception the whole of the Nineteenth Century, but above all the second half of it, must have had the effect of a mounting roar of waves tumultuously beating against one another—waves which might sometime bear down all together and bring forth untold and indescribable catastrophe.

Clairvoyant and clairaudient spirits there were who noticed the beginnings of the uproar, chiefly those men who had turned their eyes towards the most menacing and conspicuous effects of the turmoil—namely, the masses of people who were being ceaselessly cast on to the proletarian dumpheap, deprived of all status and rights, the breakdown of hitherto stable classes into social chaos. A word might well be said about these early visionaries, but the process as a whole was not arrested by their vision. It went relentlessly forward and, getting into full swing by the middle of the century, led to something unique in history: the separation of whole nations into two opposing spiritual camps without inner contact. The division did not occur everywhere with equal strength, but in certain key-places it was final, and from now on the process was further aided by propaganda. The essence of Marxism lay in completing it. The social hierarchy of earlier centuries and other cultures was, from a material point of view, often subject to far greater strains, ranging in India, for instance, from the Untouchables and pariahs to the half-divine Brahmins, and in classical antiquity from the chattel-like slave to the freeman. Nevertheless a spiritual unity always overarched these great tensions, in India it might be the belief in the possibility of being reborn into the higher castes, or in Greece and Rome the actual participation of the slaves in the spiritual world of their masters, which was expressed in the extensive practice of emancipation and the resultant rise of the emancipated. The spiritual worlds of the serfs, artisans, patricians and nobles in the early West were, of course, subsequently driven apart by the cultural hierarchy which Humanism imposed; but they were still attuned to one another in their mode of life and, though severe tensions might be set up by social pressures, they were mutually related. Not even Russia, with her oppressed and trampled peasantry, possessed a lower class which laid claim to a spiritual world of its own inaccessible to all the other classes.

This claim to a peculiar closed world on the part of those whom capitalism had cast into proletarian nonentity was the unique result, which Marx and Engels made the basis of their activity, of the interpenetration of all the revolutionary forces operating in the West since the middle of the century, that is, since the rise of an outcast proletariat in the broad mass. As men these proletarians were mere appendages of their ability to work, battered to and fro on the tides of capitalism, taken on one minute and thrown into unemployment the next, their work itself no more than a commodity. Tossed like dice, incapable of choice, they must drudge cheerlessly at the machine from morn till night, only to find on their return home to a bleak tenement as in England or, on the continent, a couple of back-rooms facing some flue-like yard, a cross-grained wife and undernourished children; not even sure of a free Sunday, with no recreations growing organically out of their lives or possessions—what else could they do but succumb to the ever-present temptation to slip off to the nearest pub and squander their meagre wages in drink? The rise of such a proletariat, flung into a veritable abyss of misery at this critical stage of its life, whose wives also were sucked dry with work and whose children no man hesitated to wear out with excessive toil in their tenderest years—these were a forcing-house in which the historical process, as represented by Marx and Engels in the Communist Manifesto of 1847 on the eve of the Revolution, could be fulfilled. This was the moment to demonstrate the whole of history in terms of evolution and the possession of the means of production, framed and determined by class-struggles, and to cry out to the rising industrial proletariat: "You, the outcasts, are the last and final stage of this evolution, yours is the task of bringing it to an end. Organize yourselves politically, economically and spiritually and then, by winning political power, you will abolish all classes in the common ownership of production. You have nothing to lose but your chains, and a world to win! Unite!"

So that in the midst of this industrial efflorescence which, internationally speaking, brought about the greatest upheaval in men's lives that history has ever seen, and in view of the formidable segregation of the proletariat the cry went forth to the world's pariahs like an uncanny premonition of things to come: "You are the only world of the future, you and you alone, if only you will conquer it. Evolution itself has placed the weapons in your hands". This is not the place to mention that there were sociologists before Marx and Engels who interpreted the revolution set going by the new century, such as Saint Simon and Comte and practical-minded socialists full of force and *élan* like Proudhon who wanted to influence the rising proletariat, or socialistically inclined reformers like Sismondi. They are all dwarfed by the propagandist power of this Marxist conception, which combined historical analysis with the strongest appeal to action in an altogether unprecedented way. Of the scientific analysis of history which Marx tried to work out over the next ten years or so, the greater part is faulty in detail. But two things stand: his conception of modern capitalism based on technology and a rising birth-rate as a centrifugal mechanism continually enlarging and re-creating its own conditions, with accumulation of capital as the driving force. Secondly, the propagandist effect on the displaced masses of the message bound up with the new doctrine, which let down an iron curtain between the self-segregating working-classes in so far as they annexed it for themselves, and the rest of society.

This annexation ensued only gradually and was by no means universal. Above all it did not include the Anglo-Saxon world, which very largely went its own way. But on the whole it meant—and how strongly this meaning affected even England is shown by Disraeli's remark about "the two nations"—that from now on Europe must begin to fall into two opposing spiritual camps, of which the lower proletarian one regarded the values held to be universal and ultimately valid in the upper camp as particularist because they emanated from ruling interests, while it itself fancied that the whole world's future values were included in its own particularisms. So that the result was not dismemberment merely, but a making relative of all objective spiritual values which were thereafter described as "ideologies", meaning screens for economic interests. This was, spiritually speaking, the blow struck at the root of the whole structure of transcendental concepts and positions held since the Eighteenth Century.

It could only be struck because these concepts, a continuation of the mathematical logicism of the Seventeenth Century, had ramified into rootless abstractions whose underlying springs of nourishment—once, as we have seen, known instinctively as immanent and transcendental powers in closest contact with life and the whole phenomenal world—had been completely lost sight of. As a result relativism, naturalism, positivism, psychologism (particularly psychologism after the collapse of the last valid structure of logical transcendentalism—the Hegelian system) all sprang up after the thirties in the ever-increasing spiritual confusion that set in with the general upheaval of life, side by side with various vulgarized or sophisticated versions of Bentham's utilitarianism, all offering, long before the onset of Marxism, the desired and loudly demanded "realistic" substitutes for the earlier and far profounder understanding of life. And the budding "Historical School", choose what form it might and whatever the notions and idealist elements with which it covered its conceptions of reality, carried within it, the more subtly and meticulously, the more scrupulously it scrutinized itself, owing to the very nature of its *positivist* frame of reference and interpretation of life, a principle that made for the complete *relativity* of all the former spiritual values which gave life a unity— little as it recognized this process for a very long time thanks to its own inherent lack of clear definitions. The confusion might end quite early on in a consistent subjectivism of the Stirner pattern, or it might, as in the case of Kierkegaard, lead from the sensation of standing on the brink of the void to a similar, if shallower, reiteration of Pascal's paradoxical plunge into faith. Be that as it may, dissolution of the universal, ideal values of life—either because men continued to profess them while ignoring their foundation, or because, looking deeper, they doubted them— this was the basic spiritual symptom of the age. But nothing struck the unity of the West so disintegrating a blow in the long run as Marxist relativism, with its consistent proclamations of an innate gulf in society that could not be bridged, and its habit of drawing axiomatic conclusions from axiomatic positions. For a long while the bourgeois world of culture paid no attention to it, yet all the time, nourished by these divisive conclusions, a second world, quite inaccessible to it, was in fact relentlessly expanding beneath its bourgeois superstructures. A world which, when one could ignore it no longer, finally burst though with the first World War into the upper strata of society and, with its end-results— the making relative not only of social ideas but of thought and knowledge as well—drove the confusion of mind, at least in Germany, to a climax in a welter of sociological over-sophistication.

Such were the consequences, in the mental and spiritual sphere, of the tidal wave which rose out of the Communist Manifesto of 1847–8.

In the sphere of actual life, however, the consequences were felt much earlier and much more strongly. In England and the

Anglo-Saxon countries the Marxist or crypto-Marxist outburst remained, for special reasons to which we shall allude in due course, at a safe distance for yet a considerable time. But in general, during this same period of capitalist efflorescence—that is, in the sixties, seventies and eighties—there at once emerged, behind the rapidly expanding and earth-conquering world which this efflorescence created, its dark shadow, which, bent on its destruction, clutched at its very life, which called itself that world's executioner, which, despite the trappings of Marxist evolution that still granted the bourgeoisie a certain span of life and a certain historical task, fell upon it at every crisis that offered and did its best by means of terrorism and acts of violence continually to undermine the existing state of things and damage what was to come.

As a result of this the bourgeois world of capitalist progress, apparently so rosy, was in reality bathed in the livid glare of what was later known, euphemistically, as "the social question", which men of deeper insight had already discerned as the revolutionary consequence of the unleashing of the acquisitive instinct, and which politicians recognized as the ever-present danger of "subversion". The danger was heightened when, in the train of world-wide commercial expansion, progress succeeded at the cost of grave crises in bringing about a general increase of prosperity after the fifties and sixties and a rise in the status of the proletariat also. This, with England setting the lead in recognizing the struggle of the trades-unions for a bigger share in the profits of production and in instituting protective measures, included attempts somehow to incorporate the proletariat in the capitalist system by various "reforms". We shall see how and why in the period immediately before and after the turn of the century this incorporation by reform had certain opportunities even outside the Anglo-Saxon countries and in the West generally. Golden opportunities! Once we have recognized it as an absolutely unique period of unceasing upheaval in all departments of life it is proper to conceive of it as not merely politically revolutionary but, from the social consequences of this upheaval and its spiritual effects, essentially as a time of chronic social revolution as well. Explosive development and a trend towards radical egalitarianism are, sociologically speaking, its most marked features, as decisive historically as the more or less general inauguration of freedom and democracy, the building of national States and the resultant vacillation between humanitarianism and power politics, cosmopolitanism and nationalism which are stressed so lovingly by the historian, certain as it is that all these other things have also left their characteristic mark on the age. But first and foremost the century is a positive volcano of revolution. Its eruptive nature allowed of peaceful interludes during which the prospects for egalitarianism seemed hopeless. But deep down in remained unchanged. Its slumber was only apparent. The tremendous crises and catastrophes which fill the first half of the Twentieth Century are the revelation and in a certain sense the fulfilment of this nature. They were only possible on the basis of that revolutionary dualism which decreed that so convulsive an age must always be seeking new paths, new outlets, always creating new situations which, coming spontaneously to a head at a given moment, must inevitably end in the very disasters that would lead to revolution, indeed egalitarianism.

All that we have written would be so much empty verbiage if we represented the little we have been able to say about the spiritual trend towards nihilism under any other guise than that which shows how and why it is related to the revolutionary tendency we have sketched, and at the same time to the social and cultural collapse in which we now find ourselves,—and to the glimpses into the depths which this collapse may perhaps make possible for us.

3. *Interludes*

If we cast our gaze backwards from the vertex of the Nineteenth Century—1848–50—and forwards on the other side to 1914 (for in reality and in spirit it extends as far as that, while, as we have remarked, its upheavals begin only in the twenties and thirties), we perceive two epochs, distinguished from each other not only by the transformation of the world that began about 1850, not only by the mighty dissemination of peoples from Europe, not only by the accelerating tempo of capitalism, technology and militarism, but above all by the radically different quality of their spiritual habitus and its variations. If up to 1850 in the practical upheavals of life everything is still experiment, still a new, tentative beginning—from the population point of view an initial thrusting into the shrinking spaces of the world,— so in the spiritual sphere everything at that time is still the echo of the period of transition, an astonished, dazzled awareness of the new vistas opened out by the newness of things. Taken as a whole, therefore, it was a time of restless fermentation in a Europe that was spatially still quite small. The second half, the period of radiation and explosion, suddenly offers wide horizons and a really new life with totally different prospects. It, and particularly the latter part of it where, in the midst of a new mutation of world and mind, Nietzsche stands like a spiritual colossus, is our especial concern, since it is there that the basic conditions of the present crisis have their direct origin.

As regards the first half of the century we shall say only this: that the proletarian world had not yet broken loose from the bourgeois world, and that the centre of gravity of the new industrial and technical development lay in England, where it had begun far back in the Eighteenth Century, and kept the lead for thirty or forty years up to the middle of the Nineteenth. But scarcely had it passed over in some measure, principally to France, when the spiritual centre of gravity also shifted from England to Paris. Paris became the intellectual experimental station of Europe, not only because of the irruption of free capitalism or the get-rich-quick slogan of Louis-Philippe, but because of all these things on the basis of that shift. This is almost truer of the thirties than of the forties, which wear a different complexion all over Europe.

Paris of the thirties was a rich, confused medley, the effects of Romanticism mingling with a new realism nourished intellectually by the revival of Natural Science (Cuvier, Geoffroy-St. Hilaire) and the fascination it exerted, and actually and factually by the awareness of the new life-principles of capitalism. The great literary exponent of the one was Victor Hugo, of the other Balzac, both at once characteristic of the new way in which the century was coming to grips with the problems of life: either to make the great values of the Eighteenth Century that sprang from a universal uprush of idealism—Humanity and Freedom— the critically untested bases of its activity, or to construct new bases out of a consciously empirical Realism (sociological in essence because of the prevailing upheavals in society), with a vague religious or quasi-religious set of ideals hovering in the background. Balzac is the chief, at any rate the first, champion of the second approach. He is a perfect product of the get-rich-quick atmosphere of the thirties which, together with the political and social, but above all the scientific turmoil of the age, influenced him profoundly. Obsessed by the sociological urge to render an exact account of his time, inspired by a longing to get to the heart of things, delighting in the "physiological" play of language and possessing as his greatest gift an unexampled intuitive and generalizing imagination, he presents, for the first time in Western literature, quite deliberately and programmatically, the "average man", and nothing more exalted than that, as the hero of an epopoeia which, in the *Comedie Humaine*, purports to embrace the whole gamut of human existence,—human averages marvellously typified, of course, and become the vehicles and mouthpieces of man's besetting passions. In this matter his realism succeeded in portraying the go-getting, the money-grubbing and the sexual licence of his age far better and more vividly than the magic and mysticism which, in his view, also belonged to reality on a higher or lower level. All the same, even Stendhal, a realist equally great and as an artist of much greater refinement and consequence than Balzac, is cast into the shade with others like de Musset and de Vigny, not to mention Dumas, by this phenomenal personage, whose new technique of studied, almost banal, realism, flirt as it might with Buonapartism, reactionary Monarchism and pietism, ushered in a totally new intellectual epoch—the epoch of literary naturalism, which here rears its head for the first time beside the naturalism already stirring in philosophy.

Like a trumpeter of the old Eighteenth Century ideals wrapped in romantic garb, Victor Hugo stands at his side, the greatest of all the word-magicians of France, so rich in word-magic, pursuing till far into the second half of the century his championship of humanitarianism and the old postulates of freedom, calmly accepting exile and proscription; while, as is well known, he owed the mark he left upon history to the romantic works, veering towards the grotesque, written during the thirties. He and Balzac are both protagonists of the onward march of the Nineteenth Century.

The forties have an altogether different complexion from the thirties with their peculiar blending of Naturalism influenced by Natural Science and social conditions, and Romanticism fed by history. For at the threshold of the forties there stands the first political organization of the working-class whose members were exclusively workers—English Chartism, its goal the radical introduction of democracy. The insurrection of 1839, following the refusal of the Charist demands, had to be bloodily suppressed, and against the intricate background of England's social development, steeped in conservatism, the movement was bound to subside in the general amelioration of the industrial worker's lot that thereupon supervened (repeal of the corn-laws, legalization of the trades unions, etc.)—and to debouch into more peaceful paths of democracy via reform and the extension of franchise. But the beacon had its effect. Suddenly people became aware of the dark side of the Industrial Revolution and mass mechanization; and the forties, which saw the birth of so many technical innovations that were eventually to create another, broader and friendlier basis for life, were consequently a time when people, still living in a cramped world, were brought sharply face to face with the human effects of the general upheaval—pauperism, as they then called the segregation of the proletariat. It was a time when the unbounded naturalism of the acquisitive instinct, given free play and aided and abetted by technics, was felt even in the upper, cultured classes as an alien, dangerous and subversive intruder; when even in England there were those who were wont to chastise it with scorpions (Carlyle) or pillory it with bitter satire mitigated only by a dash of humour, in the style of Dickens; when anarchic idealists like Bakunin travelled about the continent on the look-out for possibilities of putsches, while the only real work of social criticism that was to have any importance later was done, of course, in Paris, by men of mental verve like Proudhon and where attempts at socialist putsches had actually occurred (Blanqui's first revolt in 1839). It was a time when people first began to be affected inwardly, not merely on the political level, but in their social conscience, by the explosive and capricious nature of the great factual revolution taking place all round them, when, under the pressure of these crowding novelties, Romanticism melted like butter and even the scholastic finalization of history by Hegel creakingly collapsed, and with it the whole conceptual and doctrinal structure of German Idealism tottered on its foundations. Finer and far-sighted spirits like Kierkegaard, as we have said, drew the conclusion that, since the transcendental values of life, once supported by Idealism, were now baseless, mankind ran the risk of being brought to the brink of nothingness, and that the only thing to do was to take that logical Pascalian leap into strict and intensive Christianity. Coarser minds felt no disquietude at first. For them the turbid mixture of Idealism and Historicism that now put in its appearance, was enough. Or, if they wanted a more fundamental interpretation, they turned to something like Feuerbach's Naturalism, which saw the Ideal and the Spiritual as sheer *Nature* and with which a naïve retention of the old ideas of Humanity and Freedom as self-evident data could, and did, go hand in hand.

Marx and Engels kept this symbiosis in reserve for their propaganda which soon burst forth, borrowing its pathetic appeal entirely from these old ideas of Humanity and Freedom, although, strictly speaking, the materialist interpretation of history they had evolved since the Communist Manifesto blasted this ideal as it did all others, by making everything relative and thus devaluing it. In that second, laboriously elaborated Marxist world of a proletariat absolutely divided in fact and in spirit from the bourgeoisie, things were not proceeding so logically—for this world needed above all a practical impetus. Since, however, force of circumstances required that for a long time the only objects of Marxist interest should be the interpretation of its own situation, its own hopes for the future, the tactical seizure of opportunities and not any new intellectual constructions, we have to regard this world first and foremost as the function of a slow-flowing revolutionary stream gathering speed and spreading under the impact of propaganda and the continual development of the social upheaval, a stream from which geysers now and then shoot up as in the Commune of 1871, but on the whole deferring its main revolutionary outburst to a later date, when it would have got its forces under control thanks to "historical development", in accordance with the formula of the time: when the expropriation of the expropriators had become a simple matter owing to their numbers having been reduced by mutual competition, or to some great end-crisis of capitalism. So that the chosen goal of the toiling, subterranean masses was social and political revolution that grew in scope the longer it was deferred.

Such, then, was the situation in which the upper classes, increasingly cut off from the roots of society, had to develop mentally during the second half of the century. It was a hopeless situation from the start, concretely as well as spiritually. There is no need to stress the point. Concretely it passed through two phases: one, reaching up to the eighties, in which the new society outwardly unfolded in a mounting blaze of glory but which threatened to become hollower and hollower within, and a second, when, for reasons to be discussed later, the social threat seemed to come from below.

The period 1850–1880, during which the world was thrown open by commerce and mass emigration from Europe, the time of conquest of territory after territory which rounded off England's gigantic Empire and laid the foundations of those of France and Russia, the time which saw the concentration of peoples in the working-class and residential quarters of the rapidly growing industrial cities, the spread of credit and banking round the world, and of the news-service that accompanied trade everywhere—in short, the great inaugural epoch of planetary domestication and the technical conquest of life and nature, had for its motto, like a magically shining trade-mark, "Unlimited Prestige of Science", particularly positive Science. For as we know the names to conjure with then were Darwin, Herbert Spencer and John Stuart Mill, which last-named, though a man of deeper vision, had opened the way to the Positivism which Spencer spun out to such banal lengths of mechanistic and sociological evolutionism. Positive Science—but on the other hand it was also called History. . And thus, wherever people were too exacting to find inner orientation in the simple forms of a mechanistic interpretation of nature and society, there was a plethora of fantastical constructions offering orientation in historical images. It was, one might say, the golden age of historiography, marked in Germany by Ranke, Mommsen, the early Johann Gustav Droysen, in France by Renan, then Taine. All these men, though they might work, like Ranke, strongly influenced by ideological considerations, or be brilliant critics of society and character like Mommsen, psychologically imaginative like Renan, or obsessed with *petits faits* yet giving the best results within the framework of biography, like Taine—send out in their scrupulously substantiated descriptions potent impulses which, while largely replacing the earlier philosophical interpretations of life grounded in rationalism, still (and this is characteristic of the period) had as self-evident background the great ideas won during the Eighteenth Century—Humanity and Freedom, no matter how understood. The whole age, in its slowly separating political spheres as well as in the sphere of its bourgeois culture, still lived on the fund of experience emanating from the preceding century and continued to squander it like an inheritance without adding any new experience of its own, until finally almost nothing was left.

It is astonishing how, so soon after widespread economic prosperity had set in with world conquest and things seemed to be going a little better with the working-class (the latter appearing to have been outwardly incorporated in the capitalist system by means of the trades unions and the Co-operative Movement), the cultured bourgeoisie forgot what had shaken them so profoundly in the forties: the sight of naked acquisitiveness and its consequences. It had not altogether lost the memory of this vision in the fifties, following the revolution of 1848. But now the memory lost its outlandish quality and slowly faded from consciousness. Instead, the unshackling of the acquisitive instinct was regarded in a quite matter-of-fact way and people simply accepted the danger that side by side with this glorious bourgeois development a second world might, indeed was bound to, arise completely cut off from it and its culture, with aspirations which would imperil the continuance of its own world. Not that they did not see "the working-class question" in the external problems it posed. On the contrary this question was discovered afresh in its concrete social aspects—at least on the continent. And the perception of it everywhere gave rise to a progressive humanization of working conditions through legislation and the allowance of self-help organizations among the working-class. In Germany it led, not without severe struggles in the mind of the bourgeoisie, to the establishment, in the Society for Social Politics, of a politically influential body whose aim was to promote the necessary humane incorporation of the working-class in the social framework.

But what was happening in the intellectual sphere? Only in England did it seem that the worst was over, since a powerful economic spurt, vigorous and timely support of the working-classes by social intervention and continuous democratization on the part of the rulers had arrested not only the spiritual but also the political separation of the workers. But in Germany? The National Society whose propaganda aimed at the political unification of the country told Lassalle, who wanted to merge his Workers' Union bodily into it, that as far as it was concerned there was no working-class. And a man like David Friedrich Strauss could, even in 1872, put forward as the natural solution of the workers' problem, dependent only on their intelligence, that they should rise into the ranks of the bourgeoisie. Hence, simultaneously with outward unity, the spiritual schism of the proletariat, exacerbated by discriminative political legislation, had become fundamental, so much so that the Society for Social Politics for a long time could not contemplate accepting representatives of revolutionary Labour into its ranks, although it was working for the incorporation of the workers in the nation's unity. In France, Italy and the rest of the continent things were not quite so acute, because life there had a stronger bias towards natural or political democracy and because in those countries there were no such divisive tendencies smacking of military discipline as in Germany. But the leaven of strict spiritual separation as advocated by Marxism had force enough gradually to pervade everywhere.

Astonishing, as we have said, and only to be understood psychologically, perhaps, in the case of England, is the extent to which, notwithstanding this undermining process going on in the midst of the general frenzy of progress and expansion, the cultured bourgeoisie could still think that its own particular world was the only one that could exist and that it automatically contained all the human perfections that could possibly be imagined. This was most decidedly so in England, where the Victorian Age turned its own ingrained bourgeois mode of life into a symbol of the essentially aristocratic, impassive gentleman-type, behind which the bourgeois stuffiness that largely filled the mental atmosphere was for a long time hidden as behind a blank wall. In Germany there occurred, to speak candidly, a sort of spiritual shrinkage, seeing that the rapid process of national unification had, almost imperceptibly, substituted outward successes for inner ones, intoxicated the cultured bourgeoisie and doubtless, if one compares them with earlier periods, made them superficial,—and further, had set the petit bourgeoisie and lower classes sedulously aping them. So far did this vulgerization go that the great German historians confined themselves overwhelmingly to the retailing of national enthusiasms, with the result that one can scarcely conceive of a work like Mommsen's *Roman History*, inspired by the afterglow of the revolutionary vistas of 1848, with its magnificent descriptions of the century-long revolutionary struggle waged by the Roman proletariat, being written in the sixties or seventies in Germany. A further result was that, sole emblem of really universal synthesis of spiritual vision and historical narrative, the non-German Jakob Burckhardt towers like a lonely column in the German-speaking wilderness of the seventies and eighties. Finally, the national enthusiasms of the German bourgeoisie did not allow them to realize at all clearly how, since the campaign of 1861 and again since the rejection of the parliamentary system in 1877 by Bismarck, and because of the whole nature of his subsequent activity, their political backbone had in fact been broken, and how Bismarck's shoring up and consolidation of Germany's "realpolitisch" position by negotiation and argument had driven a wedge between the cultured classes and any responsible political action. So that in Germany they found that not only were their social roots in the lower strata, which these classes had always managed to keep intact in England, torn away, but that the political determination of their own life which in England rested on a like foundation, was also reft from their hands and themselves in point of fact reduced spiritually to the role of spectators without seeming to be aware of being flung into the corner like this. The consequences were immeasurable. For neither the bombast of Wilhelm nor the later Germany of force and violence could have arisen without them.

In France things were very different. Under the third Napoleon she had passed through the defeat of 1870 and been profoundly shaken by it; stagnation of birth-rate had set in and, owing to the separation of her eastern territories where capitalism was powerfully evolving, and from more general causes too, a marked seccession from the stream of progress. Despite her earlier revolutions there followed no similar undermining and, as no legitimism of tradition interfered as in Germany, no political castration of the bourgeoisie. In the midst of the intense and ever intensifying bourgeois way of life that was then general the intellectuals, who always had influential contacts with politics, still maintained their influence in the world at large and this, what with the universality of their projects, was really not inconsiderable. Thanks to its greater agility and animation the intelligentsia brought to birth a new world standing deliberately aloof from the bourgeoisie and repudiating its whole outlook—a world which is circumscribed too narrowly by the term "Bohemian" but nevertheless approaches it. In the final period before the first World War its emanations affected other countries: in conjunction with other factors it threw up over the whole of the continent for a short while the contours of a new, supra-national conception of life which, in its numerous manifestations, eclipsed the old bourgeois outlook.

First of all, in order to understand the secondary or reactionary movements that set in, we must enquire what the cultured bourgeoisie, stuck fast in the onflowing capitalist stream which, for all one could see in the sixties, had no discoverable limits and seemed destined to transform the earth from end to end,—what did these people do with the possibilities the new life proffered? How did they reconcile the new and the old values? How try to incorporate the latter into the former? To-day we all know: they have left us as frightful memorials of that age the "great wens" of the cities with their ribbon developments and proliferating rings; the hideous atrocities of their church architecture and other typical erections; paintings that are all drenched in the conventional "brown sauce"—a mediocre hodge-podge of sentimentality, part historical, part political; a fine record of objectivity in Science, but in literature only works that excel in local or period descriptions and can hardly hold any more general interest to-day. This much would generally be admitted about the Victorian Age nowadays, even in England. In Germany this sort of thing was first uttered, and a mirror pitilessly held up to the age, by the young Nietzsche in his two volumes of *Thoughts Out of Season* published 1873-4. He sees a Germany grown fat and complacent after the war, a Germany proud of its "culture" and what this has enabled it to achieve compared with earlier centuries. He sees, however, once the mask is torn away, only a mob of "culture philistines", people who are no longer seekers and enquirers but self-satisfied, sated, conscious epigones who, "in their inveterate barbarism", "flee enthusiasm in any shape and seek refuge in historical consciousness". And if they do not all literally separate "culture" and "life" in the unctuous Smilesian manner of David Friedrich Strauss (so rightly scarified by Nietzsche as the apotheosis of self-complacency), feeling and describing the former as a little garden of repose in which to recover from the strains of the latter, and wandering in it as "in a cabinet of wax figures", swollen with sublimities and thinking: "So let us live, so let us roam entranced!"—still, taken by and large, that is the impression they give, moderns cluttered up with an accumulation of historical and scientific facts, "walking encyclopaedias of far-off ages, customs, arts, philosophies, religions, sciences, handbooks of edification within and barbarism without", radiating tastelessness in all directions and, moving as they do "in a cosmopolitan raree-show of gods, customs and arts", the result "of their continual inner World Exhibitions of History", dessicating into "printed paper souls, incapable of any really great, creative flight, feeble personalities, massive mediocrities that become more and more mediocre", "till one's stomach turns". Therefore, cries the young Nietzsche, how shall the philosophic mind stick it in such a nation, a nation "divided into the cultured with souls that are perverted by education and the uncultured with souls that are inaccessible, a nation, therefore, that has lost the higher unity of soul and nature". And though at that time he is unable to see the social problem and its realities in true perspective, as is evident from some of his other observations, yet he can write: "Let us bear explicit witness to the fact that what is at stake is the unity of German spirit and German life, now that the contrast between form and substance, essence and convention has been destroyed". Practically or, if you will, very unpractically, the solution offered is—salvation through the great artists, philosophers, saints.

Only at one point in the German spiritual sphere of the time could a beginning be discerned for any such hope: in the great musician, poet and pamphleteer who had fled Germany as a social revolutionary in 1849 and who now, from his voluntarily continued exile in Switzerland, sent forth his great musical dramas into the world which, in their programmatic blending of music and poetry and (in the performance) educative art, were understood as the new "absolute" work of art of the future and were supposed to be of profound significance on account of their philosophical substructure. The aesthetic assessment of Wagner's

art, in which his particular fusion of legend, fantasy and expressionism rises to the heights of sensuousness, sometimes even to
theatrical bombast, must be left to professionals. There are
undoubtedly works, such as *Tristan* and the *Meistersinger* and
numerous passages in others, where eternal notes are struck in a
new way and are become imperishable. But it is no less to be
doubted that this consciously created "absolute art-form", the
antithesis of bourgeois shallowness, could be impugned as resting
on a profound, almost Schopenhauerian pessimism, or it could,
as in fact happened later, have enormous artistic success. Yet it
could never, despite the inner force of its representation, become
the redeeming spiritual expression of a national unity that did
not in fact exist and could not be created by those means; that is
to say, it could not rise to that function which Greek Tragedy
performed for a tragic age and which was given to the Greeks
once and for all time. It was a token of the nobility of youth and
restless longing for change on the part of Nietzsche to regard that
non-existent factor as, artistically, a final term instead of recognizing it as a defective premise—and to blaze Wagner's fame
abroad on that basis. At the same time Nietzsche was profoundly
right in grasping the uniqueness of Wagner's position in the smug
and optimistic world of German bourgeois culture. The uniqueness was, we must add, something specifically German. For only
in Germany, the Germany of the new Reich, amid the ruins of
all the great traditions of the German spirit, was it possible for a
single individual to stand up and actually find a prophet for his
claim that he and he alone would father forth in his works a new
German and at the same time a new Western culture. A phenomenon that was to be repeated, fatefully enough, in Nietzsche
himself.

In the France of the fifties to the eighties where, in the stages
we have sketched, the bourgeoising of life was proceeding apace
but where the cultured classes were not so cut off from the field
of political decisions, the artists had not as a general rule sold
themselves to the bourgeoisie as much as in England and Germany. Neither, on the other hand, had a similar kind of prophetic
emancipation of the bourgeois world taken place as in Germany.
The French form of emancipation which, as we have said, can
roughly be designated by the term "Bohemian", comprised a
number of diverse elements and was everywhere geared to

bourgeois normality.   In this peculiar fluid contrast between the intellectual and the merely bourgeois, France had managed, even at the time of the third Napoleon, when the uprush of capitalism and bourgeoisdom was at its strongest, not only to effect the wittiest, most intimate criticism of the bourgeois world in artistic works of a very high level but, more important, to break through on a broad front to the immemorial problems of humanity that are generally buried and hidden from sight and, for the first time and almost alone in the Nineteenth Century, to obtain a new and original vision of them.   Flaubert, with his artist's aloofness and fine-edged tool, sketched the questionable aspects of the bourgeois world, especially where it shaded off below into humdrum philistinism.   And all through Louis Philippe's reign the inexhaustible invention of the great Honoré Daumier offered a running commentary of caricature on French bourgeois life.   They were the works of a poverty-stricken lithographer earning his bread to the end of his days by his contributions—amounting to 4,000 in all—to the two periodicals *Caricature* and *Charivari*, a painter of momentous stature who anticipated many of the achievements of the later Expressionists, and who had it in him to portray grippingly not only the drudgery of the proletariat and the miserable lot of such phenomena on the fringe of society as the juggler and such-like, but also to give an unforgettable face to the deep, universal human situations and types—one has only to think of his pictures of emigrants, or of his Don Quixote.

Penetration to the immemorial facts and phenomena of the human spirit, such is also the achievement of perhaps the most astonishing artist of this on the whole superficial age, who came into uncanny contact with the realm of objective transcendental powers.   Baudelaire experienced their force in that Paris which, wrapped in the most modern garb, was growing into a capital of world-wide fame.   Extraordinarily sensitive, given to melancholy and deep brooding, he felt them from the erotic, not to say the pathologically sexual side.   He felt their dark-daemonic might and sang it in the *Fleurs du mal*.   This is virtually a break-through to the universal. Stefan George, his imitator in Germany and his equal in form and concreteness, is quite right to say of him that he won new—and he might have added, profounder—fields for poetry; and he is right also to speak of the fervent spirituality with which Baudelaire, approaching from these depths, invested the most delicate matters. Intoxicated with the Beyond Baudelaire could write of those "powers":

> Je sais que vous gardez une place au Poëte
> Dans les rangs bienheureux des saintes Légions,
> Et que vous l'invitez à l'éternelle fête
> Des Trônes, des Vertus, des Dominations . . .

This fanatic of beauty, living in an age hastening towards Subjectivism, held fast to the objective transcendental force of Beauty as to a refuge from the dark:

> Sur ton cou large et rond, sur tes épaules grasses,
> Ta tête se pavane avec d'étranges grâces;
>   D'un air placide et triomphant
> Tu passes ton chemin, majestueuse enfant.

An image like one of Michelangelo's, one thinks, rising like a redemptive symbol out of the depths of transcendental experience. And that at a time when symbol and depth lay buried under a pile of rubbish. And indeed, Baudelaire is like a solitary glimpse into the yawning pit that immediately closes again. The naturalism of Zola, magnificent of its kind, quite unbourgeois if not definitely anti-bourgeois: the wonderfully realistic characterization of Maupassant who himself touches on the dark side of things, these no longer know of such abysses. And the very lovely verse of the anti-naturalistic school of Mallarmé, Rimbaud and Verlaine does not seem, exquisite as the latter's often is, to pierce through to the level on which we meet and recognize each other as mortals, even if visions of quite other worlds disturb us.

But in this bourgeois period France trod yet another road, spiritually outside the beaten bourgeois track, which, branching off from Naturalism in its proper sense, went far beyond it and was therefore bound to end in the search for essentials, shown in all their simplicity by Daumier. I mean the road taken by the first generation of Impressionists born almost exclusively between 1830 and 1840 and, after the mid-sixties, taking their bearings from Manet. These men, feeling themselves a school, shattered the prevailing *atelier* manner with their *plein air* technique and, in the teeth of all convention, sought the direct apprehension of things in the clear light of day without any circumambulations or pretences. To begin with, their unvarnished naturalism aroused indignation and as, remarkably enough, they were regarded by their friend Zola, the man who thought he could come to the essentials through the accumulation of innumerable little "naked facts", as artistic fellow-travellers, they received a wry defence at his hands. It is true that outwardly they painted with *petits faits*, apparently resolving all objects into their light-reflexes. But with what power did they not look behind this for the essentials, the essence of things, and seek the shortest and most potent mode for its expression! It is hardly possible to render the nature of this new movement, still marked with the reserve of youth, more classically than Manet in his *Déjeuner dans l'atelier*; or a French provincial town with such economy of genius as Pissarro in his etching of the Pont de Pierre in Rouen; or to give the very breath of Paris at that time more evocatively than in the same artist's view of the Boulevard Montmartre from above, where, in a glowing sea of colour, the individual merges in the throng and yet the whole is the most concrete and actual thing in the world. These only by way of examples, showing how the impressionists, in their choice of themes, remained at one with the bourgeois life around them. Finally, borne on the same current of art, Cézanne, living like an anchorite in Aix and exhibiting scarcely a single picture all his life, found his soul in a conscious, relentless struggle for the essential core—of a person (in the pictures of his wife, for instance), of a situation (*Les Joueurs*), of a landscape, a mountain (the St. Victoire), leaving behind pictures such as that of Achille Emperaire that are among the most moving and individual achievements of great art. It is but a short step from him to the post-impressionist van Gogh, who, in his last great period of inspiration, burst the chains by which the Impressionists felt bound in their search for the essential in Nature, and thus in a grand manner ushered in a revolution in painting which tailed off rather miserably at the end, namely in Expressionism. This, however, goes beyond our central theme and we do not need to speak of it.

So that there were always, even in the periods of progress most imperilling to the spirit, forces at work in France that belonged to a sort of third world, contemporaneous with the banal world of the bourgeoisie and that of seceding proletariat; forces which, when the time came for the bourgeoisie to try to burst its confines at the end of the century, still retained a certain general significance, at least as a symptom.

Meanwhile over all Europe and thence over the world at large the historical and sociological dynamism continued its iron march. Since the beginning of the eighties it had entered on a new phase. More or less rapidly it created wholly new situations in which the eruptive forces of evolution underwent transformation and aligned themselves in a new way. At the same time more brutal spiritual collectivities gained in mass and tended to amalgamate with these evolutionary forces, thus discharging into the world a new and all-pervading atmosphere of conflict and war. Storm-clouds gathered and were apparently dispersed again, to be followed by broad periods of bright sunshine, so that they were always thrust into the background of consciousness and their gravity was realized by scarcely a soul. For reasons which are tolerably clear the future and destiny of Germany became the pivot of the world situation while—singular coincidence—in the mature Nietzsche there appeared a spiritual colossus who was busily brewing universally liberating formulae out of the existing bourgeois stuffiness, thereby accumulating a regular arsenal of explosives which, once popularized and taken all too literally, ignited and threatened the whole Western world with destruction.

We shall speak first of all of the change in sociological conditions and the spiritual transformations this entailed. Since 1850 the running tempo of cultural and capitalist expansion, which then seemed to have endless spaces and possibilities before it, had quickly girdled the earth. After 1880 mankind everywhere encountered the other side of the picture. Expanding power and the flood of goods and commodities came into head-on collision. What had once seemed a playground for unlimited free competition proved to have limits after all. In place of the demand for more and more far-flung outposts of Empire, everybody suddenly began calling for the division and distribution of the earth's surface and its key-points into spheres of interest.

Since these spheres of interest, like the allocation of colonies, could only be negotiated by settlement as between States, capitalism, which had formerly tried to rid itself of all State intervention as far as possible, inevitably fell back on the State. The result was State intervention for purposes of foreign trade or the upkeep of the home market, the guaranteeing of certain areas, the establishment of key-positions or share-quotas where interests crossed, arbitrations innumerable and, as a means thereto, congresses of world-wide scope and import. From the Congress of Berlin in 1878, which tried to regulate the balance of power in the Near East and the Balkans but did not finally succeed, to the Congo Conference of 1884 at which the division of Central Africa was decided, the succession of such congresses initiated by Bismarck's fears of war led to the Hague Peace Conferences, whither the leading statesmen all flocked in their concern—unfortunately not felt by Germany, for disarmament and the setting up of an international court of arbitration.

A convention not without grounds. For, ever since British cannon had sounded before Alexandria in 1882 for the control of the Suez Canal, the life-line of Empire, the clash of imperialisms had never ceased. It led with short lulls to what appeared from a planetary point of view to be only local wars; from the Sino-Japanese and the American Peninsular War via the Sudan Campaign, the Fashoda Interlude, the Boer War, the Japanese-Russian and the Italian-Turkish Wars to the Balkan Wars, behind which façade the rivalries of Russian and Austrian imperialisms in reality lay hid. An extraordinarily dangerous situation began to develop for Europe, which was dynamically still the focus and source of world events. Her system of balance, having functioned tolerably well for quite a considerable time, now began to exhaust itself as the centre of gravity not only of England's interests but of those of the most important continental nations too—Russia, France, Italy and finally even Germany—shifted outside Europe; while at the same time in Europe itself, which during the second half of the Nineteenth Century rested precariously on a compromise between nationalist aspirations and historic form (Austro-Hungary), certain currents arose which, backed by her imperialist tendencies, must inevitably disrupt her. I mean the racial theories that sprang from the inexhaustible fount of what purported to be scientific biology. Still sunk in unresolved controversies even in their own field, and in reality offering the mind no more than a frame for the free play of imagination, the fantastic conceptions to which such theories gave rise nevertheless did point without a doubt to real and extraordinarily important facts concerned with breeding, its variations and maintenance. These, so people argued, had been overlooked in the general picture of man hitherto, although facts of this kind must surely be quite palpable and the stress they laid on the inequality of the various races must, one would have thought, provide a very simple key to everything inexplicable in history and human life. Tendentious interest in and ostensible evidence of the facts poured in on all hands, and in the twinkling of an eye there was a ready-made popular doctrine none of whose assertions (such as the universal prejudice regarding the disadvantages of racial miscegenation) could be verified or stand the test of impartial verification, since all known races and peoples were quite obviously the result of such mixings. All the same, the less they could be proved the more fanatically—as usual—they were believed, partly because they fell in with certain instincts and partly because they appeared to offer an exact description, that corresponded to these instincts, of facts which undoubtedly existed; and also because they made a quantitative analysis of blood-mixtures possible. Moreover, as a contrast to the general democratic trend, the doctrine fitted in with the aristocratic instinct which had always set great store by "breeding", although it had not yet sunk to the level of racial theory. It was enough for the latter to give support to the self-esteem (that generally parades as "aristocractic" instinct!) particularly of nations still unsure of themselves, and to issue fierce little nations scarcely out of their swaddling-clothes and already lusting after their "baptism of fire", with a birth-certificate—and all at once its effect was there, an effect of shattering significance. For the racial doctrine now consummated its fateful marriage with unsatisfied nationalist aspirations wherever they appeared, which stimulated the growth of the consuming Nationalism we know to-day, from the historical and cultural ideas of *nationality* such as prevailed earlier. But above all it wedded itself to the imperialism that lay dormant everywhere, particularly the imperialism of the German and the Slav. And lastly it entered into a secret and illegal liaison with the forces of militarism that had become attached to these imperialisms and grown into semi-independent entities.

It is not the place here to follow the convolutions and history of the Pan-Slav Movement, which originated among the Western Slavs, was taken up by the Russian Slavophiles and debouched into the militaristic imperialism of the Czars, nor the far simpler and more direct course of Germanism, nourished ever since the seventies on Antisemitism and destined to end in arrant race-mania. We all know Grillparzer's prophetic and apprehensive prognosis about humanity passing via nationalism to bestiality. And it is true enough that increasing toughness, hatred and the most primitive pogrom instincts were both parent and child of these two movements and the atmosphere they produced. What is of historic importance for Europe is the fact that both, united in their mutual hatred, worked together not only to overturn the European East and South-east, they worked first and foremost to dislodge the vital corner-stone of any Balance of Europe that was still to be maintained, without which the whole structure was bound to fall apart into spheres of interest, as has in fact happened.

Bismarck felt this clearly and, with his far-sighted realism, advocated the retention of such State crystallizations as had been won and a policy of national limitation, seeking to banish the danger by a system of complicated alliances and back-insurances. Yet his "blood and iron" policy, though probably inevitable for the unification of Germany, proclaimed an Order of the Day that rolled across Europe and ushered in an epoch bearing the motto: Power first, last and all the time! The bulk of German professors who, to do them justice, had not always been so blind, fell down before this fetish as before a god-sent political saviour. Any and every association of ideal values with power interests (a process that life makes inevitable, since power is a basic factor and has a voice in almost all actions no matter how ideal their intention, and absolutely so where State actions are concerned) was called in the official jargon of Germany humbug, cant. People wanted Power pure and simple, Power in the abstract, without an inkling of an idea what explosions they were fostering with this glorification of an activism that, though muffled and muzzled in various ways, was formidable enough in all conscience. They flung this highly inflammable material into a world situation that was growing daily more dangerous owing to the seeds of conflict inherent in the imperialistic and military tendencies we have mentioned, without heeding the gentle warning of Jakob Burckhardt that power is essentially evil—meaning that power should not be made to serve propaganda. Yet people continued to abuse it like this and seemed not to notice how it swelled the clouds gathering over Germany which Bismarck had sought to banish, until they were ripe for a storm of unprecedented fury.

One would have thought that even if the German power-theoreticians were so blind and deaf some feeling, some uneasiness creeping over more than a mere handful of alert politicians must have arisen in the public at large, a universal consciousness that the foundations of the global order centred on Europe were on the point of being undermined, that the very core of Europe's existence was becoming daily more precarious. But in the midst of the general rattling of sabres and blaring of propaganda the exact opposite of any such feeling was, remarkably enough, the peculiarity of the twenty-four years from 1890 to the outbreak of war in 1914. The reason for this is to be found in the singular nature and inner dynamism of capitalism at this period. Never before had capitalist commercialism enjoyed such a rich harvest, gathering in all its fruits. During this quarter of a century the unceasing expansionism began to slacken off. Instead, a new and more harmonious cycle of capitalism supervened in place of the old cycles based on the extensive exploitation of the masses as analysed by Marx. The new cycle pivoted on the *increased* purchasing power of the masses resulting from the Trades Union Movement and was still further heightened by the world-wide raising of the standard of living through technology. If the winning of new markets became more difficult, the sales to areas already won in foreign lands were prosecuted at an undiminished rate, and a happy balance between domestic and foreign trade was struck owing to the mounting absorptive capacity of the home markets of Europe occasioned by the increased purchasing power of the masses aforesaid. A new cycle, therefore, resting equally on the rising prosperity of the great centres of world industry and on that of the foci of power and interest abroad. It was a healthy sort of economic cycle that seemed to offer a secure future for capitalism without the driving necessity of continual additional expansion or the earlier exploitations, and it affected all classes like a gentle rain of prosperity that falleth everywhere. Never since the advent of the Industrial Revolution had there been such an abatement of economic crises, which hitherto, as a result of orgies of over-investment followed by slumps in employment, had convulsed the whole of the Nineteenth Century in ten-year cycles, each time pitilessly throwing the workers on to the street. But after 1890 the waves began to settle down in a reasonably moderate fluctuation. And never before had the proletariat, borne along on the general surge despite the spread of Marxist doctrine and organizations, been so close *in practice* to reformist incorporation in the capitalist world, so close to an actual dissolution of its revolutionary spiritual apartness. Finally, never had the feeling that the whole world was being domesticated by the cultural forces of capitalism been so strong, or so general the unrestrictedness of personal movement when people could indulge in sight-seeing and pleasure-cruising *ad libitum*, the entire globe a single great unit which in those days could be crossed from one end to the other without a passport.

This securing and perfecting of world unification by means of culture and capitalism, together with the general rise in prosperity and diminution of social tension, gave birth to a feeling of hidden security despite the rumours of imperial problems on all sides and the universal din of militarism, racialism and nationalism—a regular ferment of disintegration. "Surely nobody will risk blowing up this closely-knit world of outward prosperity and spiritual interchange by turning these bogeys of disquiet into actual cannon shots; surely nobody will be maniacal enough to embark on the experiment of military conquest"—such was the feeling that anaesthetized the existing tensions. And whoever talks too loudly of his own power and aggrandizement, or of risks and premiums, and pursues a threatening policy, all the rest must secure themselves by uniting against him—this was the slowly evolving political maxim that resulted and was finally to end in the encirclement (dangerous because in reality it only exacerbated the tensions) of an apparently unsatisfied Germany seeking satisfaction everywhere, a veritable focus of international unrest. All this allowed a situation to develop in which a single spark sufficed to send the whole world up in flames and smother the network of prosperity and well-being in the smoke of an immense conflagration.

CHAPTER VI

NIETZSCHE AND THE CATASTROPHE

1. *Nietzsche*

Into this situation of extremest historical contradiction and under a cloud of the most menacing dangers there stepped, at the very moment when these dangers were beginning to manifest themselves, a personality of colossal dimensions whom we have already met in youth—Nietzsche, now grown ripe and conscious of his task, feeling himself called to be a spiritual destroyer, the transvaluer of all values, a man who had at his command unique powers of expression of high intellectual calibre and who could tip the trembling scales to one side or the other decisively. In his own estimation only partially a German and consciously standing aloof from everything German, Nietzsche nevertheless was a child of the German problem. He takes his stand on the crucial border-line, one might say on the very suture, of history, the crater of seething world-danger.

We have no intention of outlining the phenomenon of Nietzsche as a whole, which is more massive and more cloven almost than that of any other great man. Nor do we intend to penetrate to the full the marvellous spiritual caverns of his philosophy, sparkling and glancing with a thousand colours, or to isolate, as some have tried to do, the ultimate individual core of this most individual of philosophers and personalities, the most pregnant with fate of all Fate's vehicles of the spirit. The first is impracticable for us, and the second, quite apart from anything else, is forbidden us by our respect for his mighty destiny which the daemonism of his age cast into twilight. What we have to say in elucidation of the salient features of his historical significance which, like a storm, cleared the atmosphere with liberating and exhilarating but, on the whole, devastating effect, is roughly given below.

With him there burst upon the cultured classes who had,

particularly in Germany, by force of habit given up any idea of influencing the course of practical events by their spineless and will-less retreat into the ivory towers of contemplation, a spiritual will the like of which history had never seen, a will that spoke, and knew how to speak, to these same cultured classes. In order to grasp the effect Nietzsche had we must visualize him as a gigantic chimera: its head a speaking poet, a very considerable artist; its tail, which provided the driving and attacking power, an immense and tumultuous will, and its body a highly developed faculty for the most delicate intellectual and psychological analysis, finding an inexhaustible delight in aphoristic formulation.

Reacting to the cultural philistinism of the Germans and its clotted barbarities Nietzsche as a young man had sought salvation in the total art-forms of Richard Wagner, endeavouring to transmit in this the beginnings of a cultural unity resting on a deepening vision of the world in the Schopenhauerian manner. This youthful enthusiasm lasted only a short while, so long as he held the master in honour if not actually enjoying his intimate friendship. But after the intoxication has flown Nietzsche had to seek another great goal and conquer a world of inconquerable will in the teeth of his time. And so, after the period of his severe illness, that interlude so often described by himself of conscious critical dissection of all the old ideals and of sceptical revulsion from life, which he entitled "Voltaire" (as in *Human All Too Human*, 1876–8, and *The Wanderer and his Shadow*, 1879) there followed, after 1880, the crystallization of ideas and experiences round something wholly new in him, whose future shape was evidently not altogether clear even to himself at first. This process is laid down in *The Dawn of Day*—everywhere in that book you can see Nietzsche "on the way". Then, suddenly, a sort of revelation came in August 1881, giving rise to a time of completely new vision and new formulation and a great illuminated will, of which the crucial work is *Thus Spake Zarathustra* in 1883–5; while the essential steps thereto had already been taken in a collection of aphorisms in 1881, *Joyful Wisdom*. *Zarathustra* had come upon him like a revelation, and the first three books at least were written in a sort of continuous ecstasy. Since this in our view represents the sort of communication most characteristically Nietzschean—that is, spun round with poetry—we shall use it to outline the essentials of his message. The appropriate and probably necessary supplement to it, without poetical accessories, is to be found in *Beyond Good and Evil* (1885–6); in the Fifth Book of *Joyful Wisdom*, as in certain of the *Discourses* written in 1886 and the controversial treatise *The Genealogy of Morals* in 1887. The *Will to Power*, which he did not live to publish but whose aphorisms were for the most part arranged by him in a definite system, show him at the same intellectual level and in full control of himself. Here, however, we catch sight of those great aberrations which have made this book as popularly understood or misunderstood, a veritable powder-barrel of destructiveness. Of this we shall have to speak in greater detail later. On the other hand we can, for the purposes of our sketch, lightly leave aside the works that followed in quick succession in 1888, where a certain no longer disciplined exuberance is already apparent— *The Case of Wagner*, *The Twilight of the Idols*, and *The Antichrist*— especially as they are the culmination of earlier material in so far as they concern us at all. Whereas the *Ecce Homo*, written shortly before his collapse, is indispensable for the understanding of Nietzsche.

Taken as a whole, *Zarathustra* is without parallel in literature. Written in the form of the prophet's descent from his mountain or island solitude high above the sea in a southern land, his retreat back into this solitude and his final return from it, a message of tremendous vitality is imparted in discourses to friends, in monologues, interludes, dream-like experiences and visions. As Zarathustra wrestles with its formulation he makes it shine and glow as with a thousand lights. It is to be a message of "hardness", of "lion-like" strength. But over it is spread an air of delicate inner animation, tenderness, fragrance, and one could even add melancholy. Wonderful passages of pure poetry are scattered in and the whole book surges forward splendid with imagination and shining vision in a rhythm hitherto unknown in the German tongue. Though certain places may have the effect of a too powerful insistence on self it is in essence a grand, hard-won and bitterly felt confession, in the course of which Nietzsche's missionary zeal is applied in a hundred different ways. The message, as expressed, is often carried to extremes. Although one may accept this as a legitimate heightening of effect one still feels through it all the dark fatality of this man which we shall have to disclose to the full later, because the great act of liberation he achieved made him a like fatality himself.

To discover the nature and content of this message, its great breath and also the fateful qualities that lay in the manner of its presentation, it is as well to distinguish three things. Firstly, what one may call Nietzsche's *great rejection*, that complex of things and facts in life which he held at arm's length and which he hoped to overcome. It is from this that the direction of his message may best be understood. Secondly, the general conditions of his life and times, which were responsible not only for the clothing of his ideas but also for the limitations and one-sidedness of his vision, and which further enable one to see the causes of his later aberration. Lastly, the nature of his personality and destiny. This reveals the kernel of his message, its particular idiosyncrasy, also its extreme or eccentric qualities, its overleaping of all boundaries. In the portrait we shall sketch these three partly in isolation, partly as they bear on one another.

Everybody knows that Nietzsche himself repeatedly described as the heart and soul of his message the idea that man is something to be surpassed—the doctrine of the Superman; and, as a background to be treated only with the greatest reserve, the vision of "Eternal Recurrence" within which is to fall the "great noontide", when the Superman will be revealed.

Let us leave the latter or esoteric part aside for the moment. That man is to be surpassed is only to be understood completely as the consequence of Nietzsche's "great rejection". This, to begin with, is directed against his age and the men of the bourgeois Nineteenth Century. Later it is broadened and deepened by his Dionysian experience until it leads to the repudiation of man altogether in his present form, even the highest. Zarathustra speaks of both in the sharpest tones. Of the men of the bourgeois culture period he says, in accentuation of the charges that Nietzsche had already flung at their heads earlier: "You are the home of all paint-pots, the pied motley that is lacking in faith". "If any should strip you of your veils and wrappings, of your paint and your gesticulations, he would have just about enough left to make a scarecrow with". "This is the bitterness of my bowels, that I cannot endure you naked or clothed, you present-day men". For they are the ones who harbour in themselves and produce the man "who can no longer give birth to a star", the

"Last Man, who makes everything small and whose generations are unkillable as the ground-flea". These last men want "the ticking of a little happiness"; they want comfort. "Virtue for them is what makes modest and tame. With their virtue they have made the wolf a dog, and they have made man Man's best domestic pet". Worse: "Those apostles of submission! Wherever it is petty and sickly and abysmal they crawl like lice; only my disgust prevents me from squashing them". "Even your wickedest is petty, just as I thought". But they are also "the poison-spiders, tarantulas full of venom against everything that has power". They are the "preachers of equality", "secretly vengeful". "Distrust all those who jabber about 'Justice'; when they call themselves 'good and just' do not forget that they fall short of the Pharisee in one thing only—Power". "To-day the little people are master, preaching submission and modesty and policy and efficiency and the long boring toll of the little virtues". "The effeminate, the servile and the off-scourings of the rabble—this is now to become master of man's fate. O loathing, loathing, loathing! It asks and asks and never tires of asking how man can live best, longest, most pleasantly? That is why they are the masters to-day". And from this Nietzsche's other contention follows: that the cultured classes are world-weary. "Those who learn much unlearn all fiery longing—you hear them whispering this in the dark alleys". "Wisdom makes weary, nothing is worth while; 'Thou shalt not covet' ". "Nothing is worth while; 'Thou shalt not will' ". "But this is a gospel for slaves. Yonder is the little skiff—may it not sail into the Great Nothing?" Hatred of the increasing tameness of civilization, of mob democracy, of nihilistic pessimism born of world-weariness and mind-weariness, hatred of lassitude of the will—these were the things that exacerbated Nietzsche's original rejection of the cultural chaos of the bourgeoisie, the "scribble-rabble" and their futile historical researches, now rejected along with his own Schopenhauerian past.

But he plumbs a still deeper level of rejection. Seeing the reaction against the *fin-de-siècle* atmosphere, i.e. emergent democracy and the universal tide of outward satisfaction that leaves a welter of mediocrity in its wake, he cries that there are now the preachers of death, preachers for the "many too many". "These are the terrible creatures who go about with the beast of prey in their hearts and have no choice except lust or self-laceration". "They are the consumptives of the soul; scarcely are they born when they begin to die, and long for doctrines of weariness and renunciation. . . . 'Life is suffering', say some. . . . 'Lust is sin', say others, the preachers of death, 'let us go apart and beget no children. Giving birth is a weariness; why go on bearing? We bear only the unfortunate' ". " 'Pity is necessary', says a third. 'Take what I have, what I am. So much the less will life bind me!' . . . They want to be quit of life—what do they care if they bind others still faster with their chains and their gifts! And you for whom life is desperate toil and unrest: are you not very tired of life? . . . You can hardly endure yourselves, all your diligence is an escape and a longing for self-forgetfulness . . . Everywhere there resounds the voice of them that preach death, and the earth is full of those to whom death must be preached". Then the "mob". "To everything cleanly I am gracious, but I cannot endure the grinning mouths and the thirst of the unclean. They cast their eye down into the fountain; now only their odious grinning glances up from the fountain. They have poisoned the holy water with their lewdness, and now that they call their squalid dreams 'delight' they have poisoned words as well". "I turned my back on the rulers when I saw what they call ruling nowadays: trafficking and bargaining for power with the mob. And holding my nose I went disgustedly through all the yesterdays and all the to-days, and the yesterdays and the to-days stank of the scribble-rabble". "This is not the mouthful that almost choked me: to know that life itself requires enmity and death and agony on the cross. But once I asked and nearly choked with my asking: 'What? ! is this rabble also *necessary* for life?! Are poisoned fountains necessary and reeking fires and dirtied dreams and maggots in the bread of life?' "

It is only here that one realizes the scope and depth of Nietzsche's rejection. The creature Man, to whom all this foulness clings, Nietzsche says, must be surpassed, not only in his time-bound historical shape but altogether. Man should not rest content with the snugness and poisonous smugness of the scholars, "who sit in the cool of the shade and want to be spectators in all things". On the contrary, the whole of *Zarathustra* is a rousing summons to the will, to courage and a soaring flight to the plane on which dwells the new man.

As out of a raging sea the idea of the Superman rises out of the "Dionysian view of life". This, as Nietzsche reiterates ten thousand times, is the diametrical opposite of the Christian or any other transcendental view in the ordinary sense. It has nothing to do with the world of the "Other-Worlders", who dream of a "dehumanized human world behind this world, a celestial blank". "Cease thrusting your head into the sand of celestial things, but carry it free and proud, the earthly head that is the meaning of the earth!" For, says Nietzsche, "I call it evil and the work of a misanthrope—all that teaching about the one and the perfect, the unmoved, the self-sufficient, the imperishable. 'The imperishable'—is but a trope, and the poets lie too much. The best tropes and parables should speak rather of time and becoming; they should be a paean of praise and a vindication of all transience". This kind of earthly view sees, if it has the Dionysian perspective, that of its own nature life must be full of horror and suffering as well as of happiness and serenity; that it is a perpetual overcoming and becoming, which means a destroying and rebuilding. " 'Look', life whispered to me, 'I am that which must ever surpass itself!' " "Deep as a man sees into life, so deeply will he see into suffering". "The more man strives up towards the light, the more powerfully will his roots drive earthwards and downwards into darkness, into the depths, into evil." And, "One thing is impossible in all things—reasonableness". "A *little* reason, of course, a seed of wisdom scattered from star to star—this leaven is mixed in all things: for the sake of folly, wisdom is mixed in all things!" And further: "I am not put out of conceit with the wicked by your timidity. I am happy to see the marvels hatched by the hot sun: tigers and palms and rattlesnakes. Among men too there is a glorious brood of the hot sun, and much that is marvellous in the wicked". Therefore "you shall say 'enemy' but not 'rogue'; 'sufferer' but not 'blackguard'; 'fool' but not 'sinner' ". For "the murderer wanted blood and not plunder, he thirsted after the bliss of the knife". Finally, "Spirit is life that cuts into life: by its own torment it increases its own knowledge—did you know that? And the joy of the spirit is to be anointed, to be consecrated by tears as a beast of sacrifice—did you know that?" "Everything that is evil in the eyes of the good must come together that *one* truth may be born". So that over the whole of *Zarathustra* there floats the Song of Dionysus:

O Mensch, gib acht!
Was spricht die tiefe Mitternacht?
Ich schlief, ich schlief,
Aus tiefem Traum bin ich erwacht.
Die Welt ist tief,
Und tiefer als der Tag gedacht!
Tief ist ihr Weh;
Lust—tiefer noch als Herzeleid.
Weh spricht: Vergeh!
Doch alle Lust will Ewigkeit,
Will tiefe, tiefe Ewigkeit!

But what will the man-surpassing Superman look like, he who
carries within him and affirms the deep cloven reality of light and
dark whereof this song sings, the Dionysian reality? Or rather,
what will the "bridge"-man towards this desired Superman look
like? For there must be a new man who comprises all that has
been said in himself, for whom it is the very breath of life. Only
an altogether new man can be the meaning of existence and the
giver of meaning. "Man and the earth that is man's heritage are
still inexhaustible and undiscovered".

One has to read *Zarathustra* for onself to get the full feeling of
what Nietzsche means with his message. Nevertheless one or two
flares can be dropped here. The new man must be the bearer of
"the great health". "Behind all your thoughts and feelings there
is a mighty master, an unknown sage—it is called Self. He lives
in your body and is your body. There is more wisdom in your
body than in your subtlest learning. Who knows why your body
should need your most subtle learning? . . . The creating body
created spirit for itself as the handmaid to its will". Therefore
"I counsel you to innocence of the senses. Do I counsel you to
chastity? Chastity is a virtue in some, in many almost a vice. . . .
In those for whom chastity is difficult it is to be dissuaded. . . .
Knowingly the body purifies itself, in its struggle for knowledge
it is exalted; for the wise all instincts are hallowed, for the exalted
the soul becomes joyful. . . . Let your spirit and your virtue
serve the meaning of the earth, let all values be determined by
you anew. Therefore shall you be warriors! Therefore shall you
be creators!"

But for this what Nietzsche has elsewhere called "the pathos
of distance" and "reverence before the Self" are necessary.
"Flee, my friend, into solitude"; "hold aloof from the flies of the
marketplace"; "it is not the neighbour that I teach, but the

friend. Let the friend be a festival of the earth to you and a foretaste of the Superman". And one must be tender with one's friend: "The friend should be a master of intuition and silence; you should not wish to see everything. . . . Let your pity be intuition, to know first if your friend wants pity". And when you go into your solitude you must ask yourself: "Are you a new strength and a new authority? A first stirring, a wheel that rolls on its own? Can you compel the stars to revolve about you?" "You call yourself free? Let me then hear your ruling thought, and not that you have slunk away from a yoke". About solitaries: "So you are going to find the way to yourself! It leads past yourself, past you and your seven devils!" But he who sees his task in that light must instantly grow aerial and serene. "Untroubled, mocking, strong in deed—that is how wisdom would have us". "Those who would be light and like the bird must learn to love themselves".

In other words and in general terms: live by your own law and create it. "Let your virtue be your Self and not something alien to you, an outer skin, a veneer". "If you have a virtue and it is indeed your virtue, you have it in common with none". "Your virtue is too high for the familiarity of names". Later, in *Beyond Good and Evil*, it is said of the "superior" man that, in so far as duties grow out of them, he can only have his virtues with his equals. But in *Zarathustra* Nietzsche says, in further appeal to the will and in defence of this way of perceiving the Self: "I set this new tablet above you: Become hard". "O that you understood my word: always do what you will—but first be such as *can* will. Love your neighbour as yourselves—but first be such as *love themselves* too, such as love with the great love, with the great contempt!" "The noble-minded would create a new thing, a new virtue. . . . But the danger for the noble-minded is not that they may turn good men, but braggarts, scoffers, destroyers". Hence, "There where the storms rush down to the sea and the snout of the mountain laps water, each shall have his day and his night watches, his time of testing and recognition. Each shall be tested whether he be of my line and lineage, whether he be master of a long will, silent in his speaking, and giving in such a manner that he takes in his giving". For "when a heart flows broad and full like a river, a blessing and a peril to those that dwell in the flat lands, there is the source of your virtue. When you are exalted above praise and blame and your will commands

all things as a *loving* will, there is the origin of your virtue. . . .
You shall strive like me for the bestowing virtue". "Be chary of
accepting, choose what you shall accept—this is my advice to
those who have nothing to bestow". "Shame, shame, shame—such
is the history of man. On that account the noble mind refrains
from shaming others. Shame holds him back in the presence of
all sufferers. I like not the merciful who delight in pity: they are
too deficient in shame. . . . For in seeing the sufferer suffer
I was ashamed on account of his shame, and in helping him I
wounded his pride. Great obligations do not make grateful, but
vengeful; and when a small kindness is not forgotten it becomes a
gnawing worm". "But worst of all are the petty thoughts. Better
evilly thought than pettily thought! . . . To him who is possessed
of a devil I would say, 'Better rear up your devil! Even for you
there is still a path to greatness' ". "If you have an enemy,
requite him not evil with good, for that would shame him.
Rather prove that *he* has done *you* a good. Rather be angry than
shame anyone! . . . And should ever a great wrong be done
you, then quickly do five small ones besides. . . . Wrong
shared is half right. . . . Small revenge is more human than no
revenge at all". "It is nobler to own oneself in the wrong than
to establish one's right, especially if one be in the right". But for
the lovers of truth: "Freed from the equality of slaves, redeemed
from all deities and adorations, fearless and terrible, grand and
alone—such is the will of the truthful". "Hungering, puissant,
lonely and godless—so would the lion-will have itself". Of war
and warriors Nietzsche says: "If you cannot be saints of knowledge, I pray you at least be its warriors. . . . Seek out your
enemy, wage your war for the sake of your thoughts. And if your
thoughts succumb your honesty shall cry Victory! above them.
. . . War and courage have achieved greater things than charity.
Not your pity but your valour has so far been the mainstay of the
distressed". And thinking of military discipline as an ordering
force he goes on to say: "Revolt—that is the distinguishing mark
of the slave. But let your distinction be your obedience, and your
commanding be itself an obeying. . . . To the good warrior
'Thou shalt' sounds pleasanter than 'I will'. All that you hold
dear shall first be commanded to you. . . . But your highest
thought you shall have commanded to you by me, and it runs:
Man is something to be surpassed".

These high-lights show up the type or rather the multiplicity of types that Nietzsche's imagination requires for the next higher stage of man. He sketches certain aspects thus in *Beyond Good and Evil*: "Live," he says, "with tremendous and haughty composure. Your feelings, your 'For' and 'Against', have them and let them go at will; *deign* to feel them, ride them like horses or donkeys—for we must know how to make use of their asininity as well as their fire. Keep your three hundred facades intact—also your dark spectacles: for there are times when no man should look us in the eye, still less into our depths. Keep company, too, with that bland and roguish vice—politeness. And remain master of the four virtues: courage, understanding, compassion, solitude. For solitude is a virtue like a sublime addiction to cleanliness, which shows how all contact between man and man, all ' society', must inevitably lead to uncleanness. Somehow, somewhere, and at some time or other all community makes 'common' ".

In *Zarathustra* this type, which Nietzsche calls "the aristocratic man" in *Beyond Good and Evil*, is seen as the product of—in Nietzschean terminology—"discipline and breeding": discipline in the sense of self-culture, self-training and enhancement of will; breeding in the sense of a conscious propagation and multiplication of the result wherever possible—" you shall love the land of your children".

This is seen as a task of social organization with the Will to Power as its background. "But that you may understand my gospel of good and evil I will tell you my gospel of life, and the nature of all living things. . . . Wherever I found life I heard the language of obedience. All that lives, obeys. And this I heard secondly: whatsoever cannot obey itself is commanded. Such is the nature of living things. And this is the third thing that I heard: commanding is more difficult than obeying." More deeply still: "Listen now to my words, you wisest of men! Assay them diligently and see whether I have not crept into the heart of life, into the very roots of its heart! Wherever I found life I found the will to power, and even in the will of the servant I found the will to be master. That the weaker shall serve the stronger is the persuasion of him who would reign over one yet weaker than he: it is the one delight he may not forgo. And just as the lesser surrenders to the greater that he may have delight and power in the least of all, so too does the greatest surrender, staking his whole life for the sake of power". But the social order that would follow from this application of will is imperilled—by reason of the "fire-dragon" and "all the spewing and subversive demons of whom not only old women are afraid". "You understand well enough how to belch forth fire and darken the sky with ashes! You are the best braggarts and are sufficiently adept in the art of making scum boil. Wherever you are there is always scum to be had, and spongy, slimy, trodden-on things that hanker for freedom. 'Freedom!' you bellow with the best, but I am disabused of my belief in 'great events' so soon as there is a great smoke and shouting about them. Believe me, friend Hullaballoo, the greatest events are not our noisiest but our stillest hours". In view of all this nothing could be hoped for, in Nietzsche's opinion, from the State—"that coldest of cold monsters". Nor from fatherlands and motherlands: "Go your ways, and let the people and peoples go theirs! Darksome ways, no doubt, where not a hope gleams". And he prophesies: "A little while and new peoples will arise and new fountains gush down to new depths. For though the earthquake chokes up many fountains it creates much thirst, it brings to light also the hidden powers and secrets. The earthquake discloses new sources. In the earthquake of old nations new springs burst forth. And round him who calls out: 'See, here is a fountain for the thirsty, a heart for the languishing, a will for many instruments!' a nation will gather—that is, many united in a great effort. And there it will be proved who can command, and who must obey". But "A great tyrant might arise, a cunning monster who with his favour or disfavour might constrain all the past until it became a bridge for him, a sign and a herald and a cock-crowing. And this is the other danger and the cause of my other sorrow: if a man be of the mob his thoughts go back to his grandfather, and time stops with the grandfather! Thus the past is abandoned, for some day the mob might become master and drown all time in their shallow waters. Therefore, my brothers, a new nobility is needed, which shall be the adversary of the mob and of all tyranny and shall inscribe the word 'noble' anew on new tables. For many nobles are needed and nobles of many kinds if there is to be a new nobility. Or, as I once expressed it in parable: This is divinity— that there are gods, but no God!"

So that, side by side with his prophetic vision and his fear of mob-rule one can see Nietzsche's structural conception and the task it lays on the new "superior men", who are thought of as the new nobility in a hierarchical society and as such destined to command.

But before the new nobility can establish itself, reveal its nature and fulfil its task a transvaluation of values is needed, on which subject some crucial things are said as early as *Zara-thustra*. Obviously the Christian faith and the Redemption are abjured. "Verily there have been greater and more nobly-born men on earth than those whom the peoople call Redeemers, those raging hurricanes! And you, my brothers, must be redeemed by one greater than all Redeemers if you are to find your way to freedom". Rather, "once the people said 'God' when they looked upon the distant seas; but I have taught you to say 'Superman' ". "God is an hypothesis; but I would have your hypotheses restricted to the conceivable". "What you call world shall be created by you: let it become your reason, your likeness, your will, your love—and your delight!" But if you are creators, this is the question: "Can you be your own good and bad to yourselves and set up your will over yourselves like a law? Can you be your own judge and the avenger of your law?" "What is believed by the people as good and evil only reveals to me an ancient Will to Power. . . . Good and evil that are everlasting—there is no such thing! Everlastingly they must surpass themselves anew". "He who has to be a creator in good and evil must first be a destroyer and shatter the values. Thus the greatest evil is part of the greatest good—but such is the way of the creator". "Change of values—that is the way of the creator. . . . He who would be a creator always destroys". "Always it was lovers and creators who created good and evil. The fire of love shines in all virtue; names and the flickering of anger". "O my brothers, is not everything a-flowing to-day? Have not all the barriers and gangways fallen into the water? Who would still cling to 'good' and 'evil'? Preach me this, my brothers, in all the streets!" "But I tell you: when anything is falling, give it a final shove!"

In contrast to the customary morality Nietzsche teaches: "Love of your neighbour is the love that has gone bad on your-selves. You fly from yourselves to your neighbour and make a new virtue of it, but I can see through your 'unselfishness'. The 'Thou' is older than the 'I'; the 'Thou' has been consecrated but not yet the 'I'; therefore a man cleaves to his neighbour". On pity: "Thus speaks all great love, which surpasses even forgiveness and pity. . . . O where in the world have there been greater follies than with the pitiful? Woe to all lovers who are not exalted above their pity! . . . All great love is above pity, for it seeks to create the beloved. I offer myself to my love—*and my neighbour in myself*: such is the language of all creators. But creators are hard". Of "the three evils that have been immemorially cursed" he says: "Lust—a sweet poison to the withered, but to the lion-willed the great cordial and the wine of wines reverently treasured. . . . Lust—but I would have hedges about my thoughts and my words, lest the swine and the swill-drinkers break into my garden. . . . Passion for power—dread teacher of the great contempt, which preaches into the faces of cities and empires: 'Away with you!' until they cry with one voice: 'Away with *me*!' . . . Passion for power—which rises alluringly even before the pure and the lonely and the frugal dwellers upon the heights, glowing like a love that dapples the earthly heavens with rosy raptures. . . . O where find the right, the honouring, the baptismal name for such longing! 'The Bestowing Virtue' was the name Zarathustra once bestowed on the unnameable. And then it was, for the first time it was that he blessed *Selfishness*, the whole and holy Selfishness that wells out of the strong soul. . . . With its 'good' and 'bad' such joy in the Self is shielded as within sacred groves; with the names of its joy it banishes from itself everything contemptible. It banishes everything cowardly, saying: 'Bad—that is cowardly!' Hateful to it are those that are full of care, the sighers and moaners and pickers up of petty advantages. . . . Hateful to it and an abomination are those that will never defend themselves, that swallow down poisonous spittle and evil glances; the all-too-patient, the all-suffering, the all-contented—for that is the way of slaves. Whether they be servile before the gods and the kicks of the gods or before men and the opinions of men—it spits upon all servility, this blessed Selfishness!"

This anti-Sermon-on-the-Mount, magnificent in its way, which is amplified psychologically, theoretically, philosophically and polemically in the later works, appears in *Zarathustra* in two parts, both equally affecting: first in that cyclic coming, going, and returning already mentioned, which is at the same time Zarathustra's own struggle with his message; second in an elaborate and remarkably compassionate farewell to those people, true contemporaries, who have already marked themselves off or turned away from all that is characterized by the word 'mob'—the so-called 'higher' men. Various types are presented: two Kings, an old Pope out of service, the Magician (or Poet and Play-actor), The Man Scrupulous in Spirit who lets his blood be sucked by leeches so as to get to know their minds, and who says: "Better know nothing than half know much"; The Ugliest Man, the murderer of God: "The God who saw everything, including man, had to die! Man cannot endure that such a witness should live. . . . For he saw man's depths and dregs, all his hidden ignominy and ugliness"; then The Voluntary Beggar, who has sought refuge with the cattle: "What was it that drove me to the poorest of the poor? Was it not my disgust with the richest? But why to these cattle? Lustful greed, bilious envy, soured vindictiveness, arrogance of the mob—all these leap to the eye. It is no longer true that the poor are blessed. The Kingdom of Heaven is with these kine"; and finally Zarathustra's own Shadow: "With thee", it says, "I have wandered in the remotest, coldest worlds like a phantom haunting winter roofs and snows. With thee I have pushed into what is forbidden, the worst and the uttermost; and if there is any virtue in me it is that I fear no law. . . . With thee I unlearned belief in words and values and great names. . . . 'Nothing is true, all is permitted', I said to myself. I plunged head foremost into the iciest waters.. . . What now is left me? A heart weary and insolent; an inconstant will; fluttering wings; a broken backbone. . . . Where is my home? For this I asked and I sought, but found it not. O eternal everywhere, eternal nowhere, eternal in vain!" All these higher men who, it is clear, are parts of Nietzsche's own self that he has overcome and rejected, Zarathustra regales with his teachings of the true higher man and the Dionysian view of life which affirms suffering and evil.

But—so we must understand the extraordinary scenes that follow—these higher men of to-day do not fully comprehend him. "Their limbs lack the harkening ear", and "there is a hidden rabble in them". So in the end, with a cloud of doves fluttering round his head, a laughing young lion lays itself down at his feet and rests its head on his knee, scattering the disciples in fright: "The lion hath come, my children are nigh, Zarathustra is grown ripe, mine hour hath come! This is *my* morning, my day beginneth: arise now, arise, thou Great Noontide!"

This Great Noontide ushering in the ecstatic conclusion can only properly be understood in the light of the deliberately esoteric doctrine of Eternal Recurrence looming in the background, which Nietzsche felt as his fundamental experience. The scientific foundation of this doctrine, laid down as early as 1881 shortly after Nietzsche's first glimpse of it, does not concern us here. In *Zarathustra* itself, where it is presented in two places[1] in a dramatically heightened but half sceptical form, you feel very strongly that its spiritual significance for Nietzsche probably rests on two things. Firstly, on the revelatory concept: "And are not all things so closely bound together that this moment of time must draw all futurity after it—hence itself also? . . . The knotting of causes in which I am caught comes again, and will re-create me"; secondly and principally on the fact that it was possible for Nietzsche to say of his attitude which saw all happening as Will to Power, thus shattering the eschatological view of life: "I myself belong to the causes of Eternal Recurrence. . . . I shall come again with this sun, this earth, this eagle, this serpent, not to a new or a better life or even to a similar life, but I shall come again everlastingly to this self-same and identical life in its greatest as in its smallest things, to teach again the eternal return of all things, to speak again of the Great Noontide of earth and man, and to announce again the Superman to man". The Great Noontide, therefore, is the moment when, in the eternal cycling of things, the doctrine of the Superman can and must inevitably be announced by the Will to Power: the "can" and "must" not standing intellectually in contradiction to one another, but being one and the same.

We shall not enter into all the intellectual and spiritual problems which face us here and of which Nietzsche was obviously well aware. And of *Beyond Good and Evil* and *The Genealogy of Morals*, which appeared in conjunction with *Zarathustra* in 1885 and 1887 and put the latter's teaching on a deeper sociological, philosophical and psychological basis, we have only this to say:

[1] The chapters entitled *The Vision and the Mystery* and *The Convalescent* in Thomas Common's translation (Allen & Unwin).

that it sharply accentuates the repudiation of all the democratiz-ing and humanizing tendencies of his time. "Life is essentially appropriation, violation, the overpowering of the feeble and the strange; suppression, hardness, the forcible imposition of its own forms, mutual devouring or at least, to put it mildly, exploitation . . . precisely because life is Will to Power. Exploitation is not the monopoly of a corrupt or imperfect or primitive society—it is an integral part of the nature of life itself, an organic ground-function; it is a consequence of its own Will to Power, which is Life's will. Granted that this may be a novelty as a theory, in actual fact it is the basic factor in all history (one should at least be honest with oneself)." And in the *Genealogy of Morals* he says: "If domination and slavery are unalterable facts of life, 'morality' is to be understood as a doctrine proceeding from the power-relationships on which the phenomenon life rests". It is entirely relative; and there is, generally speaking, a "master morality" and a "slave morality". This is where the famous doctrine comes in of a "slave-insurrection in morals" and the psychological foundation of such a morality in this insurrection. It need not be repeated here. Suffice to remember that the slave-insurrection in morals, according to Nietzsche, does not begin with Christianity but with the Hebrew prophets, and is continued in the movement towards democracy which is "the heritage of the Christians". This heritage creates the morality for a herd that is given out as autonomous, "to the point of abolishing altogether the concepts of master and slave: 'ni Dieu ni maître' as one Socialist formula has it". It is this kind of herd-morality which, Nietzsche says, dominates Europe to-day, that is described in the *Genealogy of Morals* as a morality of "ressentiment", a morality "of the stew-pot of hatred" aimed at the rulers, a morality that was now creating the idea of 'evil' whereas formerly the idea of 'good' meaning well-bred, noble, and strong, and 'bad' meaning not well-bred, common, and weak, stood in opposition to one another. And because this herd-morality comes from the weak it is also the morality of pity and sympathy. At this point Nietzsche's horror of universal domestication and his Dionysian view of things become apparent together with his "will to aristocracy". He says in effect: All these champions of herd-morality who regard it as the only possible one "are united not only in their religion of pity and sympathy in so far as suffering is bound up with life (down to animal and up to 'God'—muscling in on God's pity is the prerogative of a democratic age), they are also all united in their outcry against and impatience of suffering, in their deadly hatred of suffering altogether, in their almost feminine incapacity to remain spectators, to let suffering be. United, too, in the involuntary effeminization of everything, that holds Europe in its grip and seems to threaten it with a new Buddhism". "But as a result of this there is the danger of a *mass degeneration of man*, until he is reduced to what our dolts and flat-heads of Socialists regard as the man of the future, their ideal: the debasing and dwindling of man to the perfect herd animal (or, as they put it, the man of the free society). This bestializing of man until he becomes a veritable dwarf with equal rights and demands is quite possible—no doubt about that". "But", so Nietzsche teaches from his Dionysian view-point, "man, the most valiant of creatures and inured to suffering, does not in his natural state deny suffering; he wills it, he himself seeks it, provided of course that he is shown a reason for it, a *wherefore* of suffering. The ascetic ideal of the Middle Ages was nothing but an expression of this. How the Christian torments himself with his notions about original sin, guilt and bad conscience! All this is only a sublimation of the slave morality and a long martyrdom of man, an aberration that has lasted two thousand years".

The original master-morality current among the classes responsible for rule and order and anterior to what we have known as morality since the two-thousand-year aberration, "was innocent in its identification of whatever suited the rulers, with 'good', that is to say, spiritually aristocratic, or with 'noble', that is to say, spiritually well-bred, spiritually privileged; and of 'bad' with what was alien to it, that is to say, common, inferior, of the mob. It was the morality of people who scorned 'inclusion within the social pale' that they themselves had created and constantly stepped outside, back into the innocent conscience of the beast of prey, like exulting monsters who depart from an outrageous succession of murders, incendiarisms, rapes, and tortures in high spirits as though it were only a students' rag. . . ." "At the core of all these aristocratic races we cannot fail to recognize the beast of prey, the magnificent *blonde beast* avidly rampant for spoil and victory. . . . This hidden core needs an outlet from time to time. The beast must out, must revert to the wilderness: the Roman, Arabic, German and Japanese nobility, the Homeric heroes, the Scandinavian Vikings—all are alike in this need".

Perhaps Nietzsche does not want to return altogether to this "pre-moral" morality. But he says over and over again: "Grant me just one glimpse of something perfect, pursued to an end, something terrible, tremendous, triumphant, *in which there is something to fear*". "We sense that everything is going downhill and getting more and more stupid, good-natured, mediocre, indifferent, Chinese, Christian—man without a doubt is getting better and better. Herein lies Europe's doom". Consequently "one is sick of the sight of man. What is Nihilism to-day if not that. We are tired of man. We must get beyond him". "We who see things the other way round believe that hardness, cruelty, slavery, danger in the streets and in the heart, secrecy, stoicism, temptings and devilries of all kinds, that everything evil, terrible, tyrannical, bestial and serpent-like in man can serve the raising of the species as much as its opposite; we cannot say enough when we say this much and we find ourselves . . . at the extreme end of all modern ideologies and gregarious wishful thinking—at the very antipodes of them, very likely".

The point, therefore, is to create what Nietzsche calls the "aristocratic man" and him alone, as the giver of meaning to existence and as a stepping-stone to the Superman. And when Nietzsche introduces the sketch he has already made of him in *Zarathustra* once more in *Beyond Good and Evil*, we feel how very much the contours have been determined by that horror of domestication and democratization and by his alarm over the deliberate exorcism of the shadow-side, the suffering-side of life as understood in the twofold Dionysian sense. Much that is conceived in a non-reactionary way and intellectually subtle is said in the section "What is Aristocratic?" in *Beyond Good and Evil*, quite on a par with *Zarathustra*. And how psychologically subtle he is when, speaking in another context of the probable martyrdom and inner danger of decay that beset the noble soul, he says of Jesus: "It is possible that beneath the holy fable and the lineaments of Jesus's life one of the most agonizing instances of *knowledge of love* lies hidden: a heart most innocent and eager that never had enough human love, that *demanded* to love and to be loved and nothing else, demanded it with hardness, with madness, with terrible outbursts of fury against all those who denied him love". Or when he says: "Profound suffering ennobles—it divides".

But when this inner division as a general characteristic of the aristocratic man is elevated to a "pathos of distance" *socially* justified, and when at the same time Nietzsche repeatedly demands that the gulf between the aristocratic rulers and the ruled, the "herd-men" shall not be diminished but on the contrary enlarged, we have the impression that in his all too easy caricature of socialism and democracy as in his mordant stigmatization of the broad mass of the people as mere "herd-animals" (who, remarkably enough, are supposed to be soaked in "effeminacy"),—a certain morbid exaggeration of the need to reject is very much in evidence, nourished perhaps by Nietzsche's own "ressentiment", and that it dominates him as a man in nearly every line he writes. And it is these phobias that drive his Dionysian conception of life—splendid in itself with its great affirmation of suffering and not altogether excluding "a drop of goodness and sweet spirituality"—to say through the mouth of its God Dionysus: "Often I ponder how I can advance man and make him stronger, deeper, wickeder than he is.—Stronger, deeper and wickeder? I asked in horror.—Yes, he repeated: stronger, deeper and wickeder—and more beautiful".

The "genius of heart" as possessed by "that great hidden God, the tempter-God and born rat-catcher of conscience"—the God who makes us affirm the suffering of life along with its positive side, believes, therefore, that in order (in Nietzsche's words) to advance mankind he must make them *wickeder*, which is only understandable in the light of Nietzsche's peculiar and over-riding anti-domestication phobia. For it is clear that making wickeder is something quite different from making man more affirmative of, and superior to, suffering, which is the original meaning of the Dionysian view.

And here we must pause to take note before we go further. Once the Dionysian message which, with respect to the bourgeois view prevailing in the sixties and seventies, effected a very necessary rehabilitation of the lost depths of life and showed it as an unescapable commingling of light and dark, once this message is stated in moral terms by the man who wants to be "beyond good and evil", and is turned into a demand for the fundamental affirmation of values hitherto regarded as *negative*, then, if you survey what I have recalled, the following fact emerges clearly: an extreme subjectivation and making relative of the moral values and, at the same time, a hitching of these values on to an objective Absolute. In actual fact Nietzsche cannot remain consistent.

Behind the veils of a moralism purposely left unclarified ("Morals require no understanding, they understand themselves", as Friedrich Theodor Vischer said) the whole second half of the Nineteenth Century had, wherever its worship of power was taken seriously, hence above all in Germany, in very truth made all morals subjective and relative at bottom for anyone who looked more closely. It was so among the cultured bourgeoisie. But for the rising proletarian world which, as far as its propagandist ethos went, naïvely continued to feed on the absolute ethical ideals of the Eighteenth Century, all these ideals and hence all morals had been "debunked" by Marxist historical materialism and declared "class ideology"—so that relativism was rife here too. Little as Nietzsche bothered about Marxism his *Genealogy of Morals* resembles it to the extent that for him also there are only class morals, or as he puts it, a master-morality and a slave-morality: a relativized morality that wants passionately to throw off every trace of the Eighteenth Century. Moreover it is very largely subjective. For the master-class that is to bear the new "extra-moral morality" the sociological conditions are named, the "discipline and breeding" already referred to. But the morality and characteristic attitude of this master-class is not, with Nietzsche, something self-given, the mechanical product of its social position but—since all life is based on will because it is at bottom Will to Power—a postulate willed by this class itself and preached to it by Nietzsche. It consists of new values which the new aristocrats, the creators, create. And "the whole world revolves mysteriously and silently about the creation of these new values".

And yet, is this voluntaristic subjectivism adhered to? No! For even in *Zarathustra*, when it comes to the evil that is declared so necessary, there is talk of "demons" by whom everybody can be possessed and in point of fact should be possessed. And in *Beyond Good and Evil* he expressly refers to hate, envy, avarice, lust for power—all absolute qualities—as such life-conditioning "evil" passions. Whereas on the other hand spiritual and intellectual "cleanliness" is acclaimed not only as an aristocratic virtue but as an absolute impulse—which, as a matter of fact, saturates Nietzsche's whole output and determines his personal fate. Anyone not caught in the toils of relativism and subjectivism must see, therefore, that objective values lie—and how strongly!—behind Nietzsche's work, values which he affirms or denies, or, in our terminology, "objective forces" whose positive and negative strengths are incarnate in him. What he has in mind with his transvaluation of values is in reality simply this: a shift of values and a strong modulation of their accents for a certain number of the objective powers present in man, above all such as admit of a definitely social variation by being individually emphasized or ignored. There are undoubtedly various kinds of pity and sympathy as Nietzsche himself is always stressing. The kind that comes from the overflow of a rich heart, which he affirms, and the kind that comes from no brimming inner impulse but disguises itself as a feeling of moral duty, which he rejects. Human society may be steeped in either kind in varying degrees, but the absolutely supra-personal, objective ground-stuff of any true capacity for pity, that is to say the transcendent oneness of humanity, remains completely unaffected by these relativities. The question only is, what sort of development shall we allow them? And it is quite true that one can import into the idea of "aristocratic" an accent of value which contains the greatest possible "pathos of distance" and that very "gulf" torn open by Nietzsche with such vehement zeal at the feet of the broad masses —which contains therefore the least possible amount of what we call humanity. But nobility and true humanity are essentially the very reverse of opposites. The whole of Greek Tragedy is a single example of the struggle between fate and a nobility of mind permeated with intense humanity; and what we call chivalrous and chivalry was nothing less than the synthesis—still operative even to-day in the gentleman-ideal, fortunately—of the nobility and active humanity that Christianity brought into the world.

We shall deal with this thoroughly later. But to proceed.

The Nietzsche we have tried to sketch so far is the man who influenced the young generation of the nineties, a period rich in spiritual contradictions that brings the Nineteenth Century to a close and heralds the first European and world catastrophe. To this period we shall have to return briefly later to see how Nietzsche's publications helped to give it shape.

But Nietzsche left behind him another and different wave of influence that only reached its full height between the first and second world wars. To understand this wave whose profound and—we must say bluntly—fateful effect was due to his popularization we have to bear in mind that his teachings only came to a practical head in the book that appeared posthumously at the beginning of the Twentieth Century, about fifteen years after the works hitherto discussed—*The Will to Power*. It concerns us far more than all the exaggerations and excesses contained in the somewhat undisciplined writings of the last months before his illness—The *Twilight of the Idols* and *The Antichrist*, which on that account we can disregard as *capita mortua*.

The Will to Power is an unfinished posthumous work put together for the most part by Nietzsche himself, but completed by his literary executors from the papers he left behind. We do not know whether his own hand would have moderated it or toned it down before publication. As it is, the whole work is so uniform in conception, introduces so many new and philosophically fundamental accentuations of doctrine and, in its first and last sections, carries so much of what he had said earlier to its logical conclusion, obviously quite deliberately, that we must perforce see it as on the whole a faithful expression of his intentions. The Dionysian Dithyrambs connected with it make us feel how desperately he had struggled in spirit with the extreme content of this work, after the conclusion of which he clearly wanted to celebrate what he called his "Seventh Solitude" ("Silvery bright like a fish my skiff swims into the distance") and at the first glimpse of which we feel the rightness of his words: "Down from the farthest distances a glittering star sinks slowly towards me". He himself says of this book at the time of his most intensive work, in the spring of 1888: "Almost every day I summoned up sufficient energy in two hours to review my whole conception from top to bottom; there the gigantic wealth of problems lay spread out before me clear in every line, as in relief". It is indeed a gigantic design, and he can say with some justice in the Foreword: "Great things require that we should either keep silent about them or boast—that is to say, talk cynically and in all innocence". When we are obliged to demonstrate just how fateful was the

influence of much that is in this valedictory work of Nietzsche's—
be it understood aright or only popularly misunderstood—and
how its salient features, though visible earlier, must nevertheless,
in the form given them here, be regarded as a sheer aberration
that was bound to have fateful consequences, and how this work
aspired like no other to be a guide for the future "for thousands
of years" and is yet the most time-bound of all Nietzsche's major
works—then it is well not to forget that intention expressed in the
Foreword about wanting to speak "cynically" and "in all innocence", whether we regard such an intention as good or dangerous.

The book is closely argued and has for theoretical core an
interpretation of our experience of what we call "world". Without
going into details here we can sum it up by saying that it contends
at length that there is no "Being", but only a "Becoming", which
is the only possible interpretation of the world for us. Further,
that this "Becoming" is an uninterrupted struggle of power-
monads, also called power-quanta. Power is not to be understood as the mechanical power of physics or chemistry but as
something "quasi-living": the focus or quantum of a Will to
Power. All these power foci of which the "world" consists are in
ceaseless conflict with one another, sustained by the will to expand,
the will of one to overpower the other. Life is only a particular
instance in such a struggle, a function of the nutritional process.
Every living structure is a hierarchy of similar power-foci. Man, as
a special biological case, is something imperfect—"the imperfect
animal". His peculiarity—consciousness—is wholly peripheral
as regards the hierarchy of conflicting power-foci which work
unconsciously in him and of which he consists. All the foci, even
the unconscious ones, accomplish perspectival interpretations of
existence. The conscious, human interpretation is once again
only one of numerous interpretations. There is only one perspectival knowledge, which in essence is always Will to Power:
the expansion and transformation of the contents of experience
so interpreted into logistic concepts; that is to say, the transformation of thing-forms and causality-forms into concepts of
Being and Motion. In reality, however, there is no "Being", only
a Becoming comprised in the struggle of the power-foci. Since all
knowledge is perspectival there is no "Truth" either, in the com-
monly accepted sense. Rather, "truth is the mode of interpretation without which a certain type of organic matter could not

live". "We project the conditions of our life as predicates of 'causality'; 'teleology' and 'mechanical necessity' do not exist; rather the rule only shows that one and the same event is not another event". That is, not another mode of struggle within the Will to Power but only this particular mode.

A "doctrine of affects" is given, according to which the Will to Power is "the primordial affect-form", and "all other affects" are only elaborations of it. In particular the sensations of pleasure and pain are not primary but secondary—a sort of sign-language indicating that the Will to Power affirms or denies something for a particular being. "Pleasure and pain are only concomitant symptoms; what a man desires, what every smallest part of a living organism desires, is a "plus" of power. In the struggle for its attainment both pleasure and pain ensue; as a consequence of that act of will the organism seeks resistance, needs something that opposes itself. . . . Pain, as an inhibition of our Will to Power, is thus a normal factor, the normal ingredient of every organic event. Man does not avoid it, on the contrary he needs it; every victory, every sensation of pleasure, every event presupposes resistance overcome". For the decisive point, as we have seen, is what Nietzsche proclaimed earlier: that all values which regulate man's acts or which he feels, are not objective data but are created by him; created as life-forms of his Will to Power, as manifestations of force. "An experiment might be made to see whether a scientific order of values could not be built up simply on a numerical and quantitative scale of power. All other values are prejudices". "In what respect does a value fail? Simply in respect of a quantum of accumulated and organized power". And at the same time this is understood quite physiologically: "Our holiest convictions, our evolutions with regard to the supreme values are but judgments of the muscles".

So that we have before us a close-knit interpretation of the world and life carried to the extremes of naturalism and relativism, turning against all the worlds of "Being" with unremitting polemical asperity, in particular those transcentental worlds of Being that lie behind "Becoming". But we can see how this kind of interpretation with its categories of power-quanta large and small and their impulse to expand, despite the fact that it tries to replace the Mechanism, Determinism and Causalism of Natural Science by a solely existing process of "Becoming" that is identical with the struggling monads of the Will to Power, nevertheless slips into making use of those rejected categories as the fundamental pattern of the interpretation as a whole. For what else is a self-enlarging quantum but a mechanistic concept of measure taken over from the contemporary Natural Science so abhorred by Nietzsche? But in his philosophy there is no recognition of qualities but only of quantities, which are everywhere the aforesaid quantities of the Will to Power.

Into this terrifyingly de-spiritualized view of the world, and as its theoretically most important part, Nietzsche now builds his well-known theory of morals which is the pivot of his proposed transvaluation of values since, for him, all valuations hitherto have always overtly or covertly contained a moral core. But as far as morals are concerned he is really doing something two-faced here. On the one hand he carries the "debunking" he has already undertaken in his earlier works, to its extreme limit. Moral values, he says (on top of what he has just said about values in general), are "sham-values compared with physiological ones". So in addition to debunking them he now proceeds to biologize them. On the other hand, however, his attitude is: till now—that is to say, till their debunking by Nietzsche and the appearance of the "strong men" announced by him, who consciously live without them, indeed, against them—morals have been a necessary lie. For "morals are a menagerie, instituted on the premise that iron bars may be more advantageous than freedom, even to the captives themselves; that there are animal-tamers who are not afraid of drastic measures—who know how to wield the hot iron". And, he goes on, "to be fair to morals we must replace them by two *zoological* conceptions: taming of the beast and breeding of a definite species". Indeed, "our intellectual subtlety has in the main been reached by vivisecting our consciences. We should be deeply thankful, therefore, for all that morals have accomplished so far; *but now they are only a constraint that may well become disastrous.* They themselves compel us in all honesty to a negation of morality."

Once you accept the Nietzschean deductions this is a powerful intellectual foundation, large, clean-swept, but how over-simplified! Upon it is now erected what is of the utmost importance for Nietzsche *the man of will*: a practical interpretation of his age and an equally practical prophecy.

The interpretation of his age given in all essentials in the Introduction of *The Will to Power* is a theory and a history of European Nihilism, while the last or prophetic part of the work is a theory of action. Much of what is said there is implicit in his earlier writings. But the fully mature Nietzsche here offers much that is new in many respects, particularly (thanks to the now meticulously worked-out theory of the Will to Power) those practical hyperboles that appear at the end, to understand which and how they could possibly have occurred to him, one must constantly bear in mind his primary attitude of rejection.

For the analysis of his time is wholly conditioned by it. Nietzsche characterizes his age as one of actual or potential Nihilism in that he makes use of a saying originally applied by Friedrich Heinrich Jakobi to Fichte in 1799 and of which Russian Nihilism is only a derivative, to the effect that spiritually we are all standing or about to stand before a void, which would aptly fit the situation to-day also. "What does Nihilism mean?" he asks. "It means that the supreme values devalue themselves. There is no goal and there is no answer to our questioning." Since moral valuations underlie all the higher values, and since he, Nietzsche, regards the destruction of the former as the chief task of his teaching, he sees himself as a champion of Nihilism or, as he expresses it, he realized at a certain moment that he had been a nihilist till then. In the process of disintegration which he describes as being the essence of the rising tide of Nineteenth Century nihilism (we have yet to see in what manner he conceives that this nihilism will develop or be overcome), he himself thus belongs as a consciously active agent.

He sees the process of disintegration going on at various levels. In the field of values; in the breakdown of all the highest ideals believed in hitherto, which in his eyes are all emanations of Christianity and its moral teachings so consistently opposed by him; in the whole structure of progressive civilization altogether. He speaks of "the disorganizing principles of our time: the railway, the telegraph, the centralization of an immense mass of interests in one single soul that has to be correspondingly strong and versatile; a newspaper instead of daily prayer". Hence "what is attacked most profoundly to-day is the instinct and will for tradition". And tradition means "the stretching of the will over long periods of time, the selection of such conditions and values as shall enable man to exert control over future centuries: all of which is in the highest degree unmodern". By way of substitutes there is "over-work, inquisitiveness and sympathy—our modern vices!" "A sort of accommodation to this swamping with impressions sets in: man loses the ability to *act*. He only *reacts* to outside stimuli. He expends his strength partly in getting things, partly in defending them when he's got them, and partly in opposing other people. *Profound weakening of spontaneity*". As a result "a certain deep heaviness and tiredness to balance external alertness". Socially "a copious outcrop of hybrids and middlemen of all kinds", who "make the State absurdly fat in the stomach: apart from those who actually work, 'representatives'—for instance, apart from the scholars, literati; apart from the suffering masses of the people, gabbling and puffed-up ne'er-do-wells who 'represent' that suffering, not to speak of professional politicians who do themselves proud and 'represent' suffering before Parliament with strong lungs". All this produces "cultural weaklings and abortions in comparison with the Arab or Corsair. The Chinese is a well-bred type, more durable than the European". But it is worse still on the social plane: "What has been foully calumniated is that which *separates* the higher men from the lower, the gulf-creating instincts". "It is preposterous that all Socialist theoreticians should think that there can be conditions in which vice, sickness, crime and prostitution no longer flourish. That would be passing the death sentence on life". "A society must, if it is in good heart, produce waste and refuse. But modern society is not a society at all, it has no body, it is only a conglomeration of 'shandalas'—a society that no longer has the strength to *excrete*. That is decadence. The social question is an effect of decadence. What we have always regarded as the causes of decadence are in reality its effects". At the same time "decadence in itself is not a thing to be *attacked*: it is absolutely necessary and characteristic of every age and every people. But what is to be attacked with all one's might is the introduction of the contagion into the sound portions of the organism. Are we attacking it? On the contrary. That is why we exert ourselves on the side of humanitarianism". And: "Socialism is the *tyranny* of the lowest and the stupidest carried to its extreme limits—i.e. the tyranny of the superficial and the envious . . . three-quarters hocus-pocus . . . the end-result of modern ideas and their latent anarchism. . . . Christianity, humanitarianism, the French Revolution and Socialism are one and the same thing". "The kingdom of heaven of the poor in spirit has begun. Intermediate stages: the bourgeois (because of the money-parvenu) and the worker (because of the machine)".

This situation, in which the old ideal values have collapsed and civilization stunts human beings; in which an enfeebling democratic and humanitarian movement only intensifies this stunting, such a situation is bound in Nietzsche's view to produce an age of pessimism and therefore of nihilism. "But", he says, "all nihilism is two-faced". There is the nihilism springing from enhanced power of the spirit—active nihilism; and the nihilism of spiritual decay and retrogression—passive nihilism. Simplifying the wealth of apparently contradictory things that Nietzsche has to say under this head, only hinted at here, he then proceeds to give an analysis of the last few centuries from the point of view of these two kinds of nihilism. But even in these days, says Nietzsche (and here he goes off at a tangent), there are signs of a "strengthening" which we must understand as symptoms of an active nihilism, a gratifying intermediate stage. "The same causes that bring about the stunting of man also urge the stronger and rarer spirits to greatness! Health increases; the pre-requisites for a strong body are acknowledged and gradually given reality, asceticism becomes *ironique*". And "what is attained, if anything, is a more innocent relationship to the senses, a joyous and more Goethean sensuousness, altogether a prouder feeling in regard to knowledge, so that the 'complete fool' finds little acceptance". And then comes an elaborate description of the "toughening process" that has already begun in society, in science, in morals ("principles have become ridiculous"), in politics ("we see only problems of power, the power of one quantum against another quantum . . . we perceive all rights as conquests"), in our valuation of the great ("we count passion a privilege, we find nothing great unless it includes a crime"). "In sum: there are signs that the European of the Nineteenth Century is less ashamed of his instincts". One can see with what fine feeling and with what a typically Nietzschean nuance the age of post-Bismarckian 'tough' realism is sketched—the age which the older among us have all experienced.

But Nietzsche goes further. He proceeds to a prognosis of the crisis desired by him as the result of all this. While scorning "bullock-headed Nationalism" he applauds the rising militarism, even anarchism of the time. "I exult in the progressive militarization of Europe and in its inner anarchy . . . the days of sneaking hypocrisy are numbered. The barbarian and the wild beast are acclaimed in all of us. Precisely for that reason philosophy will get a move on. One day Kant will be regarded as a scarecrow". Of Socialism he says, from the same point of view: "Even as the fidgety mole it is, grubbing under the topsoil of a society weltering in fatuity, Socialism will yet yield something useful and wholesome: it delays 'peace on earth' and the snug-making of the democratic herd-animal, it forces the European to keep a reserve of spirit, that is, cunning and foresight, not wholly to forswear the manly and warlike virtues, and in the meantime protects the European against the impending *marasmus femininus*". For the rest: "*Regimentation* has grown very strong in this democratic Europe; people who learn easily submit easily; the herd-animal —an extremely intelligent one—is being reared. Those who can command will find those who obey". "Intellectual enlightenment is an unfailing means to make people more uncertain, weaker-willed, more desirous of union and support; in brief, to develop the herd-animal in man. Self-deception on this point in democracy is extremely useful: the stunting and regimenting of man is aspired to in the name of progress!" But that is precisely what Nietzsche now applauds—for it means "the age of the greatest stupidity, brutality and wretchedness of the *masses* and the age of the highest *individuals*". So in completest hypocrisy he writes: "Beyond good and evil—but we demand that the morality of the herd be kept unconditionally sacrosanct". Much will have to be put up with, for "outwardly there will come a time of tremendous wars, explosions, but inwardly of increasing weakness (i.e. of the masses)". "So I am not afraid to prophesy one or two things, and if possible to conjure up the causes of such wars. He looks forward to "a tremendous stock-taking after the most terrible cataclysm: with new questions. . . . It will be the time of the Great Noontide, of dread enlightenment: my sort of pessimism. A mighty beginning".

Here, in this analysis of his age and in an admittedly one-sided criticism of it, there is a magnificent prophecy. And the remarkable thing about it is that the content of this prophecy and this pessimism of Nietzsche's is not held out as, nor felt to be, a grave situation that ought to be fended off if possible, but a necessary *cure*, a stage on the road to "the great health"—a process which he himself does all he can to bring on.

This is more apparent in the other, practical section of the work, the last part, which contains or indicates conclusions directly affecting life. Here our delicately balanced and intellectual Nietzsche almost vanishes behind social constructions that are highly concrete and in every respect singular. He makes bitter earnest with propositions, jibes and axioms full of ruthlessness and brutal extremism. This sort of thing: "Mankind is merely material for experiment, an unending succession of boss-shots, a pile of debris". "Nations and races form the body for the begetting of single valuable individuals, who continue the process". "Herd sense should dominate in the herd but not outside it. The leaders of the herd require a very different valuation as regards their own acts, likewise those who are independent of it, and beasts of prey". And so on and so forth. A peculiar sort of Machiavellianism full of inner untruth is then demanded. "The new virtue (of the rulers) should be introduced under the guise of the old". For, he says, "Machiavellianism *pur, sans mélange, tout vert, dans toute sa force, dans tout apreté* is superhuman, godlike, transcendental; it will never be attained by man, touched on at most".

In the concluding, practical section on "Society and the State" and "Discipline and Breeding"[1] the final conclusions from all this are drawn. "The rung you occupy on the social ladder is decided by the power-quantum you are. The rest is cowardice." The masses "are the sum of the weak". "We must think of the masses as ruthlessly as Nature does. They preserve the species". "We observe the misery of the masses with ironical sadness: we want something that *we* can do". All the same: "The workers should learn to feel like soldiers: an honorary fee, an honorary salary, but no pay". For the rest, "The workers should learn to live as the bourgeois live now; but above them, distinguished by their lack of needs, the *higher caste*, poorer and simpler, but in possession of power". He is concerned only with this higher caste or type. The workers are only the "material of transmission".

---

[1] I omit his remarks on the Will to Power as idea and art since they are of no great moment here.

And the middle classes? Here his conception is not very clear. On the one hand he expounds in conformity with his earlier writings how "the social hodge-podge" and Nineteenth Century civilization in general is bound to lead to "mob-rule" and, with the recrudescence of the *old* values, to mediocrity, to the "vision of the European of the future" as "the most intelligent slave-animal, very industrious, very modest at bottom, curious to excess, versatile, pampered, weak-willed—a chaos of cosmopolitan ideas and passions". So that he cries out in desperation: "Where are the Vandals of the Twentieth Century? Evidently they will only appear and establish themselves after violent Socialist upheavals". On the other hand he speaks in quite another tone of the middle class, the "great mediocrity" thrown up by civilization, as the necessary foundation on which the new aristocracy will stand, and the separation of such an aristocracy from it as an "outcrop de luxe". "The flattening of man must be our objective for a long time to come, because a broad basis must first be created for the stronger type of man to stand on. It is an absurd and contemptible sort of idealism that will not have mediocrity mediocre, and instead of feeling that the exceptional being is a triumph, gets indignant about cowardice, falsity, pettiness and wretchedness. *We should not wish these things otherwise*". The conclusion he draws is once again "to widen the gulf". "We should *force* the higher type to cut itself off through the sacrifices it has to make for its being". And he adds in a tone of apparent, but only apparent, mitigation: "The main objective is to open up distances, *but not to create contrasts*. Isolate the middle class and restrict its influence—the best way to keep the distances intact". For the most important thing is "a teaching that creates a *gulf*: it preserves the top and the bottom, destroys the middle". He goes on: "The progressive diminution of man is the driving force that enables us to think of breeding a *stronger race*. . . . As soon as an equalized species is attained it needs a justification: this lies in serving a higher and sovereign type that rests on it and can only rise to its true tasks on that basis. Not merely a master-race whose task is exhausted in governing, but a race with its own sphere of life, with an overflow of strength for beauty, courage, culture, manners and high spirituality; a race that *affirms* and can grant itself every great luxury—strong enough not to have need of the tyrannical imperatives of virtue, rich enough to abhor frugality and pedantry, beyond good and evil".

This new master-class which Nietzsche pictures as proceeding from a counter-movement to mediocrity and of which he says that it is to be "a forcing-house for rare and choice plants", is divided into two ruling types: the "shepherds" and the "masters" —the first being the *means* for the preservation of the herd, the second the *end* for which the herd is there at all. Both variants are to have the characteristic qualities of the "aristocratic" man who, for Nietzsche, is a step in the direction of the Superman, and thus a step beyond ordinary mortals.

This programme of social reconstruction which can be described as not only anti-democratic but a very peculiar mixture of hypocrisy and Machiavellianism, workers and everything "middling" alike being just so much raw material, is now fitted into the categories "discipline" and "breeding" from which a conspectus of the whole social future emerges. Some very remarkable prognoses are made and yet these are only the logical conclusions drawn from a work that has the quantum theory of the Will to Power as the principle of life. Nietzsche asserts: there are only nobles by birth and blood, adding, "I am not speaking here of the little word 'von' and the Almanac of Gotha—a caret for donkeys". The essential substructure of nobility is inheritance, inheritance in its widest sense. With Nietzsche it takes the form of a belief in the inheritance of acquired characteristics and the influence of tradition. But since he proposes to *create* an aristocracy he asks himself: "How can we foresee the favourable conditions in which beings of the highest worth can arise?" And he answers from his point of view: "It is far, far too complicated and the probability of miscarriage *very great*. So don't be over-enthusiastic about struggling for it. Scepticism". On the other hand (and this is the core of his doctrine of inheritance), "courage, insight, hardness, independence, responsibility can be increased, we can refine the delicacy of the balance and expect favourable accidents to come to our aid". Although he would have had (writing as he did from an intellectual standpoint that obviously recognized the importance of education) to give this pride of place, particularly intellectual education, he still wants to make marriage dependent on a medical certificate "in which certain questions must be answered by the engaged couple and the doctors regarding their family history"; and every marriage, he says, "should be seconded by a certain number of confidential witnesses drawn from the parish". An idea that so far only National Socialism has come to. Even for his "stronger" or "higher" types he gives instructions which exactly fit in with the line of events in present-day Germany. "The future as I see it," says this so intellectual Nietzsche: "a rigorous polytechnical training, military service, so that on the average everyone of the higher ranks is an officer whatever else he is". And these are to be the new forms of morality for his elect: "Faithful vows taken in Societies about what one shall and shall not do; definite renunciation of many things. See if *ripe* for it". "What do people learn in a hard school [such as he wishes?]: to command and to obey".

Against this background, on which not a word is inscribed regarding intellectual, let alone political, freedom, there rises even in his sketch of the "aristocratic" man the crucial wish-picture of the great "synthetic" man, "the milestone-man who shows how far humanity has got", and in whom "the tension of life's opposites is at its height, which is the prime condition of man's greatness. My formula for this unavoidable state of things is that man must become *better and badder*". For which reason he demands as a means whereby a stronger type may maintain itself, among other things, "the surrender to conditions in which it is inadmissible *not* to be a barbarian".

A remarkable vision of "the masters of the world", the "great men" and the "highest men as legislators of the future" then brings this practical and at the same time prophetic section of the book to a close. Of the masters of the world and their mission he says: "Slowly but inevitably, terrible as fate itself, the great task, the great question approaches: how shall the earth be ruled as one whole? And to what end should man be bred and trained as a whole and no longer as nations and races?" Moral law-givers are the chief means and for that a morality is needed which, basing itself on an undivided Will to Power and Super-power, believes that "cruelty, hardness, acts of violence, danger in the street and in the heart, inequality of rights, secrecy, stoicism, temptings and devilries of all kinds, in brief the very opposite of all the wishful thinkings of the herd are needed to edify man as a species". Such a morality, which "wants to breed man for nobility rather than for comfort and mediocrity, a morality whose purpose is to rear a governing caste, the future masters of the earth, must (so Nietzsche says once again with undisguised hypocrisy), if it is to be learnt, insinuate itself in alliance with the existing moral code and under its tenets".

On the subject of the form of society that is to support these intellectual oddities of lords of the earth he then remarks: "From now on there will be favourable pre-conditions for a more comprehensive system of rulership the like of which has never been seen. And this is still not the most important thing: international dynastic alliances have now become possible, whose task it is to rear a master race, the future 'rulers of the world'—a vast aristocracy built up on the hardest self-discipline. In this aristocracy permanence will be given to the will of philosopher-despots and artist-tyrants for thousands of years: a higher type of men who, in the ascendency of their desires, knowledge, riches and influence will use democratic Europe as their most pliable and manoeuvrable tool, so as to grasp the world's destinies in their hands, so as to be artists in men. Enough, the time will come when we shall see *high diplomacy* with new eyes". High diplomacy? one must ask. Did not these same "rulers of the world" once exist in the consanguineous Legitimist princely alliances that governed Europe up to the advent of the Democracy so anathematized by Nietzsche? Did they fulfil their task so well? Or rather, is not precisely that execrated democratic tool necessary to achieve a better result in the case of the intending new rulers of the world?

Then the "great man", the second item in Nietzsche's final vision. This man would have "the greatest multiplicity of instincts each in the greatest strength possible". "He is perforce a sceptic (which is not to say that he must necessarily appear to be one), assuming that greatness lies in *wanting* something great and the means thereto. Freedom from every sort of conviction is part of his will's strength". "He requires nobody with a sympathetic heart, only servants, tools. He associates with men always with a view to *making* something out of them. He knows himself incommunicable: he would find it lacking in taste to be familiar, and ordinarily he is not so even when one thinks he is. Unless communing with himself he retains the mask. He prefers to lie rather than speak the truth—it demands more spirit and *will*". "He has no court of law above him, on the contrary his whole nature is to acquire that unparelleled energy of greatness whereby, through breeding on the one hand and the destruction of millions of failures on the other, the man of the future may be fashioned, and *not to perish* because of the suffering that results and the like of which has never existed on earth". In this connection he adds: "In this great man the specific qualities of life are at their greatest: injustice, mendacity, exploitation. But wherever they have carried all before them it is their nature to be misunderstood at best and interpreted as a good".

On top of this typically Nietzschean portrait which, one feels, could so easily, indeed was bound to be, misunderstood, there finally stands that of the "highest man as lawgiver of the future". This lawgiver, as with Plato and in direct alignment with him, is a philosopher. The new philosopher, however, "can only arise in conjunction with a ruling caste as its highest spiritualization. Imminence of mass-politics and world government". So far there has been "a complete lack of principles for it", but the basic thought is: "The new values must first be created. Hence the philosopher must be a lawgiver. And an educator!" Despite everything "an educator never says what he himself thinks, but always only what he thinks in relation to his pupil. He must never be caught at this dissimulation, it is part of his mastery that his honesty should be believed. He must be adept in all the techniques of discipline and correction: some natures he can only advance by the lash of scorn; others, the lazy, the irresolute, the timid, the vain, perhaps only with excessive love. Such an educator is beyond good and evil, but none may know it". He must "bring about situations in which *stronger men* are needed who, for their part, require a morality (or rather, a spiritual-corporal discipline that strengthens) and will consequently *get* it". He must learn "to sacrifice many people and take his affairs seriously enough not to spare them . . . to admit rigorous discipline and violence and cunning in war". Obviously in this connection he remarks: "Roman Caesars with the souls of Christ". As regards the advent of the "highest man" he says: "After a long and costly sequence of virtue, fitness, industry, self-coercion, happy and reasonable marriages and happy accidents there will appear at last a man, a monster of power who will demand a monster of a task. For it is our power that rules us". And as to the external position of this whole tribe of philosophers hc says: "Beyond the rulers, loosed from all bands, live the highest men, and in the rulers they have their tools". A single one of them may in certain circumstances "justify whole aeons . . . one full, rich, great, whole man in comparison with countless fragmentary men". "He who establishes values and guides the will of centuries by guiding the highest natures, is the *highest man*". "I think", Nietzsche says, "that I have divined something of the soul of the highest man—perhaps all who glimpse him must perish. But those who have once seen him must do what they can to make him *possible*. Not humanity, but superhumanity is our goal".

Come l'uom s'eterna.

I have given these highly combustible sections—which, for all their grandeur, are somewhat naïve in their open hypocrisy (for it is a sign of naïveté to commit anything so esoteric in intention to print)—in such detail because their significance and influence can no longer be doubted to-day and also to be as fair as possible to Nietzsche and his glowing personal passion.

It seems to me that it is only from such an objective point of view that we can properly assess the two concluding portions of the work: "Dionysus and Eternal Recurrence". They offer in themselves nothing new; but the Dionysian view of life and its connection with the doctrine of Eternal Recurrence (which is the broad background of Nietzsche's philosophy) are both given, like everything else in the later Nietzsche—still in full possession of his intellectual faculties but theorizing to extremes—in a highly personal accent and with excessive over-emphasis. Highly personal, for instance, is the well-known sentence that underlies it all: "Dionysus versus the Crucified: there is your contrast. It is not a difference in degree of martyrdom—but martyrdom itself acquires a different meaning. Life itself, its terribleness and its recurrence bring about the agony, the destruction, the will for annihilation . . ." "Dionysus torn to pieces is one of life's promises: he will be born eternally again and come back out of the destruction". But it is excessive over-emphasis when he says of his philosophy, which is to overcome Nihilism and thus lead to the "volte-face" and the Dionysian "yea-saying to the world as it is", that yea-saying "without retreat, exception or choice": "(to it belong) the sides of life we have always denied, not only as necessary but also desirable; and not only desirable in respect of the sides we have always affirmed, as their complement or prime condition, but for their own sake, as the mightier, more terrible, truer sides of existence, in which it expresses its will more clearly". Hence "the growth of man in *terribleness* is to be understood as the concomitant of his growth in culture". "Man is the brute and super-brute; the higher man is the monster and supermonster. With man's every growth in stature and greatness he grows in depth and terribleness too: we should not want one without the other (or rather, the more completely we want the one the more completely we arrive at the other). . . . A full and mighty soul not only gets over painful, even terrible losses, privations and all manner of contempt very quickly, it emerges from these hells in greater fullness and mightiness and—this is the chief thing—with a new growth of love's blessedness". "A Goethean vision full of love and goodwill as a result".

We can see from this the actual depths of the Nietzschean view of the world, his agony and the causes of his extremism. And perhaps we can have some feeling for that special organ of his which, as he says, set in motion in him by sheer force of thought the doctrine of Eternal Recurrence, the recognition of which has, in his view, "its place in history, as a centre", and of which he asks "how it can be used as a selective principle in the service of power (and barbarism! ! !)" and whether "humanity is *ripe* for it". As a means to help us bear it he names, besides the transvaluation of values, the eternally creative principle, "not only the will to preserve the species, but the will to power; not the humble phrase: 'it is all only subjective', but: 'it is *our* work—let us be proud of it!' " At any rate he thinks that "it is not to be wondered at if a couple of thousand years are necessary to establish the contact again—what are a couple of thousand years?" And finally: "Know ye what the world is to me? . . . A marvel of power without beginning, without end, power in solid, brazen majesty . . . bounded by nothing save its own bounds, neither flowing, nor profuse, nor infinitely extended, but lodged as a definite power in a definite space, and not a space that is anywhere empty, rather power everywhere, in the play of its forces and its will at once one and many, now piling up, now sinking down, a sea of tumultuous and torrential power, eternally changing, eternally returning, with immense cycles of recurrence, in the ebb and flow of its forms passing from the utmost simplicity into the utmost complexity, from coldest, deathliest, stillest rigidity to wildest and fieriest self-contradiction, and then reverting from these plenitudes once more to simplicity, back from the play of contradiction to the delight of harmony, ever acclaiming itself in this sameness of its orbits and years, blessing itself as that which must eternally return, as a Becoming that knows no becoming-sated, no surfeit, no weariness: this new Dionysian world of everlasting self-creation, of everlasting self-destruction, this mystery-world of doubled delights, this my 'Beyond Good and Evil' without end or aim—unless end or aim lie in the happiness of the circle; without Will—unless a ring bear itself goodwill: would ye have a *name* for this world? A solution to all its enigmas? A light for ye also, ye darkest, doughtiest, most undaunted sons of the midnight? This world is the *Will to Power and nothing else*. And ye also are this Will to Power—and nothing else!"

If we take along with this half physical, half (save the mark!) metaphysical or, if you like, *existential*[1] avowal the Dionysian Dithyrambs that were probably written at the same time, with words such as: "Thy happiness makes dry round about, makes poor in love—a rainless land"; or "Self-knower—Self-executioner"; or "Guilt of necessity! Highest star of being! that no desire can reach, no negation sully, eternal Yea of life, eternally I am thy Yea: *for I love thee, O Eternity!*"—then we may perhaps get an inkling of the deeps of passionate discord from which rose the vision we have tried to adumbrate.

We do not have to investigate these depths here. Every work takes its place in the world as the work it is, has its effect and its self-given meaning, its self-allotted existence.

Were the vision we have adumbrated sheer theory, fantasy or the emotional outpourings of a quite ordinary person, or had Nietzsche's development stopped short at *Zarathustra* and the utterances of that period which are one-sided enough, in all conscience,—we would be justified in stopping there ourselves (as an earlier age did and as, if he is to be frank, the author

---

[1] Thus Karl Jaspers evidently understands it, having analysed Nietzsche essentially from this point of view in his weighty and comprehensive book: *Nietzsche—an Introduction to the Understanding of his Philosophy* (Berlin, 1936).

himself once did) and simply taking delight in the magnificent conception of this man's work; extracting from its riches what we can approve and ignoring what we must deny. We could then assimilate Nietzsche as selectively as is our custom with regard to most of what we read. But that does not apply to Nietzsche. Above all it does not apply to the later Nietzsche of *The Will to Power*. And especially it does not apply to-day, when we have experienced the effect Nietzsche has had, how he has been understood or misunderstood, what he means to-day as a spiritual element in our lives, seeing that certain terrorist dictators have made one another presents of him in luxury editions, as a comfort in time of sorrow. Nietzsche has acquired historic significance to-day. He has in fact contributed to what he himself, in *Ecce Homo*, prognosticated would be his effect—namely, to split the world's history in two.

This being so, we must take up an unequivocal position towards him. What is his work, and what its effect? We have ruthlessly to disregard all his aesthetic charm, all the fascination exerted by his mind and his expressive powers and above all by the reflections of personal fate that his work contains. What is this work? What is its place and where does it stand purely objectively? We must choose *The Will to Power*, theoretically the most consistent of his works, as the point of departure. Also, we have to make a fundamental distinction between two things: what we can term the Absolute in Nietzsche and his work, and what, being time-bound, is interpretation of his age. But the whole of Nietzsche is so saturated and stamped with his repudiation of his own age, he is so suffused by his passions in this respect and thus, in a certain sense, relativized, that the Absolute cannot be altogether separated from the time-bound, particularly since in our opinion the most absolutely Absolute in him derived precisely from that repudiation.

This final Absolute is in all probability what he called the Dionysian view of life. It was only the amazing shallowness of the contemporary world of the cultured bourgeoisie (with which he wrestled almost alone) that did not see and did not want to see the dark, or in our terminology the dark-daemonic, sides of existence. We have already mentioned the few people after Schopenhauer who were aware of these aspects and said something about them. But on the average the age had lost feeling for them.

It even ignored what Goethe, who by then had become a positive bugbear of culture in the superficial way he was understood, had left behind on this subject, toned down as it was. In all innocence, as we saw, people propagated "power-politics", turned "realist" in the Bismarckian era, gradually wearing out the (apparently) already threadbare ideals that had come down from the Eighteenth Century. Jakob Burckhardt alone "knew". The rest of the age had no eyes for the hidden and perilous qualities of existence.

And equally it was right that Nietzsche should cry out to his age—and this holds good for the 'realist' eighties too—that they did not want to know or admit that suffering is an essential part of life, that the organic process of Becoming always means suffering and destruction. To have seen this and flung it again and again in the face of his superficial age is to Nietzsche's imperishable credit. For it means that the vision of the depths that was there in Dante's, Michelangelo's and Shakespeare's time and that the Seventeenth Century still saw in somewhat different form through the eyes of figures like Pascal and Rembrandt, only to be enthusiastically covered up in the Eighteenth and finally lost sight of in the whirl of progress during the Nineteenth—was rediscovered by one who, from a distance deliberately chosen or else imposed on him by fate, viewed his times more sharply than his contemporaries could—and, what is more, was rediscovered in the form of a demand for the courage to face it squarely and not lose heart. To-day we are experiencing the most terrible things, and there is, God knows, no need for anybody to cry out to us that suffering and terror are an ineluctable part of life. It is nevertheless an accomplishment that this was seen in an age of superficiality and voiced by a man who at the same time demanded for its endurance that courage of which we stand in all too obvious a need to-day.

It is further to Nietzsche's credit openly to demand and desire a greater naturalness in life together with stricter spiritual discipline. Naturalness! We have too much of it to-day. And it may be that Nietzsche is not without complicity in this "too much". But in the stuffy atmosphere of that superannuated bourgeois cultural world, an atmosphere of narrow humdrum morality wholly untested as to its qualities and limitations and giving rise to an eroticism admitted in art but not in life, and therefore unhealthy or sickly sweet—in such an atmosphere Nietzsche's homily on "the great health" that controls the self was indeed a factor making for freedom and restoration. That homily has helped to put in the place of a bespectacled generation nervously hunched over a culture that might blow up any minute, another, a generation which grew up in a freer air after the turn of the century and gave a controlled assent to its natural instincts, the first generation of the one that surrounds us to-day, whose natural bodily expression is a delight in physical prowess and sport since it enjoys an abundance of good health, and whose intellectual characteristic it is to have curbed, under Nietzsche's influence, that vapid, flatulent gongorism that was once so much in vogue.

Neither must we omit to mention to what a remarkable extent the time shortly before and after the turn of the century was, for the cultured classes, not only a time of deepened understanding of life but also of a rise in the level of intellectual productions and of heightened demands on character, together with a broadening of horizons unknown in the previous narrow age. There can be no doubt that Nietzsche's postulate of the unprejudiced "aristocratic" man and the demands he had to make of himself exerted, like Nietzsche's whole conquest of new spiritual territories, a profound influence. If there was a danger of progressive mediocrity of mind, and if this danger was very largely banished after the end of the century, especially in Germany, the prime and deciding intellectual force that averted the danger was Nietzsche's, the man who overflowed with hatred of anything mediocre and persecuted it with withering scorn. This is a great service, for it means not only that the deep view of things was recaptured through him, but also that new heights of soul and mind were glimpsed in a genuinely new way, thanks to this rehabilitation of health and nature.

But—we must ruthlessly ask—what was the price paid? The price is everything that is time-conditioned in Nietzsche's positive attitude, and everything that, because of the aggressive position he took up, was seen in wrong perspective, underwent extreme distortion or was shattered beneath the hammer blows of his zeal, although the objects of attack may well have been valuable or humanly speaking of fundamental importance.

What is time-conditioned in Nietzsche is the whole naturalistic-relativist and subjective garb in which he presents his experience. He himself describes his ideas and postulates as "naturalistic", indeed "physiological"; and he clothes them in that wholly impossible form, which he borrowed from Natural Science, of a struggle between power-quanta, claiming that it provided the key to the nature and forms of life's changing values, the key to the world, the veritable alpha and omega of interpretation. This is the Nineteenth Century at its worst and most antiquated! It is a wholly inadequate envelope for things, externalizing and de-spiritualizing them, since things lie much deeper and only on that level really *are* what they mean. An envelope so empty, moreover, that he himself did not ultimately abide by it, considering the spiritual postulates he sets up. Further, in his case it was coupled with an extreme subjectivism, which is likewise time-conditioned,—though Nietzsche, of course, would take violent exception to the epithet "subjective", since everything is supposed to be the objective struggle of power-monads revealed "perspectivally". But this struggle is not sufficient to reveal to anybody who gives it a glance the picture of Nietzsche's "aristocratic" man, let alone all his other qualitative points of view, postulates and evocative fantasies. If all values, as Nietzsche teaches, are to be created by man—and by man, moreover, without any objective background of transcendental value—then it necessarily follows that these values are not present as objective data, but are a subjective product. Nietzsche could only see them that way, even though, with his truly *absolute* postulates of "cleanliness" and intellectual honesty as also in his whole passionate emphasis which is truly *ethical*, part of him does not adhere to this view at all.

All his affirmations and denials, so consciously italicized, sprang from the consequences of the spiritual disintegration that occurred in Europe during the Nineteenth Century. They were splinters of the collapse of the world of ideal values, a collapse that found no adequate substitute outside religion. We can say with confidence that the spiritual outcome of secularism with its historicisms and relativisms was bound to be Nihilism, as Nietzsche was quite right in thinking and which, for all that he battled with it valiantly to the end, he did not overcome.

Nietzsche not overcome Nihilism as he thought and himself wanted? We must answer: no. He could not overcome it. It

was impossible for him to do so because he was too time-conditioned. Because of this time-conditioning he inevitably got
stuck in any such attempt in that externalizing naturalism and
relativizing subjectivism, both of which he wanted to overcome
and yet consciously espoused at the same time. Like his whole
age he could not in the last resort get beyond the abstractionism
of the Seventeenth and Eighteenth Centuries even after it had
broken down, because he thought that with this breakdown of
the old ideal world of concepts or with the demonstration as to
the apparent relativity of Christian or Church morality narrowly
understood, the absolute potencies, the immanent and transcendent powers had also broken down and been destroyed—
those powers which underlie the whole conceptual world of
ideals just as they lie behind the explicit formulae of Christianity.
What an error this was! The official morality of Christianity—we cannot avoid continually emphasizing this afresh—
is nothing less than a formalized accentuation of value deriving
wholly from the preconceptual and fundamental experience
on which Christianity rests; from the experience of the transcendental oneness of mankind and from the deliberately one-sided
and passionate sublimation of this experience in its original
form. Because it is so important I am consciously repeating
what I have said elsewhere. The active "humanity" of the
Christian which was then secularized and put forth but a
stunted shoot in the Nineteenth Century "Humanitarianism"
so mocked at by Nietzsche, merely because it can be exaggerated
or turned into shallow platitudes is *no less* the expression of man's
experience of a transcendent power once discovered and thereafter become imperishable, ceaselessly active behind mankind
ever since its discovery. All those Eighteenth-Century ideals
which had apparently become so threadbare and decrepit or even
dangerous and which Nietzsche attacks so merrily are, in truth,
inklings, presentiments, perhaps over-naïve apprehensions or
value-accentuations of immediate and conscious *experience*, the
experience of the transendental powers reigning in man. Only
because the dark-daemonic *counter*-powers were turned into
abstractions and lost sight of did they become so tenuous and
apparently so remote from reality that they were no longer
capable of resisting the short-sighted Realism of the later Nineteenth Century over a wide field, but particularly in Germany.

It is true that there are different kinds of value-accentuation and thus various combinations of the values which, as Nietzsche puts it, "can be imposed on humanity". But all of them are only temporal shifts of emphasis and differences of vision, and all refer back to what I have again and again shown to be the existentially decisive, objectively actual, both immanent and transcendental power-world that shapes us. Only when we can see this world again and are ready and able to experience it in ourselves and take our bearings by it, shall we be on the road to the conquest of Nihilism, which cannot be conquered in any other way. That the shifts and accentuations of value we have in mind are ours to command, and that the differences in our valuation of the objective powers can be great enough to tip the scales either way, is obvious. We shall speak of this elsewhere.[1] The most obvious example of this, namely how great the shifts can be, is Nietzsche himself with his experiment in transvaluation.

But how time-conditioned and how dominated by peculiar phobias Nietzsche's "transvaluation" is! There is his civilization-cum-domestication phobia, for a start: civilization, he says, makes for mediocrity and softness and—this is the remarkable thing—it is precisely the masses, the Nietzschean "herd-animal" that it makes soft. Indubitably the mass mechanization of life to-day entails a tendency to mass mediocrity and above all to spiritual exhaustion. So much work that used to be done on one's own initiative and responsibility has now passed over to some de-spiritualized technical process in the "rationalized" and equally de-spiritualizing organization of the factory. And the stupefyingly dull office-work that has piled up all round us in the paraphernalia of State and industry! This is our modern fate, and it is a hard fate even if we remember that despite the mechanization a modicum of initiative and responsibility, a modicum of spontaneous inventiveness and directive activity that still *means* something and adds to the fullness of life has managed to maintain itself in the upper and lower strata alike, and is constantly taking new forms. All the same, there are losses, great losses. And they are on the increase since the "Taylorizing" of almost every type of work, even the most intellectual—not to speak of the ant-like activities of the workers themselves.

[1] In the last chapter, which examines the Absolute and the Relative in greater detail.

But a softening and enfeebling of the vital impulses? One must have a very poor knowledge of the masses and the new middle class to fear that. In the case of the workers their profession, which has peculiar problems of its own, and the nature of their work take good care that they do not become soft. And are those new middle classes in Germany, for instance, who were the main supporters of Germany's not exactly lily-handed politics which we all had to submit to during this last decade,—were those classes "soft"? The opposite is only too obvious.

Nietzsche's phobias about civilization, clearly, are more than superfluous from the point of view of "softness" and "degeneration". And after our latest experiences it would seem that we have no need to worry about the "evil", the "dark side" of life as Nietzsche meant it, everything that he called the "calumniated" counter-influences, requiring to be goaded and inflamed still further. Of double-crossing, duplicity, defamation and all the Machiavellian "virtues" so applauded by Nietzsche, down to the depths of swinishness, we have had such a sickener to-day that we hope it will rid us for centuries to come of the notion that we need cultivate evil in order to balance a too cosy life. And his clamour for war as a tonic that is necessary every now and then! Even if modern warfare that goes by the euphemism of "total", the warfare whose victims seem to be women and children for preference, had not become the orgy of bestiality we know, even if it had not sunk to fostering all our vilest and most recessive instincts and bringing them to a fine flower of superlative quality, even if it did not, as it does wherever it prevails to-day, destroy humanity and culture without trace—even if the old "gentlemen's war" still existed which now belongs to a mythical age—even so we would not need war as an antidote to effeminacy. We can learn this from this war. For were the pacifist-minded English and Americans who sacrificed themselves by thousands and tens of thousands in aerial combat and as paratroops alone, essentially worse fighters in this or any other respect than anybody else in this hideous slaughter? Nietzsche who, like most men before 1914, still thought of war as a gentleman's war, is on that account excused along with all the other champions of military heroics who were once so numerous, for thinking that he must constantly extol this "father of all things" and declaim it as indispensable. To-day, however, panegyrics of this kind are merely frivolous. And we know from our own experience, fortunately, that these injections of martial spirit are not necessary to keep up man's spiritual and intellectual strength. More need not be said on *this* problem at this juncture.

But Nietzsche raised still other problems. There is (equally time-conditioned, for it was only in the seventies and eighties that people began to feel the *pressure from below*) his fear of the "insurrection of the masses", his fear of democracy. Who can doubt to-day that an insurrection of the masses in one form or another is likewise our modern fate? But Nietzsche himself, who at a later period accepted democracy as a means of Machiavellian intent, says elsewhere that it is ridiculous to gesticulate and cry "woe! woe!" over the inevitable. Modern civilization leads to the formation of mobs. And, disregarding for the moment the human element, we would be sociologically naïve—and that Nietzsche was naïve cannot unfortunately be contested—if we believed that "mobs" capable of reading and writing and equipped with newspapers and modern news-services could possibly be preserved in their "herd-animal qualities" with "shepherds" over them or even in social forms with an effete nobility wielding exclusive power.

It is not a question of the forms the modern mass-factor assumes or can be led to assume. All Governments, however, not only the democratic but also those that take on or try to maintain dictatorial or terroristic form, are in actual fact dependent to-day on the mood, the instinctive assent or dissent of the masses, in short, the will of the people. Even in the matter of social egalitarianism, which means continuance of the mass-tendency, Governments are far more dependent on popular will when they are terroristic, dictatorial or quasi-dictatorial than when they rest on political freedom and the free consent of the masses. Everything that they withdraw from the masses in respect of freedom and self-determination they have to pay for on the *social* plane, even to the point of the complete abolition of any higher classes privileged by culture or tradition. There is no surer safeguard against one-sided domination by the masses than freedom and democracy—a fact which Nietzsche failed to see. For both these latter demand, if they are to be capable of action, a social hierarchy with leaders elected and recognized by themselves, who then automatically stand out as an élite and are acknowledged as such for the reason that it rests on the active self-determination and the feeling of the masses that the élite and the socially privileged have been created by themselves, of their own free will.

This much is patent if we observe things calmly, without polemics. But Nietzsche's phobia of the masses was at bottom—and this is the essential point—neither political nor sociological, but psychological. He infused into this phobia all his accumulated loathing of mediocrity, all his fears and concerns for intellectual and spiritual superiority, for the general level, for the heights and depths of mind and spirit that could only be won in solitude within as without—everything that had fixed the direction of his will. His will aimed at the most rigid separation from all the banality that he found in the cultured class by which he was surrounded—with the masses and their particular way of life he had hardly any contact. This revulsion and separation he then projected into the very existence of the masses and the problems they raised, which were totally different.

Thus he arrives at his ideal of "aristocracy", for which he is perpetually demanding "the pathos of distance". Thus also at his constantly reiterated demand for the widest possible "gulf" separating those superior beings whom he thought of as "the Strong", from the masses he dubbed "the herd". And here lies the most dangerous feature in all Nietzsche, the most dangerous *quid pro quo* of his whole passionate will; here the point where the question arises as to the whole sensibleness of his idea of the Superman.

Once again let us speak with the least possible accent on values, purely sociologically. First of all: throughout history it has been the case that the average human type in any given people or at any given time has taken shape under the influence exerted on the masses by the élite they themselves have formed. This is true of all historical bodies and all ages. It is true of the caste-system of India, towards which Nietzsche sometimes looks evidently with a certain envy, at least for an aristocracy or something of the kind. The élite creates the psycho-spiritual fluid and then, whether in hierarchical or non-hierarchical form, the masses mould the average type out of it. Could anything be more dangerous, therefore, I mean from the point of view of an élite, than to preach to such an élite "the pathos of distance" and the opening out of a gulf in an age like ours, when the influence of the masses is in the ascendant? That is inviting the élite to commit suicide—for sooner or later it would be blown to pieces by the social dynamic precisely as happened to the one-time privileged aristocracy, the Legitimist monarchy and everything connected with it, at the end of the Eighteenth Century. No rehabilitation of an *ancien régime*, overt or covert, as in the later Nietzsche, rather a social willing and doing that corresponds absolutely to a dynamic relationship between the masses and the élite such as is still possible to-day, a synthesis between the masses and the élite voluntarily created by both—this is the sermon preached in our ears, and not by realism alone. It is the sole means both to a spiritual raising of the masses and to a *tenable* high level for the élite itself.

Yes, to a spiritual raising of the masses! For Nietzsche's most fatal error, his most fatal *inner* aberration also, was just this: to reduce the masses to mere "material of transmission", something spiritually neutral, in his conception of life as a whole. But the masses are a dynamic factor and thus an active ingredient to be appreciated as such in any historical and cultural process. How much this is so we only see in our own. We are fantasists if we overlook this fact.

Then secondly: as regards the élite, above all (speaking in the Nietzschean categories) the élite of the "aristocratic" men, the "lords of the earth" and finally the "highest" men—those foretastes of the Superman! Is there, I ask, any possibility whatever of us mortals even conceiving these "higher" men, and is there any sense in our wanting any men "higher" than the highest that fate has given us so far in our history? Can we, as humans, imagine anything that overtops the greatest men we know, such as Dante, Michelangelo, Shakespeare, Rembrandt, Goethe, to name only a few men of the West? I confess that the project strikes me as eccentric. These men have attained a degree of inner tension, a combination of conflicting forces, a self-discipline and an intensity of living and suffering in such fullness that all Nietzsche's programmatic descriptions of the great or the highest men pale in comparison. The "milestone-men" Nietzsche is seeking and wants to create have, thank God, already *been*. And what we have to do is to recognize them as such, to use them, as

I have said, as "lighthouses" by which we can take our inner bearings if we do not possess others like them.

But in order to make this attitude fruitful for ourselves we need to re-experience the vision of the objective values and the powers that found incarnation in such men and with which these wrestled —precisely the road we have tried to break in our exposition so far.

Nietzsche lacked such a vision. That is why the Superman emerges with him as a future product of the will only to be created by man himself. Hence, also, the whole complex of desiderata not willed from any experience of the actuality of the powers and their incarnation (which we can only foster by a certain training and way of life), but desiderata that merely sprang up along with the conception of his "élite", his "aristocratic" or "lordly" higher men, such as, for instance, the consciously willed "gulf" and "distance" that make his ideal world so distorted.

Hence, finally—a point to be stressed very clearly—Nietzsche's betrayal of those fundamental forces which the West brought to birth—the combined forces of active Humanity and Freedom. Both have accompanied Western history through the centuries. And nothing was more crucial in giving it shape. The one inferred from Christianity, the other our racial heritage, endorsed over and over again by experiences drawn from the great ages of classical antiquity. The Eighteenth Century, as we saw, apprehended both as transcendental powers implanted in man. In this it rendered an immortal service, no matter that it could only apprehend them in abstract form, or at least disseminated them like that in practice. During the second half of the Nineteenth Century this discovery of Transcendence became operative over a wide field, but at the same time, owing to the absence of any new experience of the depths, it gradually grew more and more rootless. Then, towards the end, it was customary, indeed "smart" to speak slightingly of the ideas of 1789, to see only their imperfections and reverse sides which, in point of fact, were only reverse sides by reason of the precipitancy of their realization. What an injustice was done there! For whatever weaknesses, superficialities, undesirable and disastrous accretions the French Revolution and the English and American belief in democracy brought with them, the faith that upholds them both is the only universal "practical-politics" faith fir mankind, a faith born in and of the West, and in its roots, or more precisely, in its transcendental roots a real faith in the ability of man to shape his destiny on earth, offering each one of us an inspiring task. And it would be contemptible to play the apostate to this task or waver in face of it merely on account of its difficulties. Such a faith, or, in other words the profound experience of humanity that underlies it, implies no shift of emphasis that would prejudice the significance of an élite, the élite itself or even the appreciation of the great. On the contrary, only then does the question of building an élite become meaningful—within a total view of men and nations in the making. For an élite will stand out meaningfully—in the full sense of the word—above the broad masses when and only when it represents in itself the plane to which the masses can be raised with its aid. Likewise the appreciation of the great is only meaningful when they are seen as the wave-crests of life's moving sea which raises them to that height.

Only thus may both, the élite and the great, be integrated together with the masses into a future pattern of life as willed by us, a pattern that is not only practically possible, but possible without inner, spiritual strain. *Without inner strain.* Everything that Nietzsche did, saw and said, bears, despite all his passion, despite the grandeur of his conception, despite the purity of his will, the mark of such a strain. It bears the fatal flaw—which came from his aggressive attitude to the drab flatness of his age—of having demolished along with this the very foundations for a new and higher level: the broad life of the West with the ideals that have been peculiar to it since time immemorial. We can see the results of this to-day. It would be a most impertinent underestimation of Nietzsche to make his contribution to these results smaller than they are.

2. *The Period of Apparent Peace* (1890–1914) *and Catastrophe*

But before we examine these results concretely and try to outline our general attitude towards them, a brief reminder concerning the stages which led up to them after the final third of the Nineteenth Century, from the point of view of the sociological and spiritual dynamic responsible for the peculiar nature of the disaster that faces us now.

There were, as we have said, tremendous world-tensions when

the mature Nietzsche appeared on the scene, which, as soon as he began to take effect, he was bound to influence in a dangerously explosive manner after a certain moment. This moment only came in the unclarified atmosphere of tension that followed the first world war, along with the first stirrings of the catastrophe that has now descended upon us. That the moment came so late lies with the peculiar character of the period 1880 to 1914 and those portions of Nietzsche's thought which were taking effect about then, on the one hand, and with the totally different character of the first post-war period and what the popularized Nietzsche meant for it, on the other.

We shall not recapitulate here what we have already said about the first of these periods. And we have no intention of describing the period between the wars in any great detail. Much of the latter is known to everyone to-day from his own experience, and much of it cannot be seen even now in the necessary historical perspective. The following must suffice as the basis for our discussion of the contemporary situation.

The period 1880–1914, in reality charged with the greatest tensions but overspread by a feeling of security, enables us to see just what that previously mentioned slit between mind and politics means in its general consequences. We have already worked out what it meant for Germany in particular, but, different as was the inner structure of the other great European countries, it still, as a general phenomenon of the time, cast its shadow over these others as well. We shall set down very roughly how this split worked out practically and spiritually and what sort of consequences it had and was bound to have for the world at large.

The most important consequence of the split between mind and politics was a libertinism of both—that is to say, a libertinism of Power.

Politics and Power, each from then on was lacking in any kind of intellectual, i.e. spiritual control. In concrete terms, for a short while after this separation—introduced in Germany, perhaps unwittingly, by Bismarck—there still continued to sit in the Reichstag (though this, to all intents and purposes, was shorn of its power after 1878 because no longer equipped with the practical possibilities of responsible government) certain representatives of intellectual Germany, the successors to the much maligned "Professors' Parliament" of the Frankfurt Paulskirche of 1848. But already their backbone was broken. Then they vanished from it completely. Interests, that is to say, the aristocrats of the east and the heavy industrialists of the west who had vested interests in corn and brandy duties, emerged in the civil sphere together with their more or less gifted representatives, syndics and suchlike alongside the representatives of the Catholic interests (which had a special orientation of their own) and the representatives of organized labour. There was no longer any homogeneous spirit at the back of such a "gremium". Particular interests and interested points of view dominated. Simultaneously, in Austria the much scorned liberals (Nietzsche's alleged "exponents of mediocrity") opposed, with a political instinct not in the least mediocre, albeit in vain, the Danaan gift of Bosnia and Herzegovinia to Austro-Hungary—the responsibility for which Bismarck had palmed off on the Congress of Berlin—a gift that, with the power-aspirations it contained, was to become the Trojan horse for the destruction of the Austro-Hungarian Empire later on. These very reasonable liberals were succeeded by the champions of nationalist and imperialist "Pan" movements, so that both Parliament and Diet were increasingly bedevilled by conflicting nostrums until finally, so divided had the Empire become, she could be driven into that frivolously instigated conflict with Serbia, the basis of which was economic and psychological and the efficient cause Bosnia and Herzegovinia. Meanwhile in Germany Wilhelm II, on whom the one-time German intellectual traditions did not lie heavy, was able to indulge in his pompous tirades, and a pliable Parliament made up of various interests granted Tirpitz—a well-meaning fellow but quite inexperienced in politics—the money for the construction of his fleet that was to prove completely useless during the war[1]—a hazardous venture whose risks were inordinately great, far more so for Germany than for England, the intended victim. The fleet was spawned of power-political thinking; the Reichstag voted more money for armaments. Honour and profits piled up all round. But the disintegration caused by power-politics had already set in.

In France, Parliament at least managed to maintain itself on a

---

[1] The construction of the important U-boat fleet was, as is well known, left to lag far too long.

tolerably high intellectual level. But the fact that Congress could choose, in the midst of an international situation already boiling up to a climax, an inveterate war-monger and power-political intriguer like Poincaré as its President, was a sign that even in France the links between mind and politics had grown suspiciously weak—although after the brouhaha about Boulanger and the reprehensible Dreyfuss affaire one would have thought that there of all places the delirium of power-politics might have been somewhat moderated by a cold douche of intellection. Of the other countries, chiefly Russia and Great Britain, the less said the better. Power expansionism in Russia and power defence in Great Britain were the accepted watchwords of the day, dominating everything else. Hence, everywhere a libertinism of power without any higher moral or intellectual control.

And what was the quality of the intellectual sphere? Let us confine ourselves to France and Germany, probably the decisive factors for that period in things intellectual. Despite the intellectual malaise that, for complicated reasons, had temporarily afflicted France towards the turn of the century, she possessed a great philosopher in Bergson. Bergson's supersession of the mechanistic view, his doctrine of *élan vital*, which re-established the spontaneous forces in their own right, was, like much else that he did, an uncommon achievement, liberating new powers some of whose waves washed over to Germany. The so-called "pathfinders"[1] of modern France, such as Péguy, Suarez and others who contributed to the flowering of France's last literary epoch of significance and also, among other things, to the strengthening of her will to live as demonstrated in 1914, have all drunk at the quickening Bergsonian fount. And yet—that intellectual libertinism! George Sorel was nourished at the same fount, a man of the older generation but acquainted with all these people, in his general intellectual attitude not at all the revolutionary, but, nevertheless, the author of *Sur la violence*. By setting up a completely new kind of active Socialism after the Marxist model this book, together with Nietzsche, was the greatest intellectual catalyst known towards the end of the century, thanks very largely to which the Workers' Movement was turned from the paths of peaceful evolution by reform to those of revolution by violence. Parliament is an institution for

[1] So called by Ernst Robert Curtius in the *Pathfinders of Modern France*.

domestication which must be superseded by the "mythos" of active revolutionism and a genuine Workers' Movement standing on its own feet; *action directe*, formulated and propagated by an *avantgarde* tantamount to an élite; propagandist inflammation of the masses to direct action—such were the slogans. Behind this Sorelian instrument of "direct action" (still quite innocuous in its way) loomed an incipient revolutionism that took the word "violence" in its precise and literal sense and was to imbue the doctrine of an *avantgarde* with dictatorial tendencies. Such a revolutionism brought to light altogether new forces of will that threw all the old Western ideals and barriers ruthlessly overboard. There is no need to say what the two mutually antipathetic movements—each of such fatal significance for the world—were that drew sustenance from the intellectual goings-on in this essentially unworldly head whose owner could, even in old age, salute the creator of one of these two movements—Lenin—and who, in the easy circumstances of his own life, doubtless had no idea of, or did not pause to consider, what manner of "goods and possessions" quite, quite different from those of the "bourgeoisie" he was preparing for the sacrifice with his watchword "violence". But this, this kind of propaganda-mongering without considering the ultimate consequences in practice, was typical of the intellectual libertinism so rampant in the appeasement period up to 1914. It was wholly characteristic—that and the other circumstance that in bourgeois cultural circles people could with the greatest equanimity discuss and intellectually tolerate such propaganda simply as "interesting" forms of thought, something that was "in the air".

And it was the same in Germany, but in a much more "interesting" mixture considering the much greater alienation of the intellectuals as a body from all responsible and practical life. Germany was getting richer and richer. For the first time a real "leisure-class" was being deposited round about her capital-producing sphere. Simultaneously she was experiencing in the purely intellectual sphere, and assimilating it unconsciously (or if consciously, in an unaccustomed way) to her great intellectual traditions, a sort of "renascence" which burst the bounds of bourgeois-cultural stuffiness and refused, as though taking stock of itself, to keep pace with the furious tempo of mechanical progress whose destructive features had hitherto been accepted with such uncritical optimism. Taking German literature as an all-representative symptom, if the preceding period had suffered from historical and social fixations in its attitude to life's problems (can one imagine Gustav Freytag ever questioning life as such? !) and if, even in its best representatives like Theodor Fontane or the isolated Gottfried Keller, it clung fast as a general rule to fond and amiable descriptions of milieu and character—now something different emerged, a style of novel that came to grips with the real fundamentals of life (e.g. Thomas Mann), and a lyricism that drew on a timeless, depth-plumbing vision of things and sometimes gave form and utterance to them in a completely new voice. As in France, a portion of the writers in Germany also created an outward world of their own standing outside that of the bourgeoisie and the proletariat. However external it may be, this process was symbolical. Never before had there been so much conscious unconventionalism in Germany side by side with a continuance of the good old conventions, so much open interest in everything significant of life's heights and depths. Not since our classical period had we approached so close to an all-embracing view.

The atmosphere of this period would have been unthinkable without Nietzsche, the Nietzsche of *Zarathustra*. He was the real breaker of barriers, the liberator and, in many important respects, the deepener.

But what was happening from the point of view of life *as a whole*? Intellectual foci formed in various places, inwardly rich, full of the most open human relationships, capable of powerful cross-fertilization, refined, cosmopolitan in outlook. None of these foci, however, even in the cities, had the smallest relation to or the smallest influence on politics and practical life. A wall of alienation lay between. What was really going on beyond it these intellectual circles had no very clear idea for the most part. The most they did was occasionally to laugh at some of its symptoms in a smart funny paper and leave things as they were in practice. Similarly, they knew little and cared less as a general rule about what was to be done as regards the problem of the masses. It is true that there were groups that concerned themselves with making the workers decent members of society, hence with social politics. But for the sensibilities of the unfortunately very numerous persons who felt intellectually superior to all that and took their cue from the Nietzschean "pathos of distance", it was fundamentally an unimportant, an inferior if not a stupid beginning. Democracy and Socialism? The disciples of the most strong-willed and gifted German poet of the time—though not poetically the richest, perhaps—Stefan George, purported to be "a band elect"; and they felt themselves as such. They surrounded themselves with initiation rites and revelled in programmes of "rule and service" instead of getting to know or coming to grips with the grave and very real questions concerning the common future and the future of the masses. Such were the currents of the time which can only be explained by the severance of all things intellectual from the sphere of really significant practical action, that split between mind and politics, purely mental at first but destined to become very actual in its effects later on.

Even where people were not so blind and blinkered the feeling remained: "After all, nothing can be done against the swash-buckling and dilettantism of Wilhelm II in this flood of general prosperity". And on the other hand, people were rather inclined to let things slide. They were living in that feeling of security which made them believe not only that they could indulge in an unlimited "understand all, forgive all", or largesse in the noblest sense, but that such was intellectually their highest duty. They had no notion that this "understand all" attitude was, once mind and the practical world were seen as one, and however nobly intended, something quite apart, a species of libertinism—a very refined one, of course.

Behind all this and reducing it, historically speaking, to a mere intellectual episode if not to the antics of puppets, the perilous political libertinism of power-interests was steadily growing, seen with tolerable clearness by but a handful of great men as through gaps in the wall, and, against the preposterous décor of the old diplomacy, those "realist" trends now began to heave with volcanic activity, pregnant with disaster, and made all the more explosive by the evolutionary militarism that was still, on the whole, hidden from view: the forces of imperialism, nationalism and militarism were coming together in perfervid co-operation behind the scenes.

Suddenly, released by a couple of shots somewhere, the war, the catastrophe, was upon us. What had been universally felt for two years in its sultriness, what diplomatic shuffling and footling had partly provoked and partly caged as a dangerous monster, suddenly burst upon the stage. The dream was shattered overnight. The whole spiritual and intellectual world, so detached from reality, crumbled. It collapsed not only in Germany; over the entire earth it was smashed to smithereens as with a mighty hammer-blow.

Never has anything more unwanted and more unintended by those in the know descended on mankind. Never have the dark and subterranean forces let loose as though from the dungeons of Nature broken out more terribly. We do not yet know, we who stand to-day in the midst of their fury and in the thick of the second phase of that unleashing, whether they can really ever be locked up again.

A field of ruins is left, one that spiritually and intellectually overspreads the whole world and, as far as ocular evidence goes, has its centre in the wholesale destruction of men and things in Europe, first of all in Germany and round about Germany far into Russia, Italy, France, Belgium, Holland and not last England; a field of rubble beneath which lie probably 12 to 20 million dead, civilization's best blood; that contains countless wounded, mothers, wives and children of the fallen, the maimed and the homeless, and not only cities demolished *en masse* but everywhere wrecked monuments, perished documents, even the oldest and most precious, once held to be the inviolable and eternal memorials of European culture—a gruesome charnel-house reeking with the exhalations of hatred. The question as to what we are to do in the midst of this most monstrous cataclysm known to human history is addressed to us—and, speaking as a German —particularly to us Germans who, surrounded by hate to-day, were the immediate authors—we cannot shake this off—of this gigantic holocaust,—even though we also, when it began, found ourselves ensnared in a terrorism that had been cast over us, not that we were not to blame, of course. It would be pitiable cowardice not to face this question as deeply, as ruthlessly and as comprehensively as possible, an act of spiritual desertion to put the blame on to one man—for whom, indeed, no allowances need be made—and his clique. One man alone with a clique, be he a monster of elemental magnetism, of dark powers, of supreme endowment, unscrupulousness of will and almost somnambulistic knowledge of the techniques of mass corruption, can only bring about or cause to be brought about anything as monstrous as what has happened when he meets with *conditions* which gather certain powers about him and make his actions, whatsoever he does, emblematic, as it were, and acceptable for what they outwardly are and for what they inwardly mean. Of these conditions we have already spoken, giving a brief sketch of the external ones and dealing with the spiritual ones a little more precisely.

We must start with a new spiritual will if we are to come to terms with the inner and outer conditions of our life, now reduced almost to nothing; and we must modify them if we want to try to regain, spiritually—and only spiritually is it possible—a place, a dignity and a significance among the peoples of the world.

CHAPTER VII

TO-DAY AND THE TASK

More than ten years ago, about 1933, I wrote: "Only a new and universal experience of life can save us from the impending chaos". Meanwhile this chaos, having burst upon us, has—speaking for myself at least—offered us the universal, life-spanning experience in question.

If it is to be of any weight against the problems that have arisen this experience must, it is quite true, be a new experience. But what does "new" mean here? The inner experience which, without any speculation paving the way, forces itself upon us as a sudden glimpse into the subterranean depths of the outward processes surrounding us, is something we have received direct and is, as such, to be clarified subsequently by our thinking and thus made a part of our empirical understanding. It is, however, something entirely different from a philosophically acquired "terminal experience", to speak with Jaspers, since the latter can ultimately only be the result of intense philosophical speculation. Our experience, which has also to be tested by critical thought, stands as an immediate datum at the *beginning* of the process. As such, and since life is at bottom immutable and changes only in its manifest pattern, it cannot be "new" in the strictest sense. It can only be shallower or deeper, can only comprehend more of the strata of immediate Transcendence or less. Thus it is always only a new coloration of something unalterably given, a novelty that results from a variation of the historical surface pattern, from the "Becoming", which is indeed nothing but change of foreground. As with every view that advances into metaphysics here also, in complete and conscious contrast to Nietzsche's wholly unmetaphysical doctrine of Becoming which derives from the most unmetaphysical period of the Nineteenth Century and bears its features, Becoming in our view is the type, the form, the limit of every possible but in the deepest sense invariable experience of Being, and hence the mode of all its possible novelties. These can only be a recrudescence or a rediscovery of something old, something immemorially experienced, "new" only in so far as they acquire their particular physiognomy and their special tone from man's consciousness and experience in a given historical and sociological context, from the constellation of the moment. In other words: all "novelties" must come from the same depth-dimensions as the earlier ones, and the nature of the transcendental zone which touches them must, even though the mode of expression be different, be self-identical.

This being so, the earlier non-dogmatic, immediate transcendental experiences of the West were discussed, their exponents designated as "light-houses" for us to-day, and from the dogma-riddled Eighteenth Century we adduced that which we may term a supra-dogmatic break-through—not speculation, rather direct illuminative experience and understanding. None of these experiences, neither those of Michelangelo nor Shakespeare nor Rembrandt nor even Goethe, can be taken as forbidden territory to-day. They are all finger-posts, psychopomps: "High on the ancient turret stands the hero's spirit"; "spirit-greetings" they are, as Goethe says in his poem, sent out to us of to-day—and that means above all those of us who have remained young, or the younger generation.

I speak as a mere interpreter and intermediary and virtually only to the younger generation, to those of them who have had a substantial experience of what I am speaking of or who, roused to awareness, are willing and able to translate their outward experience into an inner one, an experience that plumbs the depths of their souls, which always—and this is the direction I stand for—means transcendental experience. Willing and able also to draw the necessary conclusions regardless, above all the personal conclusions. In the main I am not addressing myself to the conscious solitaries of this young generation who, though they are certainly very valuable, can hardly be considered apt for the positively tremendous task of education which lies before us and is implicit in the conclusions to be drawn. May they be preserved as highly esteemed birds of paradise for another age!

I do not know how great a part of the remaining youth or, generally speaking, of the younger generation that grew up in the first World War, that felt itself stagnating in the period between the wars and was then swamped by the events of 1933 as by a new world—their first real one, perhaps—has experienced just *what* I am speaking of, and hence is able to draw the conclusions I draw. The initial enquiries I made in 1933 were not very encouraging. Enquiries made of the still younger generation that has grown up meanwhile are for the most part indeterminate. But isolation and the impossibility of direct communication during the regime of terror from which we have just emerged may have given rise to certain habituations or to the checking of every deep feeling (such at least as might have practical results), and to that peculiar, essentially disgraceful atmosphere of "things being what they are, shall I be so lacking in taste as to fight against them?"—an atmosphere which I take to be very prevalent but which cannot, perhaps, be imputed to everybody. Be that as it may, has the bulk of our thinking youth—disregarding for the moment the glorious exceptions, the sacrifices we personally know of—felt the regime of terror for what it was and for what every earlier generation in our history would have felt it to be—a disgrace that destroyed our country's dignity? I do not know.

All the same I will try to express what has forced itself on me as something universal and with great intenseness of experience, and to tell you what I see before me. And I will say it as simply as possible.

First of all: the essence of what has happened since 1933 is not the shattering of old prejudices and their replacement by something more genuine, not the expiry of outworn ideas which were no longer able to control life in practice and the emergence of new values that would have done away with them, not the destruction of a dead by a living world—not a bit of it. All that was a façade. The zero-mark of to-day is sufficient proof of this.

Things would never have dropped to this zero had not, for the reasons already mentioned, that mentality so opposed to the older spirit of the West gained the ascendant since about 1880; that lack of depth which reached its nihilistic zenith in the later popularized Nietzsche, the ostensible conqueror of Nihilism; that anti-intellectuality which, together with the polite libertinism of mind and the brutal libertinism of power, vented its rage in the increasingly violent outburst of imperialism and nationalism. This I have sketched in outline. The idea of race, introduced into history with so much blood and beastliness, with its "one-times-one" table of heredity like a grotesque diagram imposed on a mystery as completely inexplicable now as then, is only the acme of bathos attained by the West after all its failures in profundity, the peak of pseudo-scientific tomfoolery.

I do not have to gloss over the weaker aspects of the order that was eliminated in Germany in 1933, or its fatal entanglement in the practical failures of the victorious Allies who were not only blinded by success but smitten with a veritable paralysis of any sense of reality and who denied us, a decisive factor standing in the background, every effort to build up our prestige until it was too late. Neither do I have to disguise the inner constitutional weaknesses of our own order at the time which, with its system of electoral lists, turned the central organ into an Old Age Institute for worn-out functionaries of all descriptions and, thanks to the proportional vote, into a mélange of interest-groups, simultaneously excluding young blood from any political influence whatsoever. And this, mark you, at a time when the selection of a new and competent leading class ought to have been the most urgent task for a people unaccustomed since God knows how long to any really responsible self-government. I do not have to defend this whole historically false agglomeration that, praise-worthy in principle, yet misfired in practice. I have criticized all this, while there still seemed time, openly and sufficiently, if not sufficiently drastically, perhaps, for the stopped ears for which it was intended. At any rate, this òrder was totally unable to give youth and the younger generation the feeling that the land of the future had risen from the sea.

I know also what it has meant that this whole post-war structure seemed, on top of all that, to collapse economically and socially, leaving behind, after the catastrophic crisis of unanticipated extent precipitated in 1929 by the victors in an incomprehensible fit of blindness, a world economy apparently wrecked beyond repair and a shoreless, scarcely controllable tide of unemployment. Which likewise produced no vision of any land of the future rising from the sea.

All that is true enough. And a seeking and groping, a youthful, overhasty acclamation of a novelty all too easily offered is also understandable; especially in a country, such as Germany was then, that had been spiritually and then materially pulverized under the world juggernaut, yet still felt her most vital forces unbroken. Whoever, therefore, wants absolution for 1933 can have it. But in the meantime, what about the situation to-day? We are not concerned here with external data. If anybody wants to learn what an accomplished totalitarian regime of terror developed along the lines of the most modern, close-meshed cellular organization controlling the very fibres of life and completely enslaving the people, skilfully exploiting the most primitive instincts, adept in mass psychology and with absolutely no limit as to its choice of methods, can do when it provides an orderly and order-loving people, mentally lazy, patient as lambs, with order and bread—bread which they little suspect can only be offered as the result of feverish preparations for war from the very first day, hence as a sort of war-entrée: he should make a thorough study of the first period of such a regime. And if anybody wants to learn how, the cat being let out of the bag, solemn pledges can be broken and a war of expansion embarked on for which the leaders feel that they are superior in armament and military performance, a war that could only end as a world war; if there be such who would see how this war can be allowed to grow into a frenzy of boundless expansionism, who would learn how the military qualities peculiar to a people can be spiritually coerced to a point where the latter are bled white in the interests of a governing clique not wanted at all by the broad masses and in the end clearly felt by them to be the real enemy, until the last remnants of their own life were virtually destroyed: let him study the second phase of such a regime very carefully indeed, so far as it has left him the necessary records for a secret history!

What we are concerned with is rather the psychological world contained in these processes or bursting out of them. This much can be established for certain: there certainly were spontaneous, personal factors that, making use of the various possibilities and the conditions at hand, conjured up the increasingly terrible reality that surrounds us to-day. But much as its protagonists always knew how to get themselves deliberately into the limelight as the authors of it all, we others have all felt equally clearly that there was something else at work.

People like to put it this way: the personal initiative that ultimately brought all this about fell on very fruitful ground in such and such a person. But this only takes account of the sociological conditions already noted as secondary. There was more to it than that. It was as if certain forces sprang out of the ground;

giants of action, crafty, hungry for power, which nobody had noticed before, seemed to shoot up like a crop of dragon's teeth. And a formerly unthinkable inner readiness was there in the bulk of the middle-class on whose enthusiasm, one can well say, these forces were borne at the outset. An indefinable objective *something* broke loose that swept away values taken for granted and held to be unshakable, in a universal psychic wave. A collective, supra-personal force, chained and hidden till then, suddenly burst from captivity. Once it was out it was whipped up by every conceivable means and swamped, practically speaking, *everything*.

One can, of course, try to interpret it in terms of collective psychology or personal psychology, at will, by relating it to suggestivity and all its possible conditions, variations and assumptions. But we shall never grasp the real nature of the process like this. That previously quiet, perhaps not very discriminating, but generally harmless people should suddenly turn into impudent brawlers who not only gave themselves up to frenzies of hatred, no, but with cynical realism actually sought to wreak their hate-instincts in practice, ultimately taking part in persecution, robbery and bloody murder; that hitherto reputable persons found even the vilest lying and acts of violence quite right and proper, even if they did not howl in a delirium of delight with the rest of them; that they themselves, in sober deliberation, devised mass-regulations for the brutal subjection of others and not only applauded such abominable acts, sunk to the lowest pitch of depravity, but gave them quite unnecessary support in intrigues, denunciations and calumnies of all kinds without the least feeling of meanness—these things cannot be so explained. That people who were certainly no civic heroes before but would still have regarded it as unnatural to grovel on their bellies before anybody, not only did this but even went so far as to cast suspicions, if possible, on all those who considered this orgy of servility shameful and refused to take part in the grovelling,— and, what is more, not in any access of rage, but in a refinement of cool reflection, thereby delivering the heretical thinkers, often their own relatives, up to the knife and a cruel death, all such examples being not by any means isolated, rather the expression of a quite typical sort of behaviour, namely the spread of an indescribable degeneracy coupled with that sudden readiness to witness if not indulge in extremes of brutality quite calmly—

this, like many other things that I cannot expatiate on here which suddenly appeared as a mass-phenomenon nobody would have believed possible before, is not and cannot be just a simple consequence of mass-suggestion. It was the outbreak of forces certainly collective in origin, certainly stimulable by psychology and capable of being roused under certain conditions, but forces coming from greater depths than psychology ever plumbed. It was a sudden darkening of mind that then set in, an occultation in which one felt the uncanny wing-beat of those powers whose effects one had read of in history-books as the unaccountable appearance of psychic mass-epidemics, but which one had never appreciated as real, let alone actually possible within the body of one's own people. The wing-beat of the *dark-daemonic* forces: there is no other term for their supra-personal and at once transcendent power.

For it was not only primitive, elemental, brutal powers long suppressed and hidden by training that broke forth once again, powers, therefore, which we must accept as present in all of us, deep down, as a link with the beast of prey. They were too qualified for that, *spiritually* qualified in a negative sense applicable only to man; they were, to put this qualification into words, far too *mean:*

> "Übers Niederträchtige
> Niemand sich beklage,
> Denn es ist das Mächtige,
> Was man dir auch sage",

writes Goethe—or, as we might paraphrase it:

> "About all that is dirty
> Let no one complain—
> 'Tis but the almighty
> At it again!"

But Goethe also knew of the Daemonic, even though he was not immediately connecting it with these things here. We have experienced the mysterious inner complexity of these powers. We have seen how apt they are to entwine themselves with legitimate and acceptable demands, thus bringing about, in the most distressing manner, an end-result that is detestable and shameful, while at the same time one was bound to approve certain of its manifestations, at least in the beginning. We have lived under the personal incarnation of those powers, an incarnation that ceaselessly displayed to us and the world that devastating Janus-face of the vile and the just, and that has plunged the whole world into the most terrible catastrophe it has ever known, thanks to this combination. We have suffered all this knowingly and with open eyes.

Shall we, then, be so shallow-minded as to ignore the *deeper* level that is apparent here, the transcendental and metaphysical level known to the men of earlier times, of which but *one* aspect, one of its many sides has, under our very eyes, made itself master of our lives for a spell? And if we come to grasp this level, even if only from this initial point to begin with, is *that* not the universal experience which will permit us to link up again, across a yawning chasm of nihilism, with bygone ages?

Such a link-up and the orientation that proceeds from it are not moral but transcendental. Equally they are not a private affair, they are rather, because founded in the apprehension of objective forces, universally binding on all those who have experienced such forces. They are neither comfortable nor easy, since it is of their origin to face us with decisions and to demand such decisions of us every day. And they are bound up with the apprehension and realization of yet deeper levels of Transcendence of which we have spoken continually—those which we once, in the Eighteenth Century, consciously called our own, for all that they were distorted by dogma for the most part or glossly over-simplified.

Throughout this book I have given the name "immediate Transcendence" to that which has been experienced in the presence of a terrible negative element, and can be consciously apprehended to-day and made our intellectual property. This immediate Transcendence and the whole depth-dimension of life that forces itself upon us has, as its second face—without our having necessarily to invoke a personal God—godlike features. It is at once the existence, combination and actuality of exalting and purifying powers that carry us and all humanity *beyond ourselves*, and is thus, properly speaking, transcendent and divine. No demonology of any kind is to be understood here. The Dark-Daemonic whose workings we have doubtless all felt only gives us the hem, as it were, and we ourselves have then to ring up the curtain on an all-embracing, all-permeating, omnipresent sphere of metaphysical forces lying immediately beside us and behind the phenomenal world.

To show this sphere in any systematic order is impossible, just as it is impossible to experience it uniformly, without contradictions, and give this experience without logical contradiction. What can be said of it in a general way, as far removed as possible from the emotion with which the *original* experience of it is invariably bound up, can only be in the form fragmentary indications. These are given in the last section of this book.

Meanwhile, rehearsingly and as it were rhetorically we have to go on asking questions.

Would any of us still dare to assert to-day that we can afford to lose those two great acquisitions of the Eighteenth Century—active and universal "Humanity", and "Freedom"—which we have denied? It is not a question of the outward form they then assumed, but of their substance. Is man, is humanity in its given "specificity" sprung from some transcendental level—an idea which was evidently quite unspeculative and expressed the very core of experience—or not? Is humanity, if not a "universal Being" as has been said in a beautiful metaphor, at least so "one" that only from such a "oneness" (which must in the last resort be transcendental) can a universal and fundamental feeling of fellowship—like all concentrations of it into what we call friendship, reverence, love, etc.—be understood at all? Is it *possible* for us to understand such supra-individual, basic "onenesses", which in reality comprise innumerable high-points and a wealth of configurations, but which are always inherently there and can only be discovered in their actuality *in us*? Christianity did this for the most universal of all onenesses—that worldwide coherence of human sympathy. What are we to make of these background entities and forces which only need bringing to consciousness to work like an ever-flowing subterranean river within us, where, grown *self-evident*, they help to govern our actions? How are we to understand them? Why, as "self-evidences"—evidences of the Self. For nothing has been artificially implanted or inculcated into us when the realization of human oneness becomes actual in us, that is to say, breaking in from outside or just welling up of its own accord. It is there as a part of ourselves, or more accurately as part of the substratum of our being, and hence operative and alive. (See also Chapter VIII.)

We have seen how this whole transcendental plane of being can be so buried in some people under the barren debris of brutality and vileness that no one would believe that the positive substratum of common humanity can possibly be present in such creatures and that they also are sprung, despite everything, from the same transcendental layer. But so it is. Men are many-layered. We can only understand them when we know this above all and draw the necessary conclusions in a conception of congenital forces, dominant and recessive, that constitute man and can become operative in him alternately—a point to which we shall have to return.

But to continue: the Eighteenth Century knew that man as such, because of his transcendental nature, is born to freedom. And even to-day every far-sighted person, the scientist or biologist[1] whose thought tries to fit man into the cosmic whole can only define the spiritual uniqueness of man, his special position in the total scheme of existence, by saying that he sees in him "the species born to freedom", and proving it. We shall not discuss here what is to be understood philosophically or cognitively by this given freedom. The facts are that man, he alone of all the species, by varying acts of will creates over and above the natural conditions of life his own artificial ones freely formed by himself. He creates them out of his freedom. He and he alone, therefore, knows a development of civilization and a history variously patterned by himself. Were, then, the great poetically inspired seers of the Eighteenth Century wrong when, upborne on their winged, their truly transcendental, interpretation of nature and history, they saw the specific destiny and destination of man to lie in his *self-development* towards "Humanity" through "Freedom"? Or was the apparently sober Kant wrong when he said that to pass from immaturity, or the non-use of freedom, to maturity, or the self-controlled use of it, was the goal? I think not. Both looked wittingly into the depths, whatever the veil of thought in which they wrapped their immediate experience. I only think that both, the poetic seers and the philosophers, had not yet seen the problem of man's self-development through the freedom in its full import, nor could so see it.

[1] Such as Richard Woltereck: *Ontologie des Lebendigen* (Ontology of the Living).

This problem of educating mankind to self-development through freedom and to self-government in freedom only took on its specific gravity and peculiar difficulties in the setting of *mass-freedom*—the freedom of the masses. There is a very widespread verdict to-day, apparently well-founded by events, as to the incapacity of the masses for freedom and self-determination. Books that have become famous, such as that by Le Bon[1], and accumulating experience—not to speak of the experiences we have latterly had in Germany—appear to corroborate this verdict. And yet, for all the suggestibility of the masses, for all the outbreak of daemonic collective forces in them which preclude every attempt at self-control and self-formation, coupled with the completest incapacity for judgment when faced with complicated facts, these things are still not decisive; as a *general* interpretation so negative a judgment would be mere prejudice. In the last resort it depends on temperament, on tradition, on the presence of a governing class emotionally accepted by the masses, leaders who have a general conspectus of the situation and can tune the moods of the masses to the right key or soft-pedal them; it depends, therefore, on an élite fitted for the twin tasks of psychological leadership and objective control of the situation, on the personalities that emerge from such an élite at critical moments, whether the defects inseparable from the masses in times of danger can be overcome or not. The most important, the really decisive thing, however—and this must be emphasized with the greatest force in defiance of all popular prejudice—is the average *character quality* of the masses, that is to say, of their individual men and women.

What do we mean by character quality? We mean the inflexible will to come by one's own judgment and the resoluteness to act accordingly even to one's own disadvantage.

We have seen in Germany what the lack of these two means. We have experienced how the German, who was once—in the days of the free cities (the real basis of the German revolutionary movement during the Sixteenth Century)—so stiff-necked and cocksure and jealous of his own judgment, and who, although tamed by the long reign of the Authoritarian State, still manifested genuine stirrings of the old kind right up to the revolution of 1848—was so denatured by the drilling of his three-year military

[1] Psychology of the Masses.

service, Prussian robot-like obedience and similar disciplines that he became the stiff, stereotyped, long-suffering creature of order we know to-day, almost incapable of the least move in the direction of freedom, let alone of putting it into effect. He was not always like this—indeed, as far as asserting his own will goes, quite the opposite.

And it is to take an inadmissibly narrow view of things to generalize from this or from Russia, so often cited in this connection although she may be undergoing a very fundamental change, or from one's experiences of mass-suggestion in a temperamental country like France, with her broken governing class. Anybody who has read an English war novel of *this* war dealing with the psychology of the English workers, or who has the least idea of the outlook and basic assumptions of the average North American, even one apparently cut to the pattern of the "mass", knows how utterly such a verdict would miss the point (which is not to say anything against a certain uncouthness or even coarseness that may be present in him). "Self-control" and "self-government", whoever does not know that these are not mere catchwords but fundamental *facts* born of the Anglo-Saxon character, obviously has no conception of what this war is about and should therefore keep his verdict to himself. But neither, on the other hand, should he make any generalizations as to the incapacity of the masses for freedom. At any rate he should not stand in the way of those who see that government of the masses *in freedom* is principally a question of character formation, and that it further presupposes the formation of a corresponding élite. Also, that it is facilitated by old traditions and by a temperament not too dependent on mood.

Some people—not only the advocates of a haughty "pathos of distance"—take up the attitude: "Leave the masses, let them be as they are. Where they are untouched in their historical development they should not be disturbed, the main thing is to get to work on the few, who play a leading role practically or intellectually". To this we can reply: Nobody is thinking or should think of proselytizing our European notions of freedom in areas where there still exist total cultures capable of withstanding the impact of Western consciousness, despite its disintegrating economic and political influences; highly developed cultures that fit man into the natural order quite differently from us, not as a being with an imperishable soul to be awakened but as a being completely merged in the cosmic "oneness", as in Ancient China—or as an indefinable *something* destined, in its very highest states, to "metacosmical" self-dissolution, as in India. Such cultures should indeed not be touched, though it is incumbent upon us to espouse the minimal demands of humanity, which are universally binding, here as with the primitives. It may very well be and is in fact quite likely that other great cultures of different spiritual and psychic structure apprehend the transcendental nature of man differently from us Westerners, hence arriving at different conclusions as to its realization.

But are our Western masses untouched and are they caught fast in such a different mode of apprehending the Transcendental? No! They have been brutally expropriated of the intimations of Transcendence that once existed in the West and were ready formed in Christianity only to be extensively secularized later. They have been tossed hither and thither and made homeless—you have only to think of what the last twelve years in Germany alone have done in this line, far exceeding all the buffetings of capitalism known so far. The masses have become materialistic, except for the few religious enclaves that have remained intact. They have been systematically robbed of every higher view of life and man beyond that of exclusive racial propagation and that of "nationhood", which has never in fact existed although it appeared to decide everything. In short, they have become herd-minded and debased.

Are we to leave them in this condition? More, *dare* we?

I want to speak here only to the intellectuals. We, the intelligentsia, want freedom, intellectual freedom. We know well enough that without it our initiative is broken, we are helplessly fluttering birds caught in a cage, picking up bits of food and little else, strangers to ourselves. But can there be intellectual freedom to-day except on a basis of political freedom? And is political freedom to-day, when the confused, traditionless, materialistic masses are awake and jealous of their rights and eager to assert them, is political freedom possible except as the political freedom of the masses, that is, their self-government? Of course not.

Self-government of the masses, then! And that can mean, however one varies it in practice, nothing less than this: that when and where the masses, through no fault of their own but as the result of historical circumstances, have remained largely incapable of self-government—not because of their restricted *knowledge of facts* which must be the basis of their judgment, but because of deficiencies of *character*—an alteration of both, narrowness of judgment and deficiency of character, must be aimed at. Through mass education, education through life (we learn most when we are obliged to test it all the time), and through reform of education.

And here, after a short parenthesis, we come back to what we indicated earlier as being the only possible way to shape man and hence also to re-shape the mass-man. First of all: an élite, not merely such as is qualified for political and practical leadership, but composed of persons spiritually and intellectually pre-eminent, and pre-eminent also in character, who will then, half unconsciously, act as continual models—such an élite, bringing spiritual leadership, is obviously at least as important in all fields and in all ways as the re-shaping of the masses. Beside it, there is no greater task, none more bound up with such a re-shaping. For this much is clear: there are élites and there is training for élites; now there must be élite-training for spiritual solitaries. For these, whom it is not necessary to imagine as complete recluses, rather quite normally as intellectuals from whom a fructifying rain proceeds of its own accord and is gladly received (which avoids the otherwise inevitable problem of the relationship of the élite to the masses)—for these vehicles of an influence emanating purely from their own being, certain educational facilities and means of livelihood are essential. But extraordinarily important as the salvaging of these solitaries is, they have, in their inner composition and in their immediate tasks, spiritually nothing to do with the overcoming of this catastrophe. The case is different with the other section of the élite that is to rise to practical and intellectual leadership in the new period. The catastrophe faces this section, at least in Germany, with a tremendous, indeed *the* task of the age. If the German people are to be saved from complete shipwreck in the economic and political storm that must break over them, if they are to see, beyond the bare means of subsistence, any goal for the sake of which it is still worth going on living, this goal can only—to speak with Nietzsche but in quite another sense—be "the land of their children" which they are helping to create. But this land of their children must permit the growth of a people inwardly transformed, re-converted to their old origins and thus—in so far as the old religious traditions no longer carry the necessary weight—capable of understanding life anew. Not robots, not cogs in a machine, but a people that has newly apprehended the transcendental meaning of existence, proud to live for a humanity understood in all its diversity and profundity; to live in "oneness", in a freedom grounded in Transcendence but—what has never happened in Germany before—continued into practical life and politics.

People talk or have talked so much about "culture" and what they were going to produce, or wanted to, in the cultural sphere. Let us keep quiet about it for a change, particularly as one never achieves anything in the way of culture with talk and good intentions. This is the gift of heaven and time in due season. Our business is to talk of man and to think of him as man, and of the individual man in the mass. For of such is the mass composed.

The individual, however, is as we have said many-layered, in accordance with the whole complex of congenital forces that are incarnate in him. He has these dominant and recessive forces in himself, and these can—and do—alternate in their sway.

People, the masses of any people and their characters are not uniformly arranged, not all the same at the same time, but vary as the combinations of congenital forces vary. They do so particularly over a period of time, because every individual of the mass carries in himself dominant and recessive powers whose reign or abdication varies with the time—varies, but is susceptible to influence. The variation is so strongly susceptible that the average character can be varied almost out of all recognition.

Since the hereditary forces are incarnations of supra-personal, objective, psychic or biological elemental powers, the variation can occur as it were epidemically *from outside*, through the irruption of these objective forces as life-dominants. It can, however, be accomplished *from within*, by training and mode of living. What we have described as the fearful character-mutations of the average German that have ruled over us latterly, brought about by these dark-daemonic powers breaking through, came from outside. Congenital forces, hitherto recessive, became dominant and, seizing on the greater part of the German people, transformed and gruesomely distorted them. We must guard against a second break-through and at the same time resuscitate and make dominant the forces that have almost atrophied in the average German, but were once operative in him as an unbounded urge to freedom, as independence of character, as the ability to decide his own life.

Once we have done that, once we have roused the forces of universal human oneness which are sunk in slumber, we can create the German future, its spiritual basis, and thus a new German man.

Is this not a mightily rewarding task—to create a new human type! The prime and by far the most urgent task of the German élite.

Certainly the outward pattern of life, the adjustment to political and, as far as possible, economic and social autonomy in administration will be bound to play a decisive part. But where no personal drive exists one cannot work spontaneously. The personal drive, however, must come from the way we mould our youth, from education.

And here we can say for certain: only what National Socialism has undertaken during the last few decades in Germany and, for all its perverted ends, has in fact outwardly achieved, and what, on the other hand, Soviet Russia has been able to make of the torpid moujik by means of education, namely, a proud, quick-witted and teachable industrial worker, only these things have shown what education and the indoctrination of youth can do in the way of human transformation, if tackled and carried out intensively enough. Naturally this activation in the direction of sheer rationality or primitive national instinct is easier than the one we have in mind, towards greater spiritual depth, which must always have a transcendental background. But events have proved the immense possibilities that open out before us and can instantly be understood in the light of the ideas advanced by us: that all education, be it in school or through life, can effectively set about making either the dominant or the recessive congenital forces character-fixing, or else driving them into the background, according to taste. No man can jump his own shadow. What can be fixed and made dominant by training must be there potentially. It is only a matter of raising it from the submerged state and moulding it to over-riding significance. All the innate powers we need are virtually there in the German and in the German masses. A glance at the Germans of earlier times is sufficient proof of this.

There is no danger that intensive education or "human engineering" of this kind would produce standardized patterns or types. No idea is more ill-founded in view of the luxuriant variety of "parts" that are latent in each individual. That these, made actual, should ever produce men cut to a uniform pattern is precluded, or at any rate not to be feared, once life and education have in view the development and application of transcendentally based freedom. There is nothing more inexhaustible than the multifariousness of individuals, which rests on the blending of the hereditary factors present in each. And if this multifariousness in the masses, particularly in the masses we know that are used as sheer apparatus, does not indeed lead to fully unfolded personality, rather to fragmentary creatures, animated particles with, on the whole, trivially identical needs, the same trivial recreations and almost calculable reactions—the initial stages, therefore, of that terrifying picture of the future "termite-man"—the fact is that there are great difficulties ahead of us, considering the soul-destroying effect of treating men as machines, in saving them and their souls at all, which must be operative in them somewhere. And this saving is by far the greatest human and social problem in the spiritual sphere. But if anything is to be saved of this modern mechanized humanity it must be through the awakening of their natural spontaneities, and that means above all fostering and stimulating their inborn capacities for freedom by political freedom and self-government to the greatest possible extent.

It is beyond the scope of this work and very largely beyond the competence of the author to make practical proposals for a modern form of labour organization that shall be more strongly inspired from the point of view of the development of freedom and personality, though such a way of organizing work is at least as important as the development of personality through political freedom. Only from the most detailed and specialized knowledge of modern labour processes, of the degree and limits of their elasticity and of the possibilities of integrating them with the workers' powers, could anything of any value be put forward. But by way of consolation one can nevertheless hint that neither the tailor-made and "Fordized" American worker, nor his English counterpart, is de-personalized despite all ideas to the contrary. Extreme mechanization notwithstanding, both are discriminating and most jealous guardians of their freedom and rights to self-determination, or in our terminology, guardians of their transcendentally based humanity. So de-personalization is not inevitable. Neither does it exist even where spiritual paralysis, at any rate in Germany, is much stronger to-day than with the workers, namely in the ranks of employees and official functionaries who, for a variety of reasons, have on the intellectual average become veritable herd-animals and were the mainstay of the late regime with its sheep-like tendencies. These classes have been assimilated in other countries without harm. There must be a way to re-orientate them spiritually where necessary and revive the spontaneity in them with a view to self-determination and deepened self-development.

Further, as regards the use of *practical* freedom and its connection with transcendentally based *essential* freedom. Certain as it is that, in the narrow external setting of the masses, practical or personal freedom must aim at enlarging this setting to begin with, must aim, therefore, chiefly at material betterment (wages, hours of labour, etc.), it is equally certain that self-determination in regard to these things is also a symbol: a symbol precisely of that independent "human being" which is otherwise irretrievably lost in undiluted worker-existence. Over and above every struggle for the amelioration of this and every staking of their own material life therein implied there hovers, as its presiding genius, the workers' will to free human being. It exalts this struggle and genuinely consecrates the vital stake that is bound up with it.

Of course the open struggle for material interests, that is, industrial freedom in general, has as a principle absolutely nothing to do with that virtually transcendental *essential* freedom so indispensable to mankind, the need to develop which is our particular concern. All repudiation—which is profoundly misguided—of those apparently obsolete principles of freedom comes from confusing industrial freedom—which probably is as a matter of fact largely obsolete to-day and is but an occasion for opportunism —with transcendentally based freedom, which is humanly constitutive. So that, little as the struggle for or the championing of industrial freedom as such has anything of that aforesaid "consecration" about it, nevertheless, over and above the purely material struggles of these humanly threatened workers, there is always a special quality, a trace of free action for the sake of their humanity. In this case the material use of freedom must always be judged apart from the context of ordinary industrial freedom pure and simple.

And here, growing out of the concrete situation, we have at once a clear indication of the limits and a confirmation of the nature of what we have called transcendentally based freedom, which issues in practical life and above all in politics. This is something that, for the development of our Western consciousness at least, cannot and must not be devalued and, though it has been lost to a fearful extent in Germany, must be won back again if we are to fulfil our humanity. It is a freedom whose use, whose inner and outer structure even, we have slowly to re-learn.

But it is clear, and something to be held before our eyes day and night like a shining lantern, that our task is the transformation of the German mass-man from a patient and obedient beast into an integrated type of man independent in character, upright, sure of himself, and jealous of his right to freedom. And this task, provided that a purposely intensive education to that end affords the necessary preparation, and opportunity is then given for autonomous action in practical life and politics, is not insurmountable.

Outwardly, of course, as things are now, to a very great extent it will not depend on us but rather on others whether and how this opportunity is offered us. That the Germans in the broad mass cannot be "transformed" without it, or rather, that other powers latent in them cannot become dominant and replace those now making for standardization and servility, should be kept constantly in mind by the victors. Not endless military government and occupation, not police measures and political slavery, but an opening of the door to free self-government, in conjunction with intensive education, this alone can implement the change and enable the Germans to take their place anew, and healthily and lastingly, among the peoples of the world. Whatever controls are deemed necessary for the foreseeable future, the victors should know that there is no other way to accomplish these three things at once: their own security, which they desire all too understandably; the pacification of Europe and the world; and that same unconstrained—and hence in the long run, tenable—integration, which is both humanly and morally necessary, of a great and ancient cultural people which the Germans are, into the new global whole.

But in order to set about our task we have to say just one thing more: we must try to create an élite of high intellectual calibre equipped for practical and political leadership, an élite from whose personal qualities the masses can take their bearings. At present we have nothing approaching this. Such beginnings or remnants of it as there were—the hopes of the younger generation—which had courageously resisted dictatorial tendencies and measures wherever practically possible the late regime has caused to "disappear" or, in plain language, murdered. It was very inventive in methods of silently "fixing" and liquidating the dangers that were laid up for it in these remnants of the old, or possibilities of a new, élite. These were the only people who might eventually have superseded it, and a *tabula rasa* was made of them. Here a tragedy of the most terrible kind passed off in complete silence. One day there will be many names besides the better known ones, that we should not forget. But to-day we have to start almost from scratch. And to all the older men who may return from abroad and may have been able, despite everything, to save their souls, to all who are now called or will soon be called to positions of leadership and guidance, one can only say remorselessly: "Mindful of the fearful disaster that followed the élite-less so-called 'Weimar period', your business is to look to your successors, to create a mechanism of élite-making in which personalities of intellectual eminence with a bent for politics can come to the top, every bit as much as to see that the poor, shattered German people somehow get work and bread in the immediate future and are trained up to self-government in the mass. If you do not this sufficiently and properly and, above all, unselfishly, ready to make room in good time for fresh blood, you will only succeed in bringing about yet another catastrophe resulting from the bungling of the incompetents who will then have come to power. Beware!

The men of such an élite as we have in mind will be sufficiently equipped for political action and will have practical knowledge enough to give them the broadest possible view of history and the present, but first and foremost they will know that life's highest value lies in man and his unfolding, and that this unfolding can only come from an understanding of the transcendental background of human—indeed, all—life. This alone can tell us what to do with men and what to aspire to on their behalf, how to find our way amid the conflicting forces of life, and this alone can offer us, once we have perceived their objective quality which demands a definite "yea" or "nay" from us, salvation from the bestializing vitalism of to-day, its aimless relativism and subjectivism, and, finally, deliverance from nihilism.

So one could argue did one not live in a time when, apparently dominating all inner ones, the external problems of life faced one everywhere like hideous spectres, did not all talk of spiritual matters and aims threaten to end in a hopeless cul-de-sac or in the envenomed division of one's own people, did not this people seem to be in danger once more, if perhaps in a different way, of being drawn into the abyss.

We should be quite clear about these facts, and yet at the same time we should know this: the German people can bear the excessive hardness of life that will be their lot for many years or decades as a result of the catastrophe so frivolously brought upon them; they can face the destruction of their homeland, which cannot be made good for a long time to come; they can face their poverty and distress after the disappearance of probably the most valuable of their men-folk and by far the greater part of the males of the younger generation, the pulverization of the most precious monuments of their culture and the loss of their printed intellectual reserves; they can endure their not merely political but social and economic misery and the shrinkage of the human part they play in the world outside; they can overcome this "delenda est Carthago" that has devastated their lives, together with their obligations towards others in the matter of reparations which will certainly impede any large-scale attempt at rebuilding on their own account for a very long time—ONLY if, in the vital physical and spiritual resources that are left them, they have a common *spiritual* goal, not just an external one. They must have a great impulse of will, and that can only lie in a great hope. We have tried to present the intellectual framework and, so far as lay within our power, the spiritual content, of such a hope.

Let us try to add one or two other things that may give this hope a material foundation. It is nonsensical to conceive of a country or people to-day except, materially and intellectually, within the framework of the great new planetary conditions which will arise as the result of this war and with an outline of which, because they are so crucial for the future, this book opened.

Europe, as the autonomous, material centre of world-gravity, a Europe in the old sense of equal competitive Power States, will have vanished. How the power-spheres of the Russian East and the Anglo-American West, both of which will encroach upon Europe and keep Germany above all under control—chiefly military control as far as one can see—how these will work out in practice cannot yet be ascertained despite the programmes and plans for European and planetary "gremiums" with supreme juridical powers. This must be left in great part to the oscillations and adjustments of the new power-spheres amongst themselves, and to the degree to which they inwardly bend themselves to an over-all humanitarian and really effective form of control. All prophecies on this score are otiose.

This much holds good for Germany in the first place: her role can hardly be a material one in any outward sense, but spiritually she may exert a direct influence on material conditions. If, indeed, the world of rival States as such is obsolete and the one-time competitive Powers will somehow be incorporated into a system of large world-groups all working together, hence, at best, if they remain only semi-sovereign and as a matter of historical necessity bear the stamp of larger or smaller administrative "gremiums", Germany at least in the beginning will not even be left her own administration. In addition, she will be deprived of almost all elements of leadership and guidance that could be relied upon in the coming new world. And, historically speaking, it would be only natural after the terrible things that have been perpetrated if her industrial potential were put under a control that precluded any repetition of them.

There is, perhaps, one saving thought which might make a form of control so very much in evidence that the Germans could hardly swallow it, largely superfluous, and might above all obviate a partition and the destruction of the industrial plant so vital to her existence and so capable of achievements of the highest scientific order—namely, nationalization or, better, conversion of some of the critical German war-potential industries (steel and chemicals, etc.) into public corporations functioning as units under international control.[1] Thereby account would be taken of the legitimate demand for the elimination of the political misuse of private capitalism and, at the same time, of the need for thorough-going supervision.

In this connection be it said: it is to be hoped that the Allies, despite the only too understandable feelings of hatred and the wave of popular emotionalism, will not fall into the error of separating from Germany essential territories that belong to her by language, culture and proper feeling. If they did that they would be paralysing any process of spiritual healing and transformation in Germany at the start—a process that is the precondition of world peace. Germany's natural base-potentials of heavy industry lie grouped round a centre along her periphery. A Germany virtually deprived of these and therefore hopelessly disturbed in her internal economic circulation, with her industrial masses lacking bread as a result of this disturbance, would inevitably become a starving and incurable plague-spot in the centre of Europe, infecting all about her. For Europe, fundamentally as it will lose or have to modify its political structure and significance as known hitherto, depends in all its parts on an approximate rehabilitation of its former economic structure for the tolerable well-being of its dense populations. What everybody knows for a fact, namely that Italy cannot live without deliveries of German coal and heavy industrial products, and on the other hand without the absorption of her obvious surplus of fruit by Germany, or that the Balkans can hardly get on without exchanging their tobacco and grain for German industrial goods, and so on, is only an example of the economic integration of Europe, the prosperity of one part depending on another part, for which integration Germany with her central position, large population and enormous productive capacity is absolutely indispensable. Without the productive and consumptive power of Germany neither is possible in a full and healthy manner for those other outlying areas of Europe which, as a matter of economic and climatic necessity, are an integral economic part of Germany herself.

[1] Post-war addendum: if the syndicate idea is rejected on principle as the Americans appear to have done, the only alternative is to treat these corporations as "Public Utilities", such as railways and postal services, etc., which are easy to control. Actual "nationalization" is not necessary for this.

This economic integration, by reason of its toughness and capacity to rehabilitate itself (even, despite all opposition, in the post-1918 Europe so very much altered by the dismemberment of Austro-Hungary), has now become operative as a basic European phenomenon. It had been almost completely restored to its old form and strength in the difficult years following the first world war. Because these facts are axiomatic for Europe's economy and shadow forth a crucial picture of the future that points beyond all political dismemberments, to the integration of Europe in an economic world whole, they were, as soon as they could be surveyed, thoroughly examined after the last war at my instigation and under my supervision. The two papers that resulted,[1] on European industry after the war and the economic integration of Europe, demonstrated that one has to distinguish, from the points of view in question and overleaping all political boundaries, between an industrial *nuclear* Europe and a predominantly agricultural *peripheral* Europe—the first comprising England, Germany, Belgium, Luxemburg, the Netherlands and Switzerland, the eastern areas of France and the northern areas of Italy, as well as Austria and Czechoslovakia, the second comprising the whole of the territories lying round about these. As can easily be seen, the massing of industry in the European nucleus is not an historical accident but is conditioned by the potentials of raw material and heavy industry partly located in and partly surrounding these countries and by the mines and factories exploiting them, between which or in the vicinity of which the optimum growing-points of such labour-absorbing industries as use coal and the like have developed by preference. If now, as the second paper shows, you look at the living economic circulation in this economic body of Europe, you will see that it is obvious that the industrial nucleus should be the given market for the largely agricultural areas on the periphery, just as, at the same time, they obtain their industrial articles from it (averaging 80 per cent. and 83 per cent. respectively in 1930). These peripheral areas have quite clearly not yet reached full industrial development, neither have certain subsidiary members of the industrial body of Europe, which depend wholly for their export

[1] Otto Schlier, "The Reconstruction of European Industry after the War", and Herbert Gædicke and Gert von Eynern, "The Economic Integration of Europe", Berlin, 1932. For both works portions of a temporary grant from the Rockefeller Foundation to the Institute for Social and Political Sciences in Heidelberg, were used.

market and home supplies on the prosperity of the nucleus. But this itself is a highly integrated structure geared to world economy. It is—always taking its tendency to assert itself after the first world war despite all existing obstacles, as representative—integrated in every part of the industrial processes going on in it. The various parts of the nucleus are their own best customers, since they exchange almost half their total exports among themselves. And in its turn half this exchange consists of raw materials and half-finished goods, so that it is, therefore, a movement within an integrated process of production, in which the various phases divide themselves out according to the most suitable localities and complement one another till final completion is reached. Lastly, the nucleus markets half its finished products in Europe itself; only to a comparatively small extent in the periphery on account of the latter's lesser development and inferior purchasing power; and to the second largest extent in territories outside Europe, whence it obtains 50 per cent. of its raw materials and more than 30 per cent. of its foodstuffs, paying for these with goods, transport services and revenues from foreign investments. Hence one can see clearly that Europe, politically so fragmented, is naturally and historically, but above all in its nucleus, a single unit bound by the closest and most intense economic ties, each of whose parts is intimately dependent on all the others for the full use of its potentialities. And this state of things, interestingly enough, also includes England even though she is part of the British Empire, for in 1930 she was sending 32.1 per cent. of her exports to Europe, and seemingly so autarkic France as well, whose European exports amounted to 64.1 per cent. Europe, therefore, is a body whose industrial nucleus has more vital economic ties (imports of raw materials and foodstuffs, exports of finished goods) with extra-European countries than with the periphery, which is relatively unimportant from the economic point of view; but all these peripheral areas, Central and Southern Italy, Greece, Spain, Scandinavia, etc., as well as the nuclear areas bordering on or connected with Germany, cannot prosper if Germany suffers economic collapse or atrophy.

After the last war Germany's powerfully integrated economic body was left virtually intact despite the gravest burdens. That was the cause of the comparatively rapid recovery (later interrupted by a disastrous crisis brought on by credit manipulations) not only of Germany but of Europe as a whole, which was not independent of this recovery. Nevertheless, through added political and psychological causes, the importance of Europe in total world trade has fallen in this war from 37 per cent. to 30.6 per cent.—more rapidly, perhaps, than the growing importance of the younger capitalist world by which Europe is surrounded, would have brought about on its own.

Germany's opponents have the greatest interest, notwithstanding the burden of reparations they will impose on her (this time, unfortunately, so justified), in constantly keeping before their eyes the fact that, in their own interests, they should not ruin Germany economically. The recovery of all Europe and—because of Europe's lasting significance—that of the world, absolutely depends on it. Were they to act psychologically wrong-headedly, were they, from understandable irritation, to inflict a state of things on Germany that would not be tenable in the long run, they would be acting most gravely against their own well-understood material interests. No focus of economic rottenness and misery in the middle of Europe that would necessarily infect others can serve their, Europe's and the World's interests for the future, but a German economic body burdened, it may be, with unescapable obligations which it has to discharge, yet remaining viable in accordance with its natural conditions.

For a not inconsiderable time, probably, this economic body has played itself out as the autonomous political entity it was. Germany must and should see this as the inevitable consequence of what her late leaders perpetrated against the world and herself in a fit of unholy madness. Even if Germany is eventually drawn into the circle of normal foreign relations once more, she will no longer belong to the decisive Great Powers of the world. It is to be hoped that she will one day achieve a status commensurable with her importance at the council-tables of Europe, and hence have a share in the total administration—assuming, of course, the outside control of the use of her armaments potential. But even like that she will never again become a sovereign, autonomous, competitive Power State in the earlier sense. Her existence in this sense is over and done with. That is the farewell we have to take from history as we have known it.

National cultures with *intellectually* free sovereignty, but no freely competing nation-states any more, and a hierarchy of "gremiums" or judiciary syndicates into which their economic and general policy is built—such is the new historical world-type.

Europe, and particularly its German centre, has at the same time to organize itself on a free democratic basis guaranteeing humanity and human dignity as soon as free to do so. And in addition, along with all the outwardly so urgent things it must, as inwardly the most urgent thing of all, set about educating the masses to political freedom and training an élite for political leadership. What Germany has to aim at, apart from the full maintenance of her economic unity, is the maintenance of her educational sovereignty, without which she will be quite incapable of meeting the task of her own spiritual renewal and transformation. And all foreign powers should be quite clear about this: the spirit cannot be compelled, it bloweth whither so ever it listeth. They must entrust the renewal of mind and character to the Germans themselves. Anything else would prove to be nothing but a lying in wait for revenge and a desire to push into some crack or other of the new world-syndicate or something equally disastrous, which could only lead to the worst.

The good will to self-renewal and self-transformation will be at hand in Germany after the terrible experiences she has had of her own outlook and the fearful defects in her own character up to now, if only she is granted conditions in which her good will can unfold. To create upright German men and women who want to govern themselves, and, thanks to the necessary widening of their horizon by schooling and the natural training of daily life, are capable of judgment—that can be and that will be the great wish that the Germans will keep before them after this appalling collapse.

To define some of the inner objectives of this wish (which will have to struggle with exceptionally bare material conditions) by revealing its deeper transcendental background—such, apart from the analysis of the outward sociological upheaval of life in general, was the intention of this book. In the last resort it is written above all for those who desire to dedicate themselves with me to the realization of this wish, as a spiritually active élite. Our pastors and masters so far have failed miserably. Well, now to the task of fashioning a new kind of education and a differently inspired élite. The two are intimately connected.

As a nation we shall be poor as beggars, to begin with we shall have few enough really usable teachers for the great task of national transformation, and in general we have an old and ingrained habit of education to contend with. If we want to pave the way for an intensive change of character and a widening of judgment through education, we must remind ourselves that Russia, supposed to be so culturally backward, has made an average of twenty pupils per teacher (in a State school!) into a maxim and has got somewhere. To go among the people and induce a change of character and judgment by intensive education—the urge to do this must pour like a flood through our remaining spiritual élite and our élite to be. Is there anything sweeter or more worth while than the young person as yet unspoiled by education, the young person in whom you can implant a new ideal? It was presumptuous folly to wish to create the Superman, that chimerical offshoot de luxe of the spirit; let us first create, out of his inborn depth-dimensions, Man—by evoking the recessive and repressing the hitherto dominant powers that are in him.

We must tackle this in the broadest sense and on a great scale. We have two tremendous but absolutely possible tasks: to replace the average German of to-day by another average type, and the spiritually bankrupt élite by another. Sure, man is there to be surpassed. Not by a phantom or intellectual parasite that shows its superiority by indulging in a "pathos of distance", but by a man who, in the masses, is free and rich in character, and, in the élite, full of the immanent-transcendent depths which the great, undogmatic, European prototypes once saw and experienced.

Then this human being will be able to decide for himself; then he will be able to say "Yes" and "No" for himself; then, be he never so complex, he will have a clear, unequivocal feeling within him as to what he should be as a fully developed person. Then he can live as a free citizen in human dignity, be he never so poor and possessionless. That is what we need. That is where our future lies.

CHAPTER VIII

INTIMATIONS OF TRANSCENDENCE

What is presented here is not philosophical, i.e. logically conclusive, knowledge. It is rather fragments of an interpretative order of experiences which concern the background of all experience, thus aiming at metaphysical interpretation.

This interpretation is based on empirical knowledge of the fundamental difference between the two factors constituting all inner and outer experience, the difference between the spontaneity that comes from the unseen, unfathomable background as a force incomprehensible in its very origins, and that in which it actualizes itself. We shall call the latter the "conditional plexus", in which the actualization occurs and from which it acquires its concrete expression.

This difference, dualistic as it is, has nothing to do with the difference between mind and nature or mind and matter. For both these are abstract antinomies arrived at by deduction, and are wholly controversial. Whereas our difference arises from immediate naked experience of the way in which active, spontaneous forces operate in nature and matter, while what we call "mind" is only a special expression of the spontaneity which pervades the whole of Being.[1]

Any closer details must transpire from the fragmentary interpretations of the compelling experiences herewith communicated.

1. *Transcendence in the Inanimate*
(*Essence and Experience*)

We shall call immediate or immanent Transcendence that which forces itself upon us as immediately experienced in the phenomenal world, and in ourselves insofar as we are part of it, whenever we ask ourselves what it is that we *cannot* understand in the conditional plexus.

[1] This without prejudice to any *other* mode of experience and the philosophical interpretation based on it.

In every analysis of the phenomena occurring in the outer world as well as in our own interior world, we find that we can never grasp, as something logically understandable and formulable, the actual causes of what we meet there, but only the conditions and combinations of conditions in which certain powers or forces work, powers or forces completely different in kind from the conditional plexus into which they enter, and, as far as we are concerned, absolutely mysterious in their essence.

When the physicist of the old school formulated the laws of gravity, thinking thus to "explain" the motions of the heavenly bodies, it was only our habits of thought which prevented us from seeing that nothing further was made clear except the combination of conditions in which an essentially mysterious power or force, namely gravity, somehow or other manifested itself in the phenomenal world.

The same thing happened or happens when the chemist analyses the "substances" of our world into elements, and, along with the compositional structure of these substances, establishes the affinity or non-affinity of the elements and puts it into a formula. Affinity in its turn is something mysterious for us, something that can be verified but not understood as such, for the manifestation of which in the phenomenal world all we can in fact establish is the tissue of conditions in which it works, i.e. the structure of the elements.

We need not, therfore, go to modern physics which, in its efforts to grasp the ultimate effective elementary particles of the phenomenal world, was obliged to strip off the space-time fabric of the latter, in other words, to break through the phenomenal world and its visible concreteness, completely, only to find what it sought in an *indeterminacy* whose conditions could not be fixed accurately and which it then tried to contain in a calculus of probabilities. We need not pursue these marvellous paths of enquiry which have rendered the whole phenomenal world, thanks to their empirical elucidation of it, as it were transparent, making the everywhere Invisible to a certain extent tangible for us as that world's structural element, or, one could say, permitting the Transcendence already present in the structure of what is apparently the most untranscendental thing of all—matter—to shine through. We can safely leave this way of apprehending Transcendence as manifest in the phenomenal world, since it can only be experienced with the utmost difficulty and then not in pure immediacy, to one side. Even the old, familiar, comparatively simple way which served to make the processes going on in the realm of the Inanimate intelligible to us, proves on closer inspection to be an analysis, whereby we establish the transcendental powers or forces at work in the phenomenal world (gravity, affinity, etc.) as *causes*, for which we then lay down, in our mathematical formulae of explanation, the conditional plexus of their operation, and nothing more. So that even in the realm of the Inanimate, when we try to understand its operations purely mechanically in terms of mathematical law, we find ourselves encompassed by nothing but transcendental powers or forces as the *real* causes of events. Immediate and immanent Transcendence confronts us in the Inanimate.

2. *Transcendence in the Animate* (*Biological Transcendence*)

Even in the older biology which tried to explain the Animate and its successive developments in terms of environment, that is to say, in terms of the conditional plexus surrounding it and of its reactions thereto mechanically understood, the Animate was still in its essence something altogether mysterious, altogether different from the conditional world, altogether transcendent as regards all mechanistic or causal analysis. For the peculiarities that immediately confront us as auto-plasticity, spontaneity and purposiveness in every life-carrier whatsoever were, when understood simply as mechanical reactions (modes of chemical behaviour, etc.) merely reduced to *other* a-biotic, transcendental factors. But above all, such a procedure failed utterly to do justice to the real nature of these factors, for their nature everywhere rested on the spontaneous intentions invisibly contained in them and on the utilization of matter to those ends.

The newer biology recognizes this and rejects a merely mechanistic interpretation. Proceeding as Vitalism (Driesch and others related to him) or in some other form (e.g. Richard Woltereck[1]) from the life-carriers as self-organizing units possessing an "Outside" and an "Inside" and harbouring invisible "powers" in

---

[1] *Ontologie des Lebendigen* (Stuttgart 1940).

themselves, which then, strictly purposively, mould the "Outside"—matter—as their "apparatus" and use it for their expression, this biology unequivocally describes the Animate as something immanently transcendental, from which one needs only to tear away the veil to see it as such, once one has grown accustomed to perceiving things in this way.

The successive developments of the Animate are understood in the newest biology of Woltereck, as a sequence of ever new generations of "specificants" occurring in the invisible "Inside" of the life-carriers, a sequence of ever new and ever newly differentiated "species-patterns" which find actualization in the "Outside". Accordingly, the Animate is conceived as a successive unfolding of Transcendence originating mysteriously in the Invisible but actualizing itself immanently in matter. A wealth of invisible "powers" working in the "Inside" of every life-carrier is postulated with a view to interpreting the material expression of this transcendental animation in the fullest possible way.

It is unimportant whether or not the transcendental animation of the "specificants" is thought of as being localized in space and time, being, in the former case, termed the "Inside" of the life-carrier charged with all these invisible "powers" (to keep metaphysics out of it as much as possible). Such an "Inside", a complex of invisible "specificating" powers, is obviously as mysterious a transcendental entity as the non-spatial and non-temporal "entelechy" of Driesch, which goes into matter "in the manner of a soul" and determines the living being together with its organic order, its struggles, reactions and so forth. In both views, which alone seek to do justice to the spontaneity of the Animate, we are struck by the completely different, in fact transcendental quality of *life* as opposed to the conditional plexus of *matter* used purely as a means of expression and moulded into an "apparatus" representing the "Outside" and no more.

So that, like a layer[1] lying immediately behind matter, everywhere present and moulding the different types, forms and expressions, one feels Transcendence as unceasingly actual and leaping to the eye.

---

[1] This word is chosen in full consciousness of its inadequacy. It is only a symbol for something that is of its own nature viewless, beyond space and time, a mystery which it tries to make more or less understandable in this way.

Moreover this "layer" has the peculiarity not only of creating individuals but of co-ordinating the species it brings forth—which clothe its "special" ideas in form and essence—into wholes, for whose continuation as a unity it exercises all-embracing foresight. The species is more important to nature than the individual, said the earlier biologist, observing this fact. And in view of the extravagant and sometimes exquisitely complicated methods for ensuring propagation, there come to mind as expressions of the supra-individual quality of the biological forces the well-known self-sacrifice of parents for their young and other examples of the kind. But it, the transcendental layer, goes further. Within the species or within their sub-groups it creates collectivities, such as the animal empires, in which the individuals are reduced not only functionally but even corporeally to specialized members or limbs of such self-perpetuating sub-wholes of the species. The collective organism of the termites is an extreme illustration of this. The transcendental layer in the Animate is obviously, therefore, supra-subjectival. It is the vehicle for collective powers which determine the nature, form, and co-ordinated activity of individuals.

3. *Transcendence in the Spirit*

On this basis it will now be clear what we understand by Transcendence in the spirit, or immanent Transcendence, and in what form it forces itself upon us once we have grasped its nature. This approach concerns us very closely in view of the spiritual Nihilism of to-day.

The forces of the transcendental background are, speaking purely biologically, highly capricious. Their forms, adapted to every possible set of conditions, erupt in extreme profusion, seeing that they can produce the six million species of insect. In their productivity they sometimes open out cul-de-sacs, giving rise to species which are over-developed on one side, such as the dinosaurs, and doomed to extinction. They can also produce a species like Man, who, developing gradually, has elaborate organs like the cerebrum and the eye, which together seem to provide conditions for a wholly new line of development pointing *inwards* and based on consciousness. So that the biologist thinks he can speak of a frontal change in the process—which he also regards as a *sequence*—of species-formation, a veering of it towards the spiritual.

But the spiritual forces active in the transcendental background are not just late products of evolution. That we first experience them in the unfolding of human consciousness is not to say that they are present only in human life. Once we have grasped them we see signs of their working everywhere, and we perceive that they are everywhere inmixed in the sphere of the living as a formative element, yes, that their field of action may conceivably extend even into the realm of the inorganic and the cosmic.

For active everywhere in the form-world of the living are forces which mould the species—themselves produced as it were capriciously by the vital impulse—equally capriciously into the vehicles and expressions of something supra-vital and essentially different, something which forces itself upon us and which we can only call spiritual. The peacock proud of its fan is a vehicle for something of the kind, whether it knows it or not. It is the expression of something more than merely vital. The poison-spotted viper, in outward appearance let alone in nature and behaviour, cannot be understood as *merely* vital. The dog that is faithful, the horse that is proud of its rider, likewise. And so on. The "specificants" as grasped by the newer biologist contain, overwhelming the merely vital element and moulding it from within in beauty, ugliness, malice, viciousness, courage, affection, etc., and extending up to and beyond the human realm, supra-vital qualities far transcending the perfection possible to life proper, qualities which are nothing less than the expression of spiritual forces passing into the life-carriers and shaping these in collaboration with the merely vital forces. These spiritual forces mould from within just as the biologically appropriate forces do, which aim only at appropriate perfection; but they aim beyond that kind of perfection. For them also the conditional plexus of matter is the "apparatus" of their manifestation, and, if they want to manifest themselves, the means thereto. Only thus can beauty and ugliness be understood, from within, from the zone of Transcendence whence they come; so also with spirituality which, in essence, remains purely inward and as a rule only betrays itself through its expression. We need no scientific physiognomy to appreciate this. Each of us acts and orientates himself in regard to others in precisely this way every instant. He apprehends something objective in them which manifests itself concretely. He touches a spiritual power of the transcendental background in visible form, a power which, as background, is just as supra-subjectival and, humanly speaking, just as supra-personal in this emanation as in those other manifestations of it which mould life purely vitally. The subject is its seat, its medium for a "phenomenalization" experienced outwardly or indirectly in behaviour, precisely as is the case with Driesch's purely vital entelechies and their entry into matter and sovereignty in it.

In these fragments there can and should be no attempt to survey the whole field of these hierarchically organized, omni-present spiritual forces which enter into matter and into ourselves as part of it, and, once grasped, bear down upon us in all their immediacy as supra-personal objective forces. The following must suffice as regards their nature, their differentiation from the purely vital or biological forces, and the extent to which they are bound up with them. If we stress their manifestation on the human level and the ways in which they can be experienced by us, we are not forgetting that they are emanations of the transcendental background of all life; that, indeed, they may, as we have said, operate in a manner and on a plane altogether inaccessible to us, in the inorganic and the cosmic as well.

i. *The Nature and Complexity of the Transcendental Powers*

The spiritual forces are distinct from the merely vital or biological emanations of Transcendence in that, when encountered as inner experience or outer appearance, they compel us to answer "Yes" or "No", to take up some sort of attitude, because, freed by them, we feel enlarged and lifted above ourselves, or else constricted, cut off and driven back into our own ego, sometimes with real anguish. At the same time we feel everywhere a secret communication between ourselves and them in whatsoever form they appear. As though we could, in virtue of certain possibilities innate in us, by the very fact of experiencing and apprehending them be transformed into something akin to them, become part of the objective field of power which confronts us in them. We feel them as objectively outside ourselves and yet at the same time incarnate in us, or at least the possibility of it. Our "Yes" or "No" to them seems to signify, for the time being anyway, a kind of self-transformation in us through which, according to its quality, we feel either liberated and even exalted or else cramped, isolated, cast back on ourselves to the point of agony and horror.

Our "values", as we call them, are made up of many different things. But a part of such values—once, at any rate, acknowledged as objective—is indubitably the abstract precipitate of the kind of experiences here indicated. Religion has always been aware of the background of these values, and for it the dark and dangerous powers have always been as actual as the bright, liberating ones. It saw the negative values, too, as the expression of active and existing transcendental forces. Religion never succumbed to the myopia of many philosophical systems of regarding the negative values simply as the abstract opposite or inversion of the positive values which, gained by immediate experience of the Transcendental, were thereupon one-sidedly understood as the sole source of *all* value. Herein lies the fundamental fallacy of all Idealism which equates "norm" with "value". It sees only the reflection of the positive forces and confuses abstract crystallization with power originally and immediately experienced. Which, as we have said in the historical section, the perspicacious Friedrich Schlegel realized and explicitly stated.

In their spiritual form these powers are extraordinarily complex. They are so unfathomably complex and so inextricably bound up with one another that though they may conceivably be grasped in the iridescent symbols of mythology they cannot be grasped by pure logic at all. What we call beautiful, ugly, good, bad, base, crafty, mean, sublime, etc., hardly ever appears absolutely *neat* as the expression of a transcendental force or complex of forces, but almost always in varying degrees of implication with other spiritual or biological forces. Where what we call "beauty" works upon us as a power, is it ever unmixed with something else that is inseparable from it? Only in rare instances, certainly, and in general perhaps only in the beauty that proceeds from plants. And is it not true that ugliness very often occurs as the medium for a certain kind of redeeming spiritual radiance? Antigone's love and self-sacrifice, quite obviously in her case the expression of a transcendental force ruling within her, is not merely incidentally but essentially one with the pitiless hardness she feels for her sister. The inner entanglement of love and hate so often traced by the poets of deeper vision is not an instance of psychological ambivalency but, where it occurs, the existence of a two- or many-faced bright-and-dark daemonic power. Once one has seen this one can divest more than half Nietzsche's astonishing psychological discoveries of their distortion. His famous "ressentiment", that is to say his "power-instinct in reverse", can without a shadow of doubt go with the richest, most overflowing love and goodness. Are these merely "ressentiment" for that? And for all his polish and subtlety is it not a psychologically inadmissible over-simplification for him to see perversions and inversions of the same thing everywhere, namely Will to Power, instead of seeing the infinite multiplicity and iridescence of the Transcendental invading man's emotional world and to be met with everywhere in history and life?

All our designations of value or non-value are so many conceptual labels which we affix to certain aspects of the transcendental forces manifest in the phenomenal world, forces that simultaneously reveal quite different aspects so various and interwoven and so mysteriously co-ordinated that their modality as a whole cannot be logically comprehended. It can only be felt like a gigantic wave of which we glimpse but a crest in the world of phenomena, trying to grasp it with our feeble intellects.

Even where the manifestation seems least complex, in the plant world, where we think we experience beauty pure and unmixed, and naked ugliness, this may only be, supposing our view is correct in principle, because in the plant world we cannot experience directly, cannot feel our way into, the practical urge of the plant, so to speak, as we can with the animal. This aspect remains hid from within. Externally, however, the beauty of the plant often appears bound up in a very explicit way with practical biological forces, those of propagation, namely, even though these do nothing to explain its outward form. As to the Inanimate, we can only guess. But when we experience the power that strives for beauty of expression and is active in a wonderful way in the living world of plants, experience it as a disparate and yet unifying phenomenon as, for instance, in the symphonically orchestrated carpet of flora in an Alpine valley, where it unites things that are separate both as individuals and as species; when we experience, therefore, this power as a free-floating background formatively pervading phenomena, then it often seems to us as though it embraced the Inanimate as well and raised the whole to a melody of vibrant colour and line. One thinks of the appearance of certain mountains, as Cézanne felt them, for instance. And it is like that, too, with the dark and the evil. Slime and dangerous, repulsive-looking creatures have an intangible inner kinship; similarly there is a subtle bond between the colours of an early summer day and the fauna—larks and suchlike—that belong to it. And when, on a clear, starry night our visible cosmos unveils before us, then we can imagine, sensing in its nature and configuration the presence of a sublime will, that our Milky Way is built up by something other than the foci of force made accessible to us by mathematics, or the vectors of motion and light-velocities and electromagnetic fields and world-lines which physics establishes. This "something other" may only echo in us like a bell-note. But it points to some kind of universality within that zone of daedal Transcendence which confronts us as a background not only in the living but wherever we look and dispassionately accept, and whose fullest unfolding is immediately accessible to us from within—in human life. Accessible to us from within: that is, because we are sufficiently close to the nature of the powers reigning in the invisible and unlocated background. But this does nothing to explain why they are present only *here*— the one spot that happens to be the most accessible to us.

ii. *The Structure of the Subject's Being: Nucleus of Being: Congenital forces as Incarnate Powers*

The biologist calls the vital ground-forces which he can establish, "specificants" of the subject. But he knows, of course, that being is something more than and different from the mere sum of hereditary forces. What Driesch calls entelechy is a conceptually not comprehensible but experiencable centre which, as the nucleus of being, organizes the whole. Similarly, the purely *biological* zone of Transcendence lies, as said, supra-subjectivally behind the conditional plexus of matter. Using matter as its "apparatus", in every subject it co-ordinates numerous "powers" (expressly so called by the biologist) as form-factors of subject, species and life; hence it incarnates them in the subject as from that supra-subjectival ground. Exactly the same is true of the *spiritual* accretions deriving from the background zone.

In every living being there is a not merely vital but a spiritual nucleus which is indestructible; which, given the necessary difference of structure, we perceive as something peculiar to that subject and unmistakably individual, mysteriously sprung from the background zone. And just as the *vital* congenital forces represent incarnations of supra-subjectival powers grouped round this individual nucleus in varying proportions and available to it as form-factors, so also the multitude of *spiritual* congenital forces.

The more differentiated and elaborate the structure of any given species becomes under the influence of the life impulse, the more contradictory, not merely not co-ordinated but apparently conflicting become the vital and spiritual congenital forces incarnate about the nucleus. The vital and "spiritual" reactions of a fish are simple. The "Inside" of a dog, a cat, a horse is comparatively speaking a mystery, the expressions of which, resting as they do on totally different incarnations, not even the master or mistress can always decipher or foresee.

iii. *The Uniqueness of Man*

Consciousness, as an inturned line of vision, rests, as already hinted, in all probability on the co-operation of perfected eye and developed cerebral cortex.[1] It is creative in that it permits man to confront himself with voluntary and varying images as parts of his "Outside" and "Inside", hence as "objects"; permits that tremendous unfoldment of the mental object-world and, at the same time, the projection of part of it into a changing, external "between-world" created by man himself and incomplete in its possibilities—his environment. Anything said from that environment or from other premises about the "nature" of man does not concern us here. We need only a few simple statements already introduced into the text in another connection.

[1] Woltereck.

If we wish to speak of a transcendental idea special to and specific of man, the kind of spontaneity met with everywhere in the Animate but peculiar to him, it is obvious that this idea tends towards what we call "freedom". A freedom which is primarily the consequence of the configurations of images that variously impinge on his consciousness; first and foremost, therefore, a freedom that can be seen purely externally. Because the object-images brought, so it would seem, voluntarily before his consciousness are combined, elaborated and projected outwards, there is created that "between-world"[1] peculiar to man, who thus works in freedom of vision at the conditional plexus in which he has his being. More and more—we can see to-day with what rapidity the process goes forward—he becomes the transformer of the conditional plexus of his existence, introducing what appear to be endlessly new combinations of conditions into material reality. The resultant cultural and social-structural building of environment, which creates an ever-changing world to be inwardly mastered by him and within which he emits a constant stream of new objectivations, is nothing less than the precipitate, as it were, the outward and visible sign of his being spontaneously unfolded into freedom. It is, so to speak, his freedom seen from outside. This freedom, with its perpetual variations and changes wherein he wraps himself, makes him the "imperfect animal" of Nietzsche.

Correspomding with this there is an *inner* side to the freedom born of consciousness and inturned vision. Clarity of consciousness means that man's own vital and spiritual quality also becomes an object, moreover with increasing breadth and depth as history progresses. Whatever paths he pursues for the understanding of his spirituality, religious, mythological, or freely speculative, somewhere and somehow he must, in whatsoever form he express it, discover himself as specificized in his being and moulded by that transcendental background which, mingling the biological and the spiritual, raised him and the idea specific of him out of its own spontaneity. He then discovers in this idea, as its essential feature which distinguishes him from the animal, freedom, freedom in the widest sense as begetting certain purely vital and

---

[1] This word is used here in a somewhat different sense from that in Hermann Keyserling's still unpublished book already mentioned: *From Thought to the Source of Creativity.*

practical aims, giving rise to definite spiritual decisions but also passing the practically relevant judgments, thereby transforming the purely vital aims. Turning his gaze within, therefore, he sees himself as a spiritually free being with powers of and claims to self-determination deriving from the Transcendence of his being. Wherefore it cannot satisfy him when certain philosophers, observing the development and extension of consciousness in the history of mankind, speak of "progress" in man's consciousness of freedom, but seek by some remarkable dialectical manœuvre to limit man himself as the *result* of this progress, and rob him of his self-determination. No, self-determination of the practical sort, and to-day that means political self-determination above all, is manifestly the goal of his being, the goal that confronts him when, his consciousness having broken through to the immediate background of life, he comes into contact with the Transcendence from which he grew; when he gains a clear conception of the "idea" whose spontaneity formed him.

All the same, stumbling upon this ground-layer and raising it to consciousness within him, he never experiences himself *alone*, never as an isolated subject. He can do this here as little as he can when observing the Animate as a whole. Understanding the being of any given life-carrier biologically, he will, apart from the coming upon the individual, also come upon the totality of the "species" or supra-subjectival sub-groups of the same. In other words man, freely experiencing and understanding himself as such in his own being, experiences himself as a free individual only on one side of the medal, on whose other side he finds himself stamped into the totality. He is free and part of a whole, or part of concentric rings of such totalities. But since freedom is the transcendental nucleus of his being, his advance into freedom, once he has become aware of his essential nucleus in this way, can only be on the basis of his own freedom. His freedom, deeply experienced, seeks to implement this advance somehow of its own accord.

On the vital or biological plane this generally occurs without difficulty, at any rate as regards those rings of totality whose immediately practical significance can still be felt every day, particularly as they are never experienced merely biologically but are always (in the family, the nation, etc.) strongly impregnated with spiritual qualities, with the fate-like forces of piety, tradition, language and so forth, which all act like ferments.

It was a long time before man, despite the fact that those biological totalities in general, and personal freedom at least in part, are so strongly "in his blood", consciously experienced the fusion of the two and the full consequences of this fusion— i.e. the building up in freedom of closed, supra-personal wholes in nation and State, and tested them out over and over again. We all know that it was in ancient Greece that man first became aware of these things, and acted accordingly, with results that were decisive for history. And we saw in the historical section of this book how crucial Christianity was, likewise, for the awareness of active human "oneness".

Further, the connection between man's specificity thus defined as "Humanity" and "Freedom", and the transcendental powers which rule in him and in whose midst he is placed struggling for self-determination, was discursively our theme.

And finally it may have become clear how character-formation and change of character, once we recognize that the transcendental powers incarnate in man determine his "many-layeredness", are to be understood as the dominance or recessiveness of one or the other layer of these powers in him. Which is clearly enough of some practical comfort in a situation in which everything depends on the transformation of man.

So that by now the inner connection between the vision of the immanently Transcendental herewith briefly sketched, and all the essential points we tried to explain in the main section, should be sufficiently clear.

iv. *The Absolute and the Relative*

In order to avoid misunderstandings we must add just this: the self-incarnating forces lie beyond the phenomenal world, they come from a sphere that knows nothing of its conditions, and are therefore absolute. Since we only know changes as within the geological and biological conditional plexus, in the human "between-world", and since time and space are valid only for this, these forces, being above time and space, must be unchanging like all the transcendental substrata, and therefore in the human sense of the word, eternal. Hence, it would seem, they must also have the tendency always to manifest themselves in the same way, the same forms, patterns, directions.

And such indeed is the case.

But it does not seem so at first glance. The nature of what we call good and bad, beautiful and ugly, etc., in these self-mani-festing powers, their very substance, even, varies as history shows according to place and time, from people to people, from historical body to historical body and in the latter to some extent also from period to period. Their nature and substance are not subject to slight oscillations merely, like the trembling of a magnetic needle; rather, what the Asiatic or the Indian feels as beautiful or ugly seems fundamentally different from the incarna-tion of beauty accepted by the average Westerner, and that of the Westerner of the Gothic Middle Ages seems to differ again from that of his spiritual forbear the Greek or the Roman, to give only the crudest examples—let alone all the subtler modulations traced by the art-historian, which point to the differences between the personal beauty-ideals of individual artists. Similarly on the plane of the validity of the so-called practical values. Even to-day a Chinese—not, indeed, in the conduct of his business, which is very reliable, but in the conduct of his life—holds it to be con-formable with a "superior" character not only to lie but, when opportunity offers, also to cheat. The average Russian, despite his extraordinarily kindness and helpfulness, regarded it as per-fectly natural even in pre-Revolution days (if we are to trust descriptions of it) to allow a troublesome or disagreeable old neighbour to die in such a way that one is tempted to speak of plain murder. And the Germans! Have not large sections of them regarded the shady "fixing" of people as the expression of a superior character ennobled by "blood and race" for more than a decade, whilst others were ashamed of it as insufferable vileness?

Is there anything more seemingly relative, therefore, than the ideals and conceptions of beauty and ugliness, goodness and badness, etc.?

But in the last, very crude examples this much is obvious to anybody who feels and experiences things naturally: there is wilful blindness as well as distortion of consciousness. The latter is the result of defective enlightenment (as with the Chinese and the Russians), the former consists in self-deception as to the nature of innate forces formerly recessive and now dominant (as with the Germans), which leads to "turning the blind eye" or simply to the attaching of false labels. The absolute quality of the actions and the powers themselves remains unaffected and immediately obvious to the objective eye.

Approaching closer to the heart of the matter, and finally decisive, is a second consideration, which concerns the variations aforementioned in the "physiognomy" of congenital forces which, transcendentally speaking, are the same everywhere. Here is the key: the absolute powers undergo what we can best call variation by incarnation, which, on their entry into the particular time-stuff wherein they are made manifest, automatically follows in that particular conditional plexus. If the ideal of beauty or the moral ideal, quite apart from the dominance or recessiveness of congenital forces, but purely *as such* has quite another physiognomy with the Japanese than with the Chinese and is completely different from that of the Westerner and so on, it means that the transcendental powers, absolute and unconditional in themselves, can only appear in a definite time-stuff or race-stuff. And this stuff is different historically, locally, climatically, genetically, etc. Hence they acquire their particular physiognomy in history always through the historical context in which we meet them. Since they themselves are not simple but extremely complex and not to be seized unequivocally by logic, their appearance presents a widely different physiognomy according to time and place. That is their historical variability which, however, in no wise affects the absoluteness and unconditionalness of the powers lying behind it.

For all that, however, there are limits, not conceptually definable but nevertheless present, to this variability. One thing above all: there are, let us say at once, in this variable "physiognomy" certain forms and values which are valid for all eternity; once discovered they can only be covered up again and then re-discovered, just as there are "physiognomies" which have a simpler or a more complex or a greater degree of value. German music from the Baroque to Schubert, to take an example at random, is just such an expression of obviously eternal and universally accessible character, humanly speaking. Otherwise it could not be accepted and understood to-day by Asiatics with their completely different outlook. The so-called classical physiognomy of beauty must have a similar character to a very large extent. Otherwise it could not have conquered the East as far as China, or have acted like a fertilizing force on the highest plastic utterances of the Gothic during the Twelfth and beginning of the Thirteenth Century.

Similarly Christianity's break-through to active "humanity" was, as we have seen, in reality the conscious discovery of a great, universal, transcendentally-based congenital layer in man. Something universally absolute in man was here disclosed, something which can become recessive instead of dominant but still remains just as absolute, an eternal human value.

Every development of consciousness is or can be a break-through to this kind of unchanging, and in the human sense eternal, congenital layer. And once this break-through has occurred we can never again undo the working of these powers in ourselves. Not even by covering it up in all conceivable ways. Which can also be expressed by saying: those who have a Fall behind them can never become innocent again.

GENERAL INDEX

Absolute, the: 8.
—, and Cervantes: 30.
—, and Goethe: 54.
—, and Nietzsche: 115, 134.
—, and the Relative: 139, 195, *et seq.*
"*Action directe*": 149.
Allies, the victorious, in 1918: 157.
— —, in 1945: 176, 179.
America: xiii, 1, 51.
Anti-christ, The (Nietzsche): 97, 117.
Antigone: 189.
Antiquity, pagan, and Christianity: 7.
Anti-semitism: 91.
Atomism, social, of eighteenth century: 50.
Austro-Hungarian Empire: 147, 177.

Bach, J. S.: 44.
Bacon, Francis: 32, 62.
Bakunin, itinerant putsch-maker: 77.
Balance of Europe: xii, 43, 46, 49.
Balkans, the: 147, 176.
Balzac: 75.
Baroque Churches: 44.
Baudelaire: 86.
Becoming and Being, Nietzsche's doctrine of: 118, 135, 154.
Beethoven: 44.
Bentham, Jeremy: 72.
Benz, Richard: 44.
Bergson, Henri: 148.
Beyle, Pierre: 46.
Beyond Good and Evil (Nietzsche): 97, 103, 105, 110, 113, 115.
Birth-rate in nineteenth century: 65, 67.
Bismarck: 82, 90, 92, 146.
Blanqui: 77.
Bodin: xviii.
Bohemianism: 85.
British Empire: xii, 79, 178.
Buddhism: 8.
Burckhardt, Jacob: 82, 92, 135.

Bureaucrats: 170.
Byron (*Don · Juan, Manfred,* the "Mysteries"): 59.
Byzantium: 6.

Calderon: 36.
Carlyle: 77.
Case of Wagner, The (Nietzsche): 97.
Cervantes: 30.
Cézanne: 88, 191.
"Character-quality": 164.
Character, mutation of through education: 168.
— — in Shakespeare: 29.
Chartism: 77.
Christianity, connection of with Europe's dynamism: 5.
— and Dante: 11.
— and Russia: 6.
— and Nietzsche: 111, 138.
— and Transcendence: 138, 162, 195, 198.
Clausewitz: xv.
Comte, Auguste: 70.
Congenital forces, recessive and dominant, in Shakespeare: 28.
— influence on rise and fall of nations: 29.
— and Nazi Germany: 168.
— as incarnate transcendental powers: 192, 195, 197–8.
Congresses and Conferences, age of: 90.
Co-operative Movement in England: 80.
Corneille: 36.
Critique of Practical Reason (Kant): 46.
Critique of Judgement (Kant): 48.
Croce, Benedetto (*European History in Nineteenth Century*): 55 n.
Curtius, Ernst Robert (*Pathfinders of Modern France*): 148 n.
Cuvier: 75.

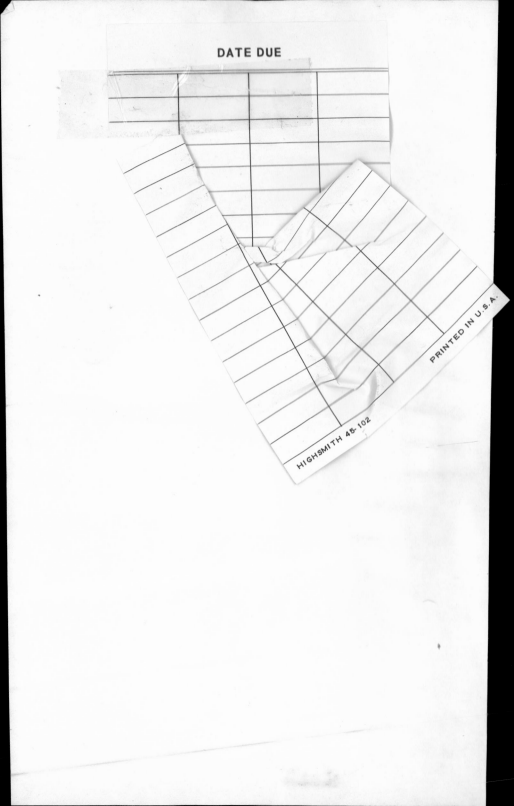

DATE DUE

HIGHSMITH 45-102

PRINTED IN U.S.A.